The New Urban Landscape

New Studies in American Intellectual and Cultural History

THOMAS BENDER, *Consulting Editor*

THE NEW URBAN LANDSCAPE

The Redefinition of City Form in
Nineteenth-Century America

DAVID SCHUYLER

THE JOHNS HOPKINS UNIVERSITY PRESS
Baltimore and London

This book has been brought to publication with the generous assistance of Franklin and Marshall College and the Andrew W. Mellon Foundation.

Second printing, hardcover, 1988
Johns Hopkins Paperbacks edition, 1988
Second printing, paperback, 1993

The Johns Hopkins University Press
2715 North Charles Street
Baltimore, Maryland 21218-4319
The Johns Hopkins Press Ltd., London

Library of Congress Cataloging-in-Publication Data

Schuyler, David.
  The new urban landscape.

  (New studies in American intellectual and cultural history)
  Bibliography: p.
  Includes index.
  1. City Planning—Environmental aspects—United States—History—19th century.
2. Cities and towns—United States—History—19th century.   3. Parks—United States—
History—19th century. I. Title. II. Series.
HT167.S285   1986   307.7′6′0973   86-7260
ISBN 0-8018-3231-4 (alk. paper)
ISBN 0-8018-3748-0 (pbk.)

A catalog record for this book is available from the British Library.

For Ruth and Gordon Cote

CONTENTS

ILLUSTRATIONS

ACKNOWLEDGMENTS

In the course of writing this book I have incurred many obligations. The Center for Studies in Landscape Architecture at Dumbarton Oaks provided a fellowship, as did the Office of American Studies and the National Museum of American Art, Smithsonian Institution. I am indebted to those institutions, and particularly to Elisabeth B. MacDougall, Wilcomb E. Washburn, and the late Joshua C. Taylor, for supporting my work. I am also grateful to Dean Bradley R. Dewey and the Committee on Grants, Franklin and Marshall College, for financial support in bringing this volume to completion.

Important as is adequate funding to enable a historian to conduct research and to write, equally so is the diligent work of librarians. Over the course of a decade I have relied on the talented staff of the Manuscript and Reference Divisions of the Library of Congress as well as personnel in several other research libraries. I have also benefited from the skill of Duncan McCollum, former archivist of the Frederick Law Olmsted Papers publication project, who conducted letter search and otherwise organized documents to make their use easier. The staff at Shadek-Fackenthal Library, Franklin and Marshall College, were most helpful, particularly David Lewis and Anne Bevilacqua.

Numerous friends and fellow historians have generously offered me their insights and made available their research materials. Among these are Jon A. Peterson, John Zukowsky, Alden T. Vaughan, Charles Capen McLaughlin, Kenneth L. Ames, Walter L. Creese, Tupper Thomas, and Patricia O'Donnell. Joy Kestenbaum, my associate in preparing a Historic Landscapes and Structures Report for Prospect Park, helped immeasurably in my research on that topic. Carolyn F. Hoffman aided in preparing this book for typesetting. Ford Peatross, Ellen M. Snyder, and Shari Berg provided invaluable service in assembling the illustrations, while Fred Sener transformed negatives into printable images.

Other colleagues and friends who have commented on part or all of earlier versions of this book include Eric L. McKitrick, Kenneth T. Jackson, Kenneth S. Lynn, Gwendolyn Wright, John F. Kasson, James L. Baughman, John A. Andrew III, Michele H. Bogart, Louise L.

Stevenson, and Jane Turner Censer. Over the last decade George B. Tatum and Charles E. Beveridge have freely shared with me their vast knowledge of the careers of Andrew Jackson Downing and Frederick Law Olmsted. Each of these steadfast friends has given a careful reading to several versions of this book, and their comments have improved it immensely. Charles Beveridge also helped select and photograph many of the illustrations.

Thomas Bender has been an exemplary editor, at once a source of support and of challenge, urging me to develop fully the possibilities inherent in my material. Similar service has been performed by members of the staff at the Johns Hopkins University Press, especially Henry Y. K. Tom, George F. Thompson, Nancy D. West, and Anne M. Whitmore.

Finally, after too many years, I thank my parents, brothers, and sisters, whose support has made writing a less lonely venture. Marsha and Nancy Schuyler didn't read many of the following pages, but they too helped make this book a reality.

To all, I am deeply grateful.

The New Urban Landscape

INTRODUCTION

This book examines the development of a new perspective on urban form and culture that evolved in nineteenth-century America as an alternative to the traditional structure and spatial organization of cities. Its focus is a continuing debate over what was the appropriate physical form for the nation's urban areas, what should be the constituent parts of the expanding cities. More specifically, the following pages analyze the creation of city parks, suburbs, and residential subdivisions in anticipation of the expansion of the urban gridiron. Promoters of these projects attempted to redirect and control American urban development at what was arguably its most crucial period—the years between 1840 and 1900—when cities were growing and changing at the most rapid rates in the nation's history, when they were becoming increasingly complex as physical and social spaces, and when they were taking the shape of modern metropolitan areas.

The task civic and cultural leaders undertook in attempting to redefine urban form was enormous. Throughout the seventeenth and eighteenth centuries most American cities had developed as economic institutions, places that existed primarily to serve the needs of commerce. Until the construction of urban transportation systems in the nineteenth century, these spaces were necessarily very compact—usually about three miles square—and noteworthy for their density of building and crowded residential patterns. Contemporaries believed that conditions of life in cities fostered the spread of epidemic disease and nurtured the seeds of discord that occasionally seemed to threaten the survival of society. As a result, many leaders of the new nation, especially those from the South, feared urban areas as threats to their republican experiment. They had studied the historical lessons of other countries and had concluded that the propertyless residents of cities were "sores" on the body politic. Distinguished spokesmen representing this group—Jefferson, Madison, and John Taylor of Caroline—celebrated the virtues of an agrarian way of life and institutionalized their distrust of urban areas by locating the national capital not in an existing city but in a new federal territory far from a metropolis.

The fears of many members of the revolutionary generation notwithstanding, during the nineteenth century cities grew—in physical size, population, and social complexity—at a rate that alarmed most contemporaries. Many newcomers to cities had migrated from rural areas, seeking jobs, escape from the loneliness of the farmstead, or perhaps the proverbial fortune promised in much of the popular literature of the period. Others had come from abroad, aggravating what historian Gunther Barth has called the "discordant features of ethnicity and race." But wherever their previous homes might have been, the changing scale of the city forced all residents to confront new, even alien, work and interpersonal relationships, to confront the sights and sounds of an accelerating urban economy as well as the remarkable cultural diversity of the urban population. This shift from country to city, from farm to factory, was perhaps the most fundamentally dislocating experience in all of American history. It demanded innovative solutions that would protect public health, provide areas for recreation to ease the psychological adjustment to a new urban environment, and redirect the spatial growth of cities.[1]

Beginning roughly in the second quarter of the nineteenth century, some leaders of a new generation, born primarily in New England and New York after the Revolutionary War, perceived these challenges and sought to redefine urban form and culture. Like its predecessor, this generation also cherished nature as the best environment, but what it meant by *nature* was quite different: instead of the plantation or the farm, these rising cultural spokesmen more and more celebrated a specific set of scenic qualities and social values they identified with a pastoral or domesticated environment, one in which man and nature had achieved the state of balance Leo Marx has termed the "middle landscape." The individuals who became promoters of the new urban landscape had witnessed the transformation of New England and the beginnings of a dramatic expansion of the nation's cities in the antebellum years, and they especially regretted what by then had become the prototypical urban form, the gridiron. While continuing to deplore the squalor and human misery of crowded, unsanitary neighborhoods, a group of talented individuals—including social reformers, physicians, religious leaders, landscape designers, and arbiters of culture—recognized the inevitability of the existence and growth of urban areas and advocated creation of more suitable recreational and domestic spaces. Drawing upon the rhetoric of sanitary reform and of republicanism, as well as a belief in the moral superiority of nature and domesticity, these individuals gradually shaped a comprehensive view that recognized both the limitations and the promise of city life. Theirs was the vision of a new and civilized urban landscape, a more openly built urban environment that combined the morality they attributed to nature and the enriching and refining influence of the nascent cultural institutions that were making the city more and more attractive as a place of residence. The result of their efforts is a heritage of urban parks and suburban communities, which represent attempts, admittedly imperfect, to recast the shape of America's cities in the second half of the nineteenth century.[2]

This new conception of the city was not entirely novel, of course, for even in antiquity the poet Martial had celebrated the pleasure of *rus in urbe*, the country in the city. Like their classsical predecessors, the rich and powerful in Renaissance Italy and Augustan England sought to combine urban advantages and rural surroundings. Occasionally this took the form of a city house with extensive gardens, but more often it required the maintenance of at least two residences. The same pattern appeared in colonial America, where structures such as Captain John McPherson's Mount Pleasant, located in what today is Philadelphia's Fairmount Park, served as summer retreats from the heat and bustle of the city and from the epidemics that devastated the populace with alarming rapidity.[3]

The conception of the city as a new urban landscape that evolved in nineteenth-century America differed from its precursors in three principal ways. First, to a greater degree than in western Europe, with its long tradition of metropolitan centralization, the idea of creating a more openly built urban environment began as a repudiation of the commercial city. Popular writers, aspiring statesmen, clergymen — virtually anyone seeking an attentive middle-class audience — could find one by damning the city and attributing to its temptations the degradation of a moral society. These latter-day jeremiads blamed the conduct of trade and manufacturing, which necessitated compactness of building and crowded living conditions that cultural leaders considered a grave threat to social order.[4]

Second, this new conception of the city and its possibilities was middle-class in orientation. With the rise in urban property values during the nineteenth century, the density of building and stress of apartment and tenement life seemed to undermine traditional values associated with family and community. An anonymous writer in *Putnam's Monthly* captured the impact of new urban conditions at mid-century when he noted that in the city "families rise and fall continually like the waves of the ocean." To counter this instability promoters of public parks created communal spaces for family outings, places where the naturalistic landscape offered relief from cramped, dark, poorly ventilated dwellings, and where rural scenery might sooth the "nerves and mind" of visitors. Similarly, the most enlightened builders of suburbs consciously shaped surroundings that would avoid the congestion of cities and provide an environment more conducive to the ideal of home as domestic refuge. These middle-class foundations of the new urban landscape contrasted sharply with a contemporary development in European city planning, the imperial parks and boulevards of Baron Haussmann's Paris.[5]

Third, advocates of the new urban landscape broke with older patterns of city form by attempting to achieve the differentiation of space and land use within the metropolis. Because workers needed to live near their places of employment, in the colonial and early national years cities usually mixed commercial and residential functions on the same block. Too often this resulted in the congestion, filth, crime, and disease that contemporaries feared. But beginning in the 1830s, urban transportation systems made possible the separation of workplace and domicile, thereby creating the potential for eliminating what reformers considered the worst environmental failings of the older commercial city.[6]

The conception and creation of the new urban landscape began in the antebellum years, when more and more Americans recognized that existing recreational spaces within cities were hopelessly inadequate. As a result of urban growth the gridiron spread relentlessly over once rural areas on the periphery, thereby increasing the distance separating country and city; as urban congestion worsened, the scenic associations of the pastoral or domesticated landscape became more and more logical as correctives to the changing environment of the city. At first, proponents of the new urban landscape found an alternative to traditional city form in the "rural" cemeteries that were created beginning in the 1830s. These cemeteries incorporated naturalistic scenery and their design emphasized a curvilinearity that stood in clear contrast to the straight lines and right angles of the gridiron. However pleasant, such cemeteries did not address fundamental problems of urban form: they were didactic landscapes, full of monuments that offered visitors moral lessons as well as moments of contemplation. Moreover, these cemeteries were at best only semipublic institutions and were located so far from the city as to make it all but impossible for working people to escape to them from their neighborhoods.

Thus, during the 1840s and 1850s proponents of the new urban landscape applied the lessons of cemetery design and crusaded to create large public spaces within the city. They began with the notion that the country was somehow inherently superior to the city, that what the urban environment most needed was a large recreational ground—a park. Nevertheless, even advocates of parks differed over what form these spaces should take. Many looked to Europe, where the park had begun as a landscaped area adjacent to a country house, and where, traditionally, public parks served as repositories for monuments and cultural institutions. But a landscape filled with temples and statuary was not "the country," not completely the antithesis of urban sights and sounds, and gradually the somewhat undefined concept of park evolved and took on an American expression. It became, in Frederick Law Olmsted's work, as completely as possible a naturalistic landscape, one consciously designed to shut out the urban environment, by subordinating all necessary structures to the realization of broad reaches of scenery, and to provide the elements of a rural setting that, he felt, met the psychological and social needs of residents of the city.

New York's Central Park was the first major attempt to achieve these goals. Almost immediately after its construction, however, Olmsted recognized that even so large a public landscape was not equal to the task of refining and civilizing a city. Because of the high cost of urban land, Central Park was located far to the north of the built area of Manhattan and was virtually inaccessible to the people who most needed it. Consequently, Olmsted and his contemporaries urged the creation of parkways and park systems that would extend the benefits of parks to all neighborhoods of the city. By the end of the century, under the leadership of Olmsted and his colleague Charles Eliot, the park system became a comprehensive metropolitan solution to the recreational needs of the modern city.

The new urban landscape also included the suburb, which began as an escape from the city but became an important element of a comprehensive new urban form. If a gridiron city provided few locations appropriate for residential development compatible with the culture of domesticity, Olmsted recognized that large areas had to be platted in advance of urban growth. Indeed, by 1879 he had concluded that "a large part of the ideas of a city, which have been transmitted to us from the period when cities were walled about and necessarily compact and crowded, must be put away." The application of the gridiron to domestic areas, Olmsted believed, inflicted on inhabitants of the city a degree of suffering not exceeded even by the barbarism of the "most brutal Pagans." In place of the old urban structure he envisioned a modern city that included the morality of nature as well as the economic functions of urban life. Such a city would combine "more compact and higher building in business quarters" with "broader, lower and more open building in residential quarters." Olmsted and a group of talented contemporaries applied the lessons of urban growth, mass transportation, and differentiation of urban space. They struggled to create a new city with a compact commercial center, spacious parks for recreation, openly built residential subdivisions, and suburban communities—each an integral and interdependent part of the modern metropolis. This restructuring of the urban environment was essential, Olmsted realized at the end of the 1870s:

"Our country has entered upon a stage of progress," he wrote, "when its welfare is to depend on the convenience, safety, order and economy of life in its great cities."[7]

A concern for maintaining social order pervades much of the writing of Olmsted and his colleagues, in large part because these promoters of parks and suburbs thought of themselves as reformers. They believed, as did advocates of penitentiaries and other asylums and celebrants of the new culture of domesticity, that the physical spaces humans occupy influence their patterns of behavior. Thus the question of city form was not merely an aesthetic one but involved a statement of political and social ideology. As a result, understanding the goals and methods of these reformers within the nineteenth-century context in which they acted is essential. Were these men, as some historians have asserted, blatantly exercising social control? Were they imposing their own values and standards of behavior on newcomers to the city? Were the kinds of recreational and domestic spaces they provided the sort that urban residents actually needed? To be sure, Frederick Law Olmsted believed that a large naturalistic park was essential in modern cities because it offered opportunities for the quiet contemplation of natural scenery, and he felt that parks should intentionally encourage such activity. Indeed, Olmsted considered this function so important that he attempted to exclude other, more active, uses from his parks. He also arranged and policed the landscape in a way that expected restraint and decorum from park users. Undoubtedly his conception of the park differed from that held by many residents of the cities in which he worked. But, tempting though it has proven to some historians, to attack these reformers and to dismiss parks as examples of social control ignores the more positive aspects of their creators' motivations.[8]

Andrew Jackson Downing, Olmsted, Calvert Vaux, Charles Eliot, and other planners whose works this book analyzes attempted to create landscapes that they hoped would promote the highest potential of civilization in America. Downing, for example, asserted in 1850 that "the higher social and artistic elements of every man's nature lie dormant within him, and every laborer is a possible gentleman, not by the possession of money or fine clothes—but through the refining influence of intellectual and moral culture." He confessed that public school education was not enough, and to raise Americans to a higher level of civilization Downing advocated a program of "popular refinement," which involved the creation of a whole series of institutions—publicly supported libraries and museums as well as parks and gardens. If implemented, he predicted, these institutions would "banish the plague spots of democracy."[9]

Similarly, Olmsted believed that conditions in Northern cities failed to measure up to the potential of a republic. In a letter to his life-long friend and founder of the Children's Aid Society, Charles Loring Brace, Olmsted sketched the outlines of a comprehensive reformist program: "We need institutions that shall more directly *assist* the poor and degraded to elevate themselves. Our educational principle must be enlarged and made to include more than these miserable common schools. The poor & wicked need more than to be let alone." He urged Brace to continue his work with New York City's children, and advocated the creation of a range of organizations that would provide for the poor "an education to refinement and taste and the mental & moral capital of gentlemen." The park, he thought, would be for the residents of the city, "an oasis[,] an arcadia, in the desert of brick & mortar."[10]

Calvert Vaux, an English architect who came to the United States in 1850 to work as Downing's partner and who later collaborated with Olmsted on a series of important public landscape designs, shared this orientation. He believed that raising the level of civilization in America was so important to the "*social* progress of the spirit of republicanism" that he advocated governmental encouragement of the arts. In *Villas and Cottages,* his handbook of residential design, Vaux explained the role of architecture in promoting refinement and taste in America. He believed that the success of Central Park was "of vital importance to the progress of the Republic," and asserted that the park-maker's task was "the translation of the republican art idea in its highest form into the acres we want to control."[11]

Admittedly, this reformist crusade attempted to raise the level of civilization in America. It hoped to induce immigrants and lower-class residents of cities to emulate the behavioral patterns, the refinement and culture, of an educated class. Some historians will find this damning. Yet even if they were conservative or elitist, the words and works of promoters of the new urban landscape convey a positive vision of what American society could become and reveal a deep commitment to the nation's republican destiny.

This vision of the new urban landscape reflected a desire to redirect the course of urban culture and city form in nineteenth-century America. As a conception it evolved, became more complex and comprehensive, in response to the physical and demographic growth of cities. As a creation it was subject to the pull of state and local politics and, even in the 1850s, to the dynamics of machine rule. Ultimately, of course, the new urban landscape did not totally remake the city, as some of its promoters had hoped, nor did it eliminate such longstanding problems as poverty, crime, and disease. Indeed, its promoters, while recognizing the essential commercial foundations of urban life, never gained control over the design of business districts. Unable to alter the shape of older neighborhoods as well as the

commercial center, advocates of a new urban landscape created recreational and domestic spaces on the periphery of cities. They could
not remedy inequities in the existing social structure, or provide
housing and play facilities for the poor, which compromised their vision of the new city. Despite this very real limitation, in its attempt to
reconcile the increasing economic dominance of cities with traditional values of home, family, and nature, the new urban landscape
was one of the most creative and enduring contributions to civilization undertaken in nineteenth-century America.

PART ONE

Changing Conceptions of Urban Form

CHAPTER I

FLAWED VISIONS: THE LESSONS OF WASHINGTON AND NEW YORK

The Capitol wants a city.
— FREDERICK MARRYAT

. . . this cramped horizontal gridiron of a town without towers, porticoes, fountains or perspectives, hide-bound in its deadly uniformity of mean ugliness. . .
— EDITH WHARTON

At the beginning of the nineteenth century the United States was predominantly agrarian. Cities were small in physical size and few in number, while the urban population was trifling compared to its rural counterpart. Perhaps it was symbolic that in 1800 the seat of the national government moved from Philadelphia, largest and most cosmopolitan of America's cities, to a new federal enclave, soon to be designated the "city of magnificent intentions," in the marshes and swamps along the Potomac River. The decision to relocate the capital so far from a metropolitan center undoubtedly expressed one ideological conviction shared by many members of the revolutionary generation, that agriculture was the most virtuous way of life and that cities were necessary evils. The creation of a new national capital also forced American leaders, quite self-consciously, to plan a city that would be compatible with national aspirations and republican institutions.[1]

The government's move to what later came to be known as Washington, D.C. was preeminently a political decision, but it also involved issues of major cultural importance to the new nation. The Residence Act (July 16, 1790), which determined the general site of the capital, was a component of the well-known compromise by which Alexander Hamilton gained approval for the federal assumption of debts incurred by the states during the Revolutionary War. But the Residence Act was itself a significant compromise. Most obviously, the creation of an independent "territory" of Columbia attempted to circumvent the competition of cities and states for the

Figure 1. Plan of the City of Washington, D.C., by Andrew Ellicott after Pierre Charles L'Enfant. Engraving by Thackeray and Vallance for *The Universal Asylum and Columbian Magazine*, March, 1792. (Courtesy, Geography and Maps Division, Library of Congress, Washington, D.C.)

prestige and economic benefits that would follow designation as the national capital. The cession of land by Virginia and Maryland to form the federal district also gave the new government dominion over itself, thereby ensuring freedom from potential conflict caused by overlapping national and local jurisdictions. And, of course, the selection of the geographically central Potomac site was a sectional compromise which, contemporaries hoped, might strengthen the Southern states' attachment to the nation.[2]

In a larger sense the creation of the District of Columbia reveals a deep cultural ambivalence about cities and their place in what Americans considered "Nature's Nation." The grandiose plan prepared by Major Pierre Charles L'Enfant (fig. 1) suggests an attempt to create a European-scale capital, replete with the classical imagery that announced America's claim to a republican tradition. But despite the

Changing Conceptions of Urban Form

desire to build a capital worthy of the future greatness of the nation, and despite the appeal of republican iconography, many of the founding fathers rejected the conception of the new city as a metropolis. They had, after all, recently engaged in warfare to resist the centralized authority of one metropolis, London, and the persistent localism of the thirteen new states was unmistakable.[3]

Thomas Jefferson personifies this ambivalence: comfortable in the fashionable society of Paris and fond of the amenities of urban life, he nevertheless questioned the place of cities in American culture. In *Notes on the State of Virginia* he asserted, "We have no townships." With Enlightenment rationalism Jefferson took an empirical approach to the subject. English "*laws* have said there shall be towns," he observed, "but *nature* has said there shall not, and they remain unworthy of enumeration." In his estimation Virginia's geography and economy made unnecessary the development of cities and towns such as those in New England and the middle colonies: her numerous rivers, shipping channels connecting distant plantations with European centers of trade and culture, served as the life lines of a decentralized agrarian society. In this Jefferson posited an alternative vision of American development, one determined not by Old World institutions but by the abundant natural advantages of the New.[4]

More important, Jefferson realized, European experience taught that cities were dangerous threats to republican institutions because they housed large numbers of the dependent poor. Historian Edmund S. Morgan has explained the seeming paradox of slavery and freedom in colonial Virginia as a result of this fear of the landless poor. He interprets Bacon's Rebellion of 1676 as the culmination of economic discontent on the part of a large group of freemen, formerly indentured servants, who, because of cost and prior settlement, had experienced difficulty acquiring arable land except on the frontier. Ironically, Virginia had inherited a problem it was helping England solve, an overabundance of impoverished workers. Most Virginians had come to share a philosophical distrust of the propertyless laborer, who lacked the political independence required of all good and true republicans. In the aftermath of Bacon's Rebellion, leaders in the Old Dominion looked more favorably on racial slavery, for it provided a means of eliminating the need for indentured servants, who eventually would swell the ranks of an armed, poor white class. So great was this fear of the dependent poor that Virginians could find the solution of permanent Negro slavery acceptable in practice even if abhorrent in theory.[5]

Like the Commonwealthmen, Jefferson associated the propertyless laborer with economic dependence. In the most famous passage in *Notes on the State of Virginia* he wrote, "Dependence begets subservience and venality, suffocates the germ of virtue, and prepares fit tools for the designs of ambition." If the landless classes constituted a threat to republican virtue (which John Adams defined as a "positive passion for the public good"), the independent farmer personified the true republican. "Those who labor in the earth," Jefferson declared, "are the chosen people of God, if ever He had a chosen people, whose breasts He has made His peculiar deposit for substantial and genuine virtue." Indeed, Jefferson equated the state of agriculture with the moral health of the nation: "generally speaking, the proportion which the aggregate of the other classes of citizens bears in any State to that of its husbandmen, is the proportion of its unsound to its healthy parts, and is a good enough barometer whereby to measure its degree of corruption."[6]

Jefferson's well-known strictures against cities appear not in "A Notice of the Counties, Cities, Townships and Villages" but in the chapter devoted to "The Present State of Manufactures, Commerce, Interior and Exterior Trade." While in the abstract and at a distance he recognized that cities were essential to civilization, Jefferson dreaded the impoverished laborers who congregated in commercial and manufacturing centers. Advising his countrymen to "let our workshops remain in Europe," he declared that the "mobs of great cities add just so much to the support of pure government, as sores do to the strength of the human body." Similarly did Washington and Adams fear the "tumultuous populace of large cities."[7]

An incident that occurred in Philadelphia in June of 1783 reinforced this fear in revolutionary leaders and may have contributed to their decision to locate the national capital so far from a large city. In that month a group of Pennsylvania soldiers marched on the State House while Congress was in session and demanded their pay, which was long overdue. After the tension had passed, Congress moved out of the city and reconvened in more hospitable quarters in Princeton, New Jersey. The soldiers' "affront" to Congress undoubtedly strengthened the argument for an independent federal territory, preferably one beyond the influence of urban mobs.[8]

The location of the new federal city established the nation's self-image as an agrarian republic and its design attempted to avoid settlement by propertyless workers. The capital would be located not in an existing city but on a new site, surrounded by the agricultural districts of Maryland and Virginia. The magnificence of L'Enfant's Baroque street system disguises the way in which the city plan embodies this ambivalent attitude toward urban life. L'Enfant's grand design made no provision for industry and, by requiring that all houses and buildings be constructed of brick or stone, attempted to ensure that all residents would be men of property. Despite rhetoric claiming that the capital would soon become a thriving seat of commerce and civilization, Washington instead became a boarding house city vir-

Changing Conceptions of Urban Form

tually no one found attractive. Like eighteenth-century Williamsburg, the new capital was a capital in name only: the principal, almost the only function of the federal city was to house the government.[9]

The location of the capital in Washington, D.C. marked a break with the pattern of urban development dominant throughout the colonial era. Cities are, first and foremost, economic institutions. They exist primarily to serve the demands of commerce. The location and plan of the new capital, however, attempted to avoid the density of building and the character of the populace found in the traditional commercial city.

But in the absence of sound economic foundations, the subsequent development of the nation's capital was an abysmal failure. The scale of L'Enfant's projected city was matched only by the parsimony of a government that refused to spend the money necessary to implement the plan—with disastrous results. According to historian Henry Adams,

> When in the summer of 1800 the government was transferred to what was regarded by most persons as a fever-stricken morass, the half-finished White House stood in a naked field overlooking the Potomac, with two awkward Department buildings near it, a single row of brick houses and a few isolated dwellings within sight, and nothing more; until, across the swamp, a mile and a half away, the shapeless, unfinished Capitol was seen, two wings without a body, ambitious enough in design to make more grotesque the nature of its surroundings.

For members of the government the new city was noticeably lacking in urban form and in the amenities of urban life. The Irish poet Thomas Moore vilified Washington in 1804 as

> This embryo capital, where Fancy sees
> Squares in morasses, obelisks in trees.

Henry Adams pithily noted, "Never did hermit or saint condemn himself to solitude more consciously than Congress and the Executive in removing the government from Philadelphia to Washington." L'Enfant's design remained a vision of future greatness: the nation's capital developed into a mean, slatternly place virtually no one found attractive, and the government existed "at a distance and out of sight" of the rest of the country.[10]

Visitors to the new federal territory rightly called it the "city of magnificent intentions," but the disparity between L'Enfant's conception and the government's ability and determination to execute the plan was enormous. The Capitol and the President's House remained unfinished, members of Congress clustered in boarding houses, the streets were unpaved, and recreational and sanitary facilities were virtually nonexistent. To make matters worse, British troops burned the public buildings in the summer of 1814—after which there was talk of moving the capital back to Philadelphia—and the city's rebuilding program collapsed during the economic panic of 1819. Thus during the 1830s and 1840s visitors continued to be shocked by the dismal physical appearance of Washington. Charles Dickens characterized the city in terms of "spacious avenues, that begin in nothing, and lead nowhere; streets, miles long, that want only houses, roads, and inhabitants; public buildings that need but a public to be complete, and ornaments of great thoroughfares, which lack only great thoroughfares to ornament." The subaltern E. T. Cook ascribed to a French lady the observation that the capital resembled "a town gone on a visit to the country." Even the sympathetic New Englander Theodore Dwight could remark that the "magnificence of the plan is evident to every eye, and so is the want of power to complete it."[11]

The isolation of the Potomac site did, however, eliminate the threat that the "mobs of great cities" would soon dominate the government. Dickens noted that this location for the capital "very probably" was chosen because it was "remote from mobs." Theodore Dwight added that in Washington "local interests and influences are not likely to engross and control the attention of the government in so great a degree as they have often done in large cities; and there is no mob to overawe or even to threaten their freedom." Unsurprisingly, the most astute observer of nineteenth-century America, Alexis de Tocqueville, concluded that because the government was situated in Washington the nation had no true capital. This he judged "one of the first causes of the maintenance of republican institutions in the United States."[12]

Perhaps most significantly, the location of the capital on the banks of the Potomac River determined that the United States would become a polycentric nation. Tocqueville rightly defined a capital as the city "whose direct or indirect influence is felt over the whole extent of the country." National capitals were metropolises, places like London, Paris, or Vienna. At once the political, economic, and artistic centers of their respective countries, these cities provided for the concentration of intellectual, financial, and governmental resources and served as points of diffusion for truly national cultures. But while metropolitan leadership might be appropriate in European countries, experience taught that a dominant capital would pose an immediate threat to the survival of the American experiment. Tocqueville represented conventional wisdom when he asserted that the "preponderance of capital cities. . .exposes modern republics to the same defects as the republics of antiquity, which all perished from not having known this system." Alas, survival exacted a price, and the Washington he visited was not a thriving metropolis but an "arid plain"

Changing Conceptions of Urban Form

covered with a few handsome buildings and the scattered villages denominated a city. Washington was a poor choice as the nation's capital because in its conscious repudiation of the commercial city it was artificially located and because the government lacked the resources and will to develop it adequately. "Unless one is Alexander or Peter the Great," Tocqueville concluded, "one must not meddle with creating the capital of an empire."[13]

The nation's first grand attempt at city planning failed because, in rejecting the commercial city and a European tradition of metropolitan leadership, the revolutionary generation cast America's honorific imagery in terms of a decentralized agrarian republic. Cities were conceded to be necessary, but they were hardly thought of other than as necessary evils. As a result, throughout the nineteenth century the belief that the United States was, and should remain, an agrarian nation made it difficult to deal effectively with problems attendant to urbanization.[14]

L'Enfant's plan for the capital, which superimposed a Baroque axis on a rectangular gridiron, was an attempt to create a monumental civic space. But in forsaking traditional urban functions Washington became a one-dimensional city in which officials of the government were artificially separated from leaders in other fields of endeavor. And because it was developed so haphazardly the L'Enfant plan would have little influence on the design of other American cities. Throughout the rest of the nation, city builders returned to the more traditional form of the gridiron.

The development of New York represents the reassertion of commercial functions as the basis for urban form and culture. In the aftermath of the Revolutionary War residents there began the arduous task of reconstructing a city twice burned during a lengthy British occupation. New York's recovery was remarkable, and in 1785 the city government acted to provide for future growth by surveying the common lands lying north of the populated quarters. Casimir Goerck's map of that year divided into rectangular blocks those outlying properties. Eleven years later Goerck submitted an additional plan, the "Map of the Common Lands," which solidified the rectangular pattern and provided for north-south streets one hundred feet wide and east-west streets sixty feet wide.[15]

These surveys, however, established street plans only for municipally owned lands. By 1806 the Common Council recognized the need for a more comprehensive plan that would control the development of the city by "laying down as well the individual as the Corporate property." On February 3 of that year the council approved the draft of an act to accomplish this and engaged a surveyor to prepare such a plan. But because any proposal to divide private lands by

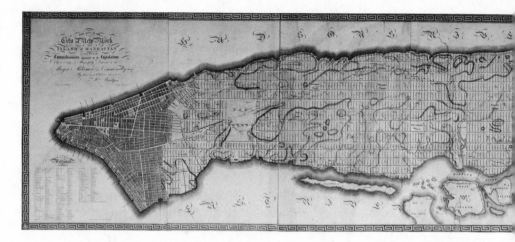

streets would arouse heated resistance from individual owners, the council shifted its strategy and requested the state legislature to appoint an impartial commission to devise a suitable street arrangement. By entrusting the plan to three men of unimpeachable character, the city hoped to place above local politics and individual claims the provisions for future growth. To prevent costly and time-consuming litigation by dissatisfied landowners, and to facilitate the "rise of frequent subdivisions of property," the Common Council requested that the commissioners be granted powers to make permanent, arbitrary decisions. By an act of April 3, 1807, the state legislature gave the city these responsibilities, appointed Gouverneur Morris, Simeon DeWitt, and John Rutherford commissioners, and entrusted to them "exclusive power to lay out streets, roads and public squares when the same shall be built upon." In addition, the law established criteria for street openings and determined that the commissioners' plan "shall be final and conclusive."[16]

The first problem confronted by the commissioners was to determine an overall scheme for their design. L'Enfant's 1791 plan for Washington suggested one alternative, as did the recent replatting of Edinburgh, but the commissioners rejected "those supposed improvements by circles, ovals, and stars," claiming that such plans sacrificed convenience and utility for embellishment. Instead they reasoned that the city would be "composed principally of the habitations of men, and that straight-sided and right-angled houses are the most cheap to build and the most convenient to live in." Having thus determined that the gridiron would be the most suitable plan for New York's needs, the commissioners attempted to make adjustments that would respect existing property lines. Finding no equitable or acceptable solution, they allowed no deviation from the plan's rectangular uniformity.[17]

Changing Conceptions of Urban Form

Figure 2.
Plan of New York City, 1811, by Gouverneur Morris, Simeon DeWitt, and John Rutherford, Commissioners, John Randel, Surveyor. (Courtesy, Eno Collection, Art, Prints & Photographs Division, The New York Public Library; Astor, Lenox and Tilden Foundations, New York City.)

The commissioners submitted their plan to the city in 1811, four years after they had begun work. In addition to determining an overall grid, they set aside three major spaces for public use, areas for a municipal reservoir, a parade ground, and a marketplace. As none of these functions was mentioned in their 1807 instructions, the commissioners demonstrated some foresight in anticipating future needs. Less fortuitous was their neglect to reserve grounds for public recreation. Because of the high cost of land, and because the rivers surrounding Manhattan Island already served recreational purposes, they made no provision for a public park or garden.[18]

The Commissioners Plan of 1811 (fig. 2) provided that avenues running north and south be one hundred feet wide and that streets running east and west be sixty feet wide (excepting fifteen wider streets intended to facilitate crosstown traffic). But, the intent of the commissioners notwithstanding, New York's gridiron created a number of structural problems that became evident as the city grew in physical size. Although a gridiron does not have to be as compact or as inflexible as New York's 1811 plan, its crosstown streets were so narrow as to be dreadfully inadequate, and its provision for blocks without alleys effectively consigned service traffic to roadways. The size of each block, two hundred by eight hundred feet, created many very valuable corner lots, but it also resulted in building sites almost one hundred feet deep. And because of the high cost of urban land, when constructed most of the city's houses necessarily would be very narrow, sometimes as little as twelve or fourteen feet wide. Moreover, the inflexible gridiron, which treated all parts of the city equally, ignored topography—a major consideration at a time when carts were pulled by horses—and left no sites for noble buildings or for groups of related structures. Perhaps most important, in imposing this street arrangement on Manhattan the 1811 plan failed to provide for potentially different patterns of land use and ensured that, as the center of population moved uptown, congestion inevitably would follow.[19]

The Commissioners Plan extended the rectangular gridiron as far north as 155th Street, a distance of more than seven miles from the built area of the city. This was totally unrealistic (even the commissioners admitted that it provided "space for a greater population than is collected at any spot on this side of China") because the plan far exceeded the traditional and then feasible limits of a city's size. Until the development of urban transportation systems later in the century, most cities were approximately three miles square, circumscribed in extent by the distance an individual could walk conveniently. Nevertheless, the commissioners explained, they carried the plan to 155th Street—far beyond the geographical extent of the "walking city"—because they foresaw the development of the more desirable land at Harlem before that of the lowlying area to the south. They did not lay out streets in the northernmost reaches of the island because they feared that such a plan "might have furnished materials to the pernicious spirit of speculation."[20]

Despite this last suggestion, the Commissioners Plan of 1811 was a monument to the primacy of commercial and speculative values. Underlying the plan was a particular conception of the city, one in which the urban dynamic was defined not by the streets or public buildings but by the waterfront and adjacent warehouses. Street traffic was directed toward the rivers to the east and west because trade was the principal source of the city's wealth and because property values far outweighed considerations such as public health and recreation. John Randel, secretary and surveyor to the commissioners, later boasted that the plan's major contribution to the city was "the facilities afforded it for *buying, selling,* and *improving* real estate on New York Island."[21]

Washington and New York represent two alternative directions for the development of urban form and culture in nineteenth-century America. One was a monumental civic space, consciously designed to avoid the failings of the commercial city and to exemplify republican values; the other was avowedly and arbitrarily a commercial metropolis. In retrospect neither city plan was appropriate: L'Enfant's "city of magnificent intentions" was too grandiose for the young republic, while the Commissioners Plan of 1811 would prove too limited in conception to meet the various spatial requirements of a modern metropolis.

Washington's development during the three decades preceding the Civil War demonstrates both the fragility of its standing as the capital and the implications of polycentrism for the nation's cities. To be sure, Washington experienced a modest construction boom in the

1830s, when a series of fires necessitated replacing several important governmental structures. The Greek classicism of Robert Mills' Treasury, Thomas U. Walter's Post Office, and Alexander Jackson Davis's and William P. Elliott's Patent Office all added immeasurably to the city's attractiveness and fundamentally altered the scale of public buildings. Indeed, though the earliest federal projects had intentionally been designed on a residential scale, those of the 1830s came to dominate the city's skyline. In the following decade James Renwick, Jr., added yet another landmark, the Tudor Gothic structure on the Mall that houses the Smithsonian Institution.[22]

But, as Tocqueville rightly noted, a few public buildings do not constitute a city, and because of its location and foundering economy Washington lagged behind most eastern cities in its rate of growth. According to geographer Allan Pred, the years from 1840 to 1860 marked "the beginning of a major shift in the principal functions of most important urban centers, a related breakthrough in the importance of manufacturing in the national economy, and the two highest decennial rates of urbanization ever recorded in U.S. history." Unlike most northeastern cities, however, Washington did not experience a major diversification of functions or economic activity: its largest employers were the government and government-related firms, and overcapitalization of the Chesapeake and Ohio Canal severely restricted the amount of money available for investment in other civic projects. The city did record impressive demographic gains in these two decades, but its population in 1860 was only 61,122—less than one percent of the nation's total urban population. Most of those residents came from the southeast, one of the least urbanized areas of the country. Thus, at the time when the largest American cities were wracked by growth and change, the federal government was totally unprepared to offer leadership, either by action or by example.[23]

By contrast, New York experienced sustained, dramatic growth in these decades. Construction of the Erie Canal, the beginning of regularly scheduled transatlantic packet service, and the extension of railroad networks all contributed to New York's domination of the national economy. At the ceremonies marking the opening of the Erie Canal in 1825, Governor DeWitt Clinton described improvements in transportation as "the revolution of a century." The city's growth proved Clinton wrong only in understatement in his prediction that by 1900 "the whole island of Manhattan, covered with habitations and replenished with a dense population, will constitute one vast city." But because New York's leaders failed to conceive of the city as more than an economic institution, they were unable to curb speculation while promoting urban growth. The limitations of this particular vision of the city became evident in succeeding years, when streets once laid out only on paper became busy thoroughfares, when wharves and warehouses lined the waterfront and eliminated the choice recreational areas the commissioners who platted New York so admired in 1811. Moreover, increasing property values and a spiraling rate of demographic and economic growth resulted in staggering levels of congestion. The sheer mass of pedestrians, carts, and carriages strangled traffic on the rectangular street system, and demand for habitable space on lots one hundred feet deep produced that bastard child of the gridiron, the tenement house. New York's plan was obsolete before the built area of Manhattan extended even as far north as 42nd Street.[24]

During the antebellum years the city's merchants and civic leaders attempted to meet the challenge of urban growth through two of the most ambitious public works projects undertaken in nineteenth-century America. The Croton Aqueduct system (initial stages completed in 1842) provided a supply of pure water that enabled the thirsty city to continue its physical expansion, and Central Park (begun in 1857) offered carefully contrived scenes of rural beauty as the antithesis of the crowded, rectilinear urban environment. But however visionary these achievements, however genuine their contributions to the health of the city, neither the water supply nor the park changed the shape of the metropolis. Property values were too high and questions of equity too intractable to permit major alterations in the arrangement of streets. The gridiron remained inviolable and inflicted on future generations of New Yorkers what Frederick Law Olmsted judged the worst city plan ever invented.[25]

The gridiron became the norm in American city planning in the nineteenth century. As historians Richard C. Wade and John R. Stilgoe have pointed out, the rectangular street arrangement—whether New York's or Philadelphia's—became the national landscape and, especially when set against the backdrop of wilderness, symbolized rationalism and urban form. The gridiron promoted the frequent division of property and was admirably adapted to urban expansion. It was, in short, the most dramatic expression of the commercial forces that have shaped American urban development. But in its very predictability and inflexibility the gridiron too often sacrificed appropriate civic space and scale to the engine of commerce.[26]

The two most important American city plans undertaken at the turn of the nineteenth century differed radically, both in design and intent. Washington, D.C. was the product of a manifest hostility toward urban life, and especially of the fear of mobs. Designed to avoid the congestion and disorder of the commercial city, the plan of the nation's capital marked a turning away from traditional urban form. By contrast, New York, the epitome of the commercial metropolis, was shaped by the trenchant economic realities of the nineteenth century. Ironically, in neither city did its creators envision or

Changing Conceptions of Urban Form

make provision for the various types of land use and the differing social and economic needs of an urban population: Washington was an artificial city, totally divorced from the economic foundations of urban life; New York imposed on residential areas a street plan more appropriate to commercial districts. Both city plans were products of eighteenth-century rationalism; both were failures when measured by a different definition of urban form and culture that emerged in the middle of the nineteenth century.

As the pace of city growth accelerated, as the problems of urban congestion were aggravated by the inflexible gridiron, the case for a new urban landscape became compelling. Some cultural leaders began to learn anew the lessons of urban form. In 1811 the gridiron had been so widely accepted as the optimal street arrangement for a commercial city that the plan received only perfunctory treatment in the press—even though it had a dramatic impact on existing property lines. But as construction swept northward on Manhattan Island, destroying pastoral farms and densely wooded hills, the rationalism of the gridiron began to seem more and more irrational. Increasingly those spokesmen dissatisfied with the gridiron criticized it for depriving residents of daily contact with nature.

Thus, during the nineteenth century a nation without a tradition of metropolitan leadership attempted to refine and civilize its cities by creating more openly built urban environments. This conception of the new urban landscape combined commercial functions with the traditional New England ideal of community, the new culture of domesticity, and the belief that nature could soften the harsh demands of city life. The new city that its promoters envisioned would contain a compact business district as well as a series of discrete residential neighborhoods and spaces for civic monuments, for educational, social, and cultural institutions, and for public recreation. It would be a comprehensive city, at once thriving and humane, commercial and domestic. But as a concept the new urban landscape would have to overcome the traditional bias against cities, and therein lay its first great obstacle.

CHAPTER II

TOWARD A REDEFINITION
OF URBAN FORM AND CULTURE

So it happens that, though Mr. Greeley so frequently and eagerly exhorts the young men of the country to go to the West, the young man observes that Mr. Greeley himself stays in the city of New York; and he follows the example of his adviser and does not take his advice.
— EDWARD EVERETT HALE

The location of the nation's capital in Washington, D.C., and the subsequent placement of most state capitals not in their largest cities but in geographical centers had profound implications for American urban culture. By artificially separating seats of government from the country's metropolitan areas, the revolutionary generation enshrined as cultural norms the agrarian ideal and an accompanying philosophical distrust of cities. Moreover, the growth of urban areas in the first half of the nineteenth century in some ways confirmed the worst fears of Jefferson and his contemporaries. The density of building in the walking city bred high rates of crime and disease. With the introduction of urban transportation systems, the gridiron spread inexorably over the surrounding countryside, thereby depriving city residents of contact with nature. Similarly, the rise of the industrial city threatened to bring the worst aspects of the British factory system to American shores, and the presence of the urban mobs Jefferson had warned against in 1785 seemed to portend the failure of America's republican experiment.[1]

Given the conditions of life in the city during the antebellum era, it is not surprising that what historian Anselm Strauss has called a "dichotomy in American thought" between urban and rural values persisted as a central cultural fact during the nineteenth century. For succeeding generations the moral contrasts ascribed to country and city retained potent ideological implications. But this does not mean that nineteenth-century Americans were necessarily as anti-urban as they have sometimes been portrayed. In their influential book, *The Intellectual versus the City*, Morton and Lucia White trace what they consider a "powerful tradition of anti-urbanism in the history of American thought"– one that extends from Thomas Jefferson and his contemporaries to the modern architect Frank Lloyd Wright, who died only three years before the book's publication in 1962. The Whites argue that there is "no persistent or pervasive tradition of romantic attachment to the city" in American literature or philosophy. The authors speculate that this repudiation of urban culture "by figures who represent major tendencies in American thought" continues to affect attitudes toward the city in our own time.[2]

To be sure, the tradition the Whites describe was a prominent aspect of American culture throughout the nineteenth century. Not only the "nation's most celebrated thinkers" cast doubt on the desirability of cities; so too did countless lesser writers, popular orators, ministers, and celebrants of woman's sphere. Nevertheless, the Whites overargue their case by positing country and city in a kind of Manichaean dichotomy. As a result, their analysis leaves little room for an appreciation of the complex pattern of accommodation many Americans made to the realities of urban life, however distasteful or shocking they considered the city. Nor do the Whites account for the millions of people who, for various reasons, wrote with their feet rather than with pens by moving from farms or from abroad to the nation's cities. The dominant ideological strain may have been what historian Henry Nash Smith terms the "myth of the garden," a celebration of the superiority of agrarianism and the West over the urban East. But not everyone believed what they read in promotional tracts or dime novels. The image of the city frightened many nineteenth-century Americans, but it attracted and inspired many others.[3]

Indeed, careful analysis of the printed record and unpublished sources reveals the beginnings of a fundamental change in the way Americans perceived the city in the first half of the nineteenth century. Two developments help explain this change. One was a subtle restructuring of the agrarian ideology, a changing perception of nature that was an American expression of Romanticism. The other was the tenuous beginning of what Gunther Barth has identified as "modern city culture." Taken together, the refashioning of traditional agrarianism and the nascent appreciation of some aspects of city life led to a redefinition of urban form and culture and made possible the creation of the new urban landscape.[4]

In its clearest formulation – in the writings of such men as Jefferson and John Taylor of Caroline – the agrarian ideology was a program of social organization. Jefferson's affection for agriculture, for example, was predicated on the political belief that farmers possessed the independence that would guarantee the survival of the nation's republican institutions. Many nineteenth-century Americans similarly judged a rural way of life to be most compatible with republican virtue. Andrew Jackson Downing, writing in the 1840s and early 1850s for enlightened inhabitants of agricultural districts as well as city dwellers with a taste for country pleasures, described farming as the "bone and sinew" of the nation. Pointing out that agriculture produced annually more than twice as much wealth as all other occupations combined, he called cultivators of the soil the "great industrial class" of the New World. Like Jefferson, Downing hoped that the United States would remain predominantly agrarian.[5]

A host of other writers echoed traditional claims for the primacy of agriculture, as publishers across the United States issued a dazzling array of books, magazines, almanacs, and pamphlets devoted to the subject. For example, a contribution to Downing's monthly, *The Horticulturist*, described farming as the most essential of all occupations and as the criterion of civilization everywhere on earth—as did the youthful Frederick Law Olmsted, who advised his brother to abandon academic study and instead take up farming. Rural pursuits, he reasoned, "tend to elevate and enlarge the ideas" and offer the able practitioner the opportunity to cultivate "taste and sentiment" as well as crops. Farming was a way of life, the most virtuous way of life, not simply a means of earning a living. And its rewards transcended economic values: the "charms of rural life," asserted a correspondent to the *Christian Examiner*, "are among the purest and most lasting pleasures which gladden the human heart."[6]

By the second quarter of the nineteenth century, however, the traditional defense of agrarianism was full of rhetorical flourishes that bore little resemblance to the practice of farming. The agrarian stability Jefferson envisioned had been replaced by what James Fenimore Cooper termed a "spirit of unrest," which characterized most rural communities in the two decades preceding the Civil War. From North and South, owners of small farms and large plantations moved inexorably westward, attracted by the lodestone of fertile land and economic opportunity. Tocqueville observed:

> In the United States a man builds a house in which to spend his old age, and he sells it before the roof is on; he plants a garden and lets it just as the trees are coming into bearing; he brings a field into tillage and leaves other men to gather the crops; he embraces a profession and gives it up; he settles in a place, which he soon afterwards leaves to carry his changeable longings elsewhere.

Cooper, who after an extended absence in Europe returned during Jackson's presidency, was similarly distressed by American mobility and instability. His character Paul Powis lamented that a "disposition to change is getting to be universal in this country," a development he

Changing Conceptions of Urban Form

considered "one of the worst signs of the times." In *Home as Found*, Cooper's "commodore" of Lake Otsego described Templeton's farmers as "unlucky fishermen, always ready to shift ground." Downing also recognized with dismay the "great tendency towards constant change, and the restless spirit of emigration, which form part of our national character."[7]

The transition from subsistence to commercial agriculture contributed to this "spirit of unrest." Although farmers living near cities had long sold their produce to urban customers, two new developments dramatically expanded the opportunities for marketing crops. One was the accelerated growth of cities, which increased the demand for produce; the other was the transportation revolution, which enlarged the geographical area able to provide foodstuffs to the urban population. The transportation revolution added new concerns of price fluctuation and competition from distant regions to such traditional risks as weather and crop productivity. This evolution in the rural way of life sounded the death knell of the agrarian ideal, for what may once have been a stable, industrious enterprise was becoming a speculative venture. Perhaps more important, the rise of commercial farming directly affected attitudes toward nature. Historian Robert Gross's studies of Concord, Massachusetts, in the mid-nineteenth century demonstrate that Transcendentalism was at least in part a response to the rise of a market economy.[8]

The agrarian ideology celebrated the "charms of rural life," forgetting that the farmer's lot was hardly one of refinement and ease. Unfortunately, few writers escaped the bounds of a literary convention that extolled a pastoral existence: most champions of a rural way of life failed to see—or at least to describe—the loneliness, monotony, and drudgery of the farm. Yet the instability abhorred by Cooper and Downing, and the pathos of Thoreau's John Field, were at least as real as the perfunctory recitations of rural virtue. Sidney George Fisher, an urbane Philadelphia diarist with a keen taste for country pleasures, lamented that a "man of any education cannot live among farmers in this country. The moment you leave the neighborhood of a city," he asserted, "you are in the midst of barbarism, except in a very few spots in America."[9]

Few spokesmen would have gone so far as Fisher in describing farming as a new form of barbarism, but increasingly, during the first half of the nineteenth century, traditional agrarianism dissolved into nostalgia and an appreciation for natural scenery. As the landscape became more and more domesticated, artists and writers celebrated not the rigors of agriculture—which, after all, necessarily required alteration of the environment—but the beauties of "Dame Nature." The pages of literary magazines filled with "reveries" in the Hudson Highlands, and members of the eastern cultural elite began flocking to such popular resorts as Cozzens' Hotel and the Catskill Mountain House to partake of the scenery. Not only the elite enjoyed such pleasures. Hartford merchant John Olmsted took his son Frederick on "tours in search of the picturesque," and the son later recalled how deeply the perception of nature affected his father and shaped his own life:

> On a Sunday evening we were crossing the meadows alone. I was tired and he had taken me in his arms. I soon noticed that he was inattentive to my prattle and looking into his face saw in it something unusual. Following the direction of his eyes, I said: "Oh! there's a star." Then he said something of Infinite Love with a tone and manner which really moved me, chick that I was, so much that it has ever since remained in my heart.

Nature, then, became a source of inspiration, a place not for hard work but for contemplation, for tranquility and renewal.[10]

Thus by mid-century a subtle reworking of the agrarian ideology was evident: critics had begun to fault the city not only in Jefferson's political and social terms but also because it was not "the country." Urban growth was especially regrettable because it deprived residents of daily contact with nature. Predictably, these new critics reasoned that the absence of nature in cities was the source of poor health, poor morals, and insanity. Tocqueville, for example, was told that "madness is commoner" in America than elsewhere, while Swedish novelist Fredrika Bremer found that the bustle of New York produced in its inhabitants "restless, deeply-sunk eyes" and "excited, wearied features." The American Medical Association's Committee on Public Hygiene similarly concluded that conditions in cities resulted in the "destruction of human life," and some years later Frederick Law Olmsted attributed to cities a harmful impact on the "nerves and minds" of their residents.[11]

Many writers at mid-century invidiously compared the city with the country, a place they esteemed for its contributions to health and morality. The authors of *Village and Farm Cottages* enumerated advantages to health among the "peculiar and beneficial influences of rural life." Moreover, they claimed, in the country "moral influences are much better than those of the city, as the air is much more salubrious." A writer in the *Horticulturist* described a rural existence as especially desirable because it offered relief from the "din and turmoil of the city." In a series of designs for inexpensive cottages published in 1848, the architect Thomas Thomas, Jr., attempted to make it possible for laborers and their families to escape the tenements and the "unhealthy and immoral influences of city life."[12]

Keepers of the new agrarianism invariably portrayed rural life as the virtuous counterpoint to the city. Henry Ward Beecher, for exam-

Changing Conceptions of Urban Form

ple, praised the farm for training men to industry, self-reliance, morality, and enterprise and claimed that cities were "only saved from physical degeneracy, by large annual draughts from the rural population." Lewis F. Allen, the prolific writer on agricultural subjects, asserted that

> from the farm chiefly springs that energetic class of men, who replace the enervated and physically decaying multitude continually thrown off in the waste-weir of our great commercial and manufacturing cities and towns, whose population, without the infusion— and that continually—of the strong, substantial, and vigorous life blood of the country, would soon dwindle into insignificance and decrepitude.

Success in urban enterprise, however, was not enough. A writer in the *Atlantic Monthly* predicted that the nostalgic child of the farm would evoke "the vision of the old homestead, . . . a picture of rural life, so homey, yet so beautiful, that the heart will breathe a sigh upon it, and the voice will say, 'It were better so.' "[13]

But, of course, it would not be so. Folklore, literary convention, and Frederick Jackson Turner's frontier thesis notwithstanding, relatively few nineteenth-century Americans moved from cities to farms. Instead, the children of agricultural districts migrated to cities and there joined the immigrants, who were swelling the population of urban areas. The rate of urban growth was alarming. In 1790 there were only twenty-two towns with populations greater than twenty-five hundred (the criterion then used by the census bureau to define an urban area), and only three cities exceeding twenty-five thousand. By 1830 three cities had surpassed fifty thousand, and New York housed more than one hundred thousand residents. Worse, the pace of growth was accelerating: Stuart Blumin and Allan Pred have pointed out that the years from 1820 to 1860 marked the greatest decennial rates of increase in the urban population in American history.[14]

Even more ominous was the rise of the industrial city. The first large-scale manufacturing establishments had been located on rural sites and had relied upon a transient female labor force. By the 1840s, however, these towns were becoming cities. Soon after its founding, the industrial complex at Lowell, Massachusetts, had been praised as a beacon of republican prosperity, yet within twenty years it had grown from a sleepy New England village into the fourteenth largest city in the United States. Unsurprisingly, in Lowell many of Jefferson's worst fears were realized: an increasing visibility of poverty, the emergence of a landless, propertyless working class, and the growth of slums and urban diseases.[15]

The sheer numbers of newcomers to the cities taxed the ability of municipal governments and philanthropic organizations to meet the increased demand for services. Population growth so outstripped the construction of new residential units that many New Yorkers lived in boarding houses or in very undesirable conditions in the crowded older neighborhoods. The density of building, the invention of the tenement house, and the proliferation of saloons and brothels resulted in what historian Kenneth T. Jackson has called an "increase in urban nuisances" and a decline in the quality of life. The problems of the city were real, not rhetorical, and nothing better symbolized them than street congestion or the poverty and squalor of New York's most notorious slum, the Five Points area.[16]

Nevertheless, the flourishing of urban cultural institutions in the decades preceding the Civil War enhanced the attractiveness of cities. Boston's Athenaeum, the Free Gallery of the Art Union of Philadelphia, and New York's American Art-Union, Dusseldorf Gallery, and National Academy of Design displayed contemporary painting and sculpture. Moses Kimball's Boston Museum and P. T. Barnum's American Museum appealed to people more interested in exotic curiosities; they also helped socialize newcomers to an urban way of life. The performing arts were thriving: playwright William K. Northall wondered in 1851 "if there be a city in the world of the same size and population which can exhibit a theatrical prosperity equal to New York." Impresarios established opera houses and academies of music, and Jenny Lind and other European artists sang to packed audiences throughout the country. Libraries, lyceums, and fraternal organizations enriched the intellectual and social life of cities and towns. These cultural institutions—vehicles for the realization of what Downing termed "popular refinement"—achieved their greatest measure of success in urban areas.[17]

Although much of the popular literature continued to depict the horrors of the "evil city," during the 1840s and 1850s an increasing number of religious, literary, and artistic leaders realized that the growth of urban areas was not an unmitigated evil. The Reverend Edwin Hubbell Chapin addressed the competing claims of country and city in a series of sermons published in 1853 under the title *Moral Aspects of City Life*. In this he paid due fealty to the virtues of a rural existence and admitted that the city "encloses all forms of corruption," that its "splendor is overlapped by poverty and crime." Chapin nevertheless located in cities the "symbols of civilization—the measures of human progress." Among the benefits associated with urban areas he enumerated "the departments of culture—the schools and lyceums" and "achievements in the worlds of matter and mind." Throughout his sermons Chapin praised the city's complexity, its diverse, anthropomorphic manifestations, as the closest physical approximation of human nature. In short, he wrote, "the interest of the city is as superior to that of the country, as humanity is to nature; as the soul is to the theatre in which it is enacted." There is a "moral significance" to urban life, Chapin concluded, because "that which is strongest and noblest in our nature is illustrated in the city."[18]

Other spokesmen joined Chapin in celebrating the cultural potential of urban areas. Philadelphia librarian and antiquarian John Jay Smith found cities to be "great storehouses of Art and Knowledge," while attorney Frederick W. Sawyer described cities as "leaders in almost every thing that has been done for the amelioration and improvement of the condition of man." A writer in *Putnam's Monthly* went so far as to equate the development of them with the "history of the civilized world." At a time when a majority of his contemporaries were appalled by urban growth, this writer intrepidly claimed that the "world's progress in civilization, in art, in knowledge of 'things human and divine,' [had] been mainly caused and promoted by and through the agency of great cities."[19]

Still, most Americans at mid-century found the prospect of an urban nation troubling. The increasing importance of the city as an economic and cultural institution, however, attracted even people with strong attachments to the farm. Historian R. Richard Wohl has demonstrated the duality of the "country boy" myth in nineteenth-century literature to be a portrayal of the city as a corrupting Babylon and, somewhat incongruously, an arena in which rural virtue gained entrepreneurial success. This tenuous juxtaposition, a lurid depiction of immorality in the city and the triumph of the old agrarian order over the new, suggests the degree to which urban imagery plagued the keepers of the Jeffersonian conscience. Dreaded though the perils of the city might be, not even the experience of "Arthur in Babylon," a tale of virtue corrupted, could stem the growth of the urban population.[20]

The migration of millions of Arthurs from farms and from abroad in the 1840s and 1850s created obvious problems, many of them intractable, but it also created unprecedented economic and cultural opportunities. Even in its new formulation the agrarian ideology remained formidable, but the growth of urban cultural institutions had made the amenities of city life tempting indeed. Thus in the two decades preceding the Civil War the intellectual and cultural response to cities and their place in "Nature's Nation" became increasingly complex. Instead of an outright rejection of cities, as the Whites maintain, a pattern of ambivalence, characterized by grudging acceptance and accommodation, emerged in American thought.

Ralph Waldo Emerson personifies this new duality in attitudes toward country and city. Much of his published writing predicted that rural life would have a powerfully "sanative" influence and would encourage the development of new virtues among the American people. In his 1844 essay "The Young American," which heralded the compatibility of Transcendentalism and technology, Emerson exclaimed: "Whatever events in progress shall go to disgust men with cities and infuse into them the passion for country life and country pleasures, will render a service to the whole face of this continent." Because he believed that land was physic and food for mental and physical growth, Emerson considered the farm an asylum for those who failed in urban society.[21]

Despite this almost ritualistic paean to the new agrarianism, Emerson betrayed his ambivalence toward the pastoral idyll and the attractions of urban life in his *Journal*: "I wish to have rural strength and religion for my children, and I wish city facility and polish." For Emerson, the railroad, the master symbol of rapid urbanization, held out the possibility of the best of both worlds, providing opportunities for Americans to become acquainted with the boundless resources of the continent, and to build rural gardens and homes while maintaining frequent intercourse with the city. According to historian Michael Cowan, Emerson thus emerges as "one of the chief proponents of reconciliation" between the romantic hostility toward the urban experience and the growth of cities.[22]

Edward Everett Hale likewise considered the competing claims of country and city. Admitting that "our intellectual and moral faculties are urged to the highest point of culture by the intense competition of large towns," and acknowledging the "elegant refinements, the liberal institutions, the noble charities, [and] the creative, industrious, the world-encompassing energy, of the cities," he nevertheless believed that the "contagion of vice and crime produce[d] in a crowded population a depravity of character." But despite his belief that the "want of centralization" in America produced a more virtuous people, Hale spent almost his entire adult life in Boston. His fealty to the agrarian ideal notwithstanding, Hale would not move away from the large cities that made him "tremble for the future."[23]

The landscape painter Thomas Cole professed a romantic preference for the country over the city, but he too revealed an ambivalence. His 1836 "Essay on American Scenery" praised "*rural nature*" as an "exhaustless mine" of poetic and painterly inspiration, "an unfailing fountain of intellectual enjoyment where all may drink & be awakened to a deeper feeling of the works of genius & a deeper perception of the beauty of our existence." Cole spent the greater part of each year at his country house in Catskill, New York, and from there made frequent sketching trips to the nearby mountains as well as more extended tours "in search of the picturesque." He represented the annual prospect of returning to New York for the winter season as wearisome, professing to be happiest in the country and perceiving the city with a "presentiment something like of evil." To friend and fel-

Changing Conceptions of Urban Form

low painter Asher B. Durand, Cole prescribed an existence similar to his own: "You must come & live in the country," he advised, as "Nature is a sovereign remedy," and "in the country we labour under more healthy influences" than in the city.[24]

Cole's series of allegorical paintings, *The Course of Empire* (completed 1836), served as a vehicle for expressing his attitudes toward country and city. On five canvasses he portrayed the progress of civilization from a savage to a pastoral state, then to an urban one, and finally, destruction and reversion to the primitive. The pastoral state (fig. 3), embodying the balance of man and nature, was obviously the best; man and nature in their unbalanced, urban state (fig. 4) was the worst. Cole's cyclical interpretation of the progress of civilization expresses a variation of the agrarian ideology, with destruction seen as the price exacted of an urban society that dominates nature.[25]

And yet, despite his ritualistic proclaiming of what his first biographer, Louis L. Noble, calls a "love of rural life" and a "natural aversion to the city," Cole's correspondence with Durand suggests a different reality. During the summer of 1836 he addressed more than a dozen letters to his fellow painter, pleading for the favor of a visit. Here one glimpses another side of the rural ideal, the loneliness of the country and the positive attractions of urban life and society. Although he described himself as a fine example of the *"effects of country air,"* in encouraging Durand to foresake the city Cole admitted, "if you would pitch your tent near me I should also be benefitted." Praising country life even while longing for city news and city friends, Cole, like so many other nineteenth-century Americans, was trapped by the stereotyped definitions of country and city.[26]

The early career of *litterateur* and social dandy Nathaniel Parker Willis offers still another illustration of the degree to which the reformulated agrarian ideology captivated nineteenth-century Americans. In the early 1840s Willis retired to a secluded glen in the Susquehanna Valley, where he hoped to spend the rest of his days. From this "altar of life-long tranquility" he wrote devastating critiques of the city and lauded the virtues of rural life. "What surprises me most in the past," he declared, "is, that I should ever have confined my free soul and body, in the very many narrow places and usages I have known in towns." In *Letters from Under a Bridge* Willis parried the questions of friends who asked how long he would be "contented in the country." *"Comment, diable!"* he replied, and asked instead how they could be "contented in a town." But, like Cole, Willis soon tired of his self-imposed seclusion and urged literary friends to take nearby farms on the Susquehanna, to "cluster about this—certainly one of the loveliest spots in nature." Without society the attractions of his pastoral idyll soon diminished, and Willis reported that "inevitable necessity drove him again into active metropolitan life."[27]

From the "Editor's Easy Chair" at *Harper's New Monthly Magazine*

Figure 3. *The Course of Empire: The Arcadian or Pastoral*, by Thomas Cole, 1836. (Courtesy, The New-York Historical Society, New York City.)

Figure 4. *The Course of Empire: The Consummation of Empire*, by Thomas Cole, 1836. (Courtesy, The New-York Historical Society, New York City.)

George William Curtis astutely assessed the ambivalent relationship of country and city in American thought: "The poets and other people who have been so enthusiastic about the country have lived in the city," he asserted, "and wrote their eulogies within brick walls." To Curtis it was obvious that the great triumphs of civilization were achieved in cities, that a more accurate portrayal of rural life would emphasize the "silence, the seclusion, the drudging toil, the long monotony of the year, [and] the mental idleness" of the farm. The poetic descriptions of agriculture and of rural pursuits, he concluded, hardly appealed to the plowboy or the milkmaid.[28]

Nathaniel Hawthorne also illustrated the rather somber reality of the agrarian existence. The "peril of our new way of life," he wrote of Brook Farm in *The Blithedale Romance*, "was not lest we should fail in becoming practical agriculturists, but that we should probably cease to be anything else." Rigorous labor "left us mentally sluggish in the evening," and the great minds of the associational enterprise "were fast becoming cloddish." Predictably, when the protagonist, Miles Coverdale, returned to Boston he placed city and country in a new perspective. "Whatever had been my taste for solitude and natural scenery," he exclaimed, "yet the thick, foggy, stifled elements of cities, the entangled life of so many men together, sordid as it was, and empty of the beautiful, took quite a strenuous hold upon my mind. I felt as if there could never be enough of it." What Coverdale learned at Blithedale was that the realities of agricultural labor were rather different from the rural pleasures described in pastoral idylls, and afterward he found city life much more attractive. Thus, while observing the various activities of the hotel lobby, Coverdale concluded: "All this was just as valuable, in its way, as the sighing of the breeze among the birch-trees that overshadowed Eliot's Pulpit."[29]

Curtis and Hawthorne were correct in asserting that the awareness of the natural environment celebrated in the painting and literature of the mid-nineteenth century was an urban phenomenon, one that differed markedly from traditional agrarianism. It was an expression, in historian Perry Miller's words, of "a fundamental opposition of Nature to civilization." Taken together, however, the new attitude toward nature and the appreciation of urban cultural institutions held out the possibility of uniting the best aspects of each. After all, what was wrong with the city was that it was not "the country." As a conception, the new urban landscape sought to remedy that failing by bringing into the city large expanses of rural beauty. It was a crusade to create a new urban form, one that introduced nature as a means of countering the overcivilization of the city.[30]

But not just any landscape would be appropriate. By mid-century the term *country* conveyed a specific set of scenic values associated with a pastoral or domesticated landscape. Unitarian minister Henry

W. Bellows explained that this celebration of nature was an urban expression of nostalgia for the country. Because of the task of subjugating the wilderness, he pointed out, backwoods farmers hated trees. City dwellers, on the other hand, trapped by the relentless gridiron and surrounded by walls of brick and brownstone, sought to preserve or create within their midst the antithesis of urban conditions, the country. Thus developed a great but understandable irony of the nineteenth century. Settlers on the frontier employed the rectangular street plan to convey at least the appearance of urban civilization, while residents of cities on the eastern seaboard attempted, through the creation of public parks and suburbs, to restore aspects of the countryside.[31]

The new urban landscape was a creative synthesis of the divergent values associated with country and city in nineteenth-century American culture. In the absence of a tradition of metropolitan leadership, this simultaneous redefinition of agrarianism and urban culture was the source of the most original developments in city form in the antebellum years. Many urban reformers felt, as Henry P. Tappan claimed, that "life in a great city is, at best, a war with nature"; their creative energies attempted to shape vicarious or actual escapes from the urban environment. To mitigate, or perhaps to camouflage and thereby make more tolerable, a necessary evil, landscape architects designed parks that would "combine the rural with the artificial in cities." Olmsted, one of the designers of New York's Central Park, believed that an urban public park should "resemble a charming bit of rural landscape, such as, unless improved by art, is never found within the limits of a large town." The park was consciously designed and created to be the country within the city.[32]

For those who, like Emerson and Willis, wanted to enjoy both the pleasures of the country and the attractions of urban society, or for those who wanted a rural upbringing for their children but found it necessary to work in the city, real estate promoters developed communal spaces for homes on the urban periphery, connected to the city by railroad, steamboat, omnibus, or ferry. As early as 1823, Hezekiah Pierrepont advertised lots on Brooklyn Heights as desirable places of residence for New York's workers because the site combined "all the advantages of the country with most of the conveniences of the city." Twenty-five years later Downing could write: "Hundreds of thousands, formerly obliged to live in the crowded streets of cities, now find themselves able to enjoy a country cottage several miles distant,—the old notions of time and space being half annihilated." Thus nineteenth-century Americans attempted to resolve the competing claims of country and city by creating a new urban landscape, by bringing into or near the metropolis the physical aspects of the country. After all, George William Curtis noted, "the pleasantest life is the union of the two."[33]

CHAPTER III

THE DIDACTIC LANDSCAPE: RURAL CEMETERIES

... the first really elegant public gardens or promenades formed in this country...
— ANDREW JACKSON DOWNING

The first physical expression of the evolving definition of urban form and culture in antebellum America was the development of rural cemeteries. These were usually created by nonprofit stock companies and were the first large spaces near cities laid out in the "natural" or "picturesque" style of landscape gardening that were open for public visitation. Although at first the justification for rural rather than urban cemeteries was concern for public health and the inadequacy of downtown space for burial, these cemeteries became rural retreats frequented by city residents in search of contemplative recreation, didactic landscapes whose scenery and monuments instructed visitors in morality and respect for the dead. Their popularity thus marked the confluence of two important ideas: the new attitude toward domesticated nature emerging in landscape painting, literature, and the debate over urban form; and the need for publicly constructed and maintained parks to bring country into the city.

The idea of burying the dead outside city limits had roots in antiquity, of course; the Romans had carefully separated the worlds of the living and the dead. The law of the Twelve Tables forbade interment in cities, and great heroes were buried in honored places along the Appian Way or in other suitable rural locations. But for centuries in the Western world Christians had buried their dead *ad sanctos,* in consecrated grounds adjacent to churches. Because churches were the focus of community life, most cemeteries were located in cities and towns. The medieval dead coexisted with the living, and the cemetery was a public place. In addition to its use as a facility for interment, the cemetery served as an "asylum" for meeting friends, for dancing, for gambling, and for various events. Only in the late Middle Ages did the Church forbid such profane activities, and at least until the late eighteenth century the churchyard cemetery remained a neighborhood institution.[1]

Several factors contributed to the abandonment of urban interment. One, certainly, was a changing conception of death. Throughout Western history most corpses had been buried in large common graves, and, as these became crowded, remains were disinterred in order to make room for the more recently departed. Near the end of the eighteenth century, a new concern for the dead, which French historian Philippe Ariès ascribes to "the survivors' unwillingness to accept the departure of their loved ones," led to criticism of the Church's burial practices and a desire for individual and permanent grave sites. The accumulation of the dead in churchyards had become intolerable, both because of this newfound piety toward the departed and for considerations of public health. In 1765 the Parliament of Paris issued a decree closing all urban cemeteries and ordering the transfer of corpses to new burial grounds outside the city.[2]

The closing of some churchyards resulted simply in the transfer of bodies to other urban cemeteries, which then became overcrowded. In the first decade of the nineteenth century, however, Parisians established four municipal cemeteries in the city's outskirts, Montmartre, De Vaugirard, Mont Parnasse, and Père la Chaise. According to Ariès, "eighteenth-century authors of cemetery plans wanted cemeteries to serve both as parks organized for family visits and as museums for illustrious persons." Père la Chaise, the most famous of the four, became a popular resort for Parisians and an obligatory tourist stop for foreigners. Originally the private pleasure grounds of the Jesuit priest Francois d'Aix de la Chaise, the estate was purchased in 1804 by the Prefect of the Seine for use as a public cemetery. One American visitor described Père la Chaise as "the most attractive spot in France," and another noted, "Parisians are accustomed to visit these silent abodes of the dead on Sunday, as a promenade."[3]

Although Père la Chaise eventually would serve as a model for America's rural cemeteries, churchyard interment continued to be the custom in the United States until the 1830s. As in France, this was largely the result of tradition. People who buried members of their family in a churchyard did so anticipating that they would someday lie next to them. Moreover, removing the dead from daily contact with the living implied a want of respect for the departed and might leave the remains, unprotected in a rural environment, subject to violation. No doubt, as existing burial grounds filled up and fell into disrepair this tradition became less compelling; but for some it must have represented a formidable psychological barrier to the creation of rural cemeteries.

In order to overcome the inertia of tradition, advocates of rural cemeteries pointed out that most urban burial grounds were over-crowded and poorly maintained. When Congregational theologian Timothy Dwight visited the Connecticut town of Guilford in 1800, he criticized the shameful neglect of the dead. There he found the center square "deformed by a burying ground," unenclosed by fence and thus trampled by man and beast. The sad state of the cemetery, he concluded, indicated "so little respect in the living as to eradicate every emotion naturally excited by the remembrance of the deceased." John Jay Smith reported that Philadelphia's old Friends Grave Yard had become so crowded that he "found it impossible to designate the final resting place of a darling daughter," while Joseph Story asserted that most cemeteries were "crowded on all sides by the overhanging habitations of the living" and were enclosed by fences "only to pre-serve them from violation." Cemeteries had become places of gloom, "objects of disgust and terror" that exacerbated the normal grief associated with death. "Why," asked Washington Irving, "should we thus seek to clothe death with unnecessary terrors, and to spread horrors around the tombs of those we love?" Instead, he reasoned, graves "should be surrounded by every thing that might inspire tenderness and veneration for the dead, or that might win the living to virtue."[4]

Moreover, by the 1830s the growth of American cities had made economically desirable land that formerly had been set aside for cemeteries, so bodies were exhumed and moved to less advantageous locations. "Philadelphia has been increasing so rapidly of late years," Smith wrote in 1835, "that the living population has multiplied be-yond the means of accommodation for the dead." He witnessed the desecration of the German Reformed graveyard, when "bodies were dug up in a brutal manner & removed." A crowd of enraged by-standers acted to "prevent the bodies from being thrown into a trench" and broke the laborers' tools. According to Smith, this har-rowing scene led some Philadelphians to feel that as ground became "more and more valuable" they would see "many such acts perpe-trated." New York's potters' field was filled and converted into Wash-ington Square, and the old burying ground near Philadelphia's Franklin Square was covered over and made into a promenade. In the 1850s Frederick Law Olmsted reported that the value of real estate in New York City had created a "pertinacious demand for a division of Trinity churchyard"; Herman Melville's fictional Church of the Apos-tles Cemetery "was invaded for a supplemental edifice"; and the Daily Tribune described the vacating of the Twenty-fifth Street burial ground as "another instance of the insecure resting place of the dead within the City limits." Recognizing the impact of urban growth, proprietors of rural cemeteries located them at what they deemed a safe distance from cities, and added in their charters of incorporation statutory provisions guaranteeing the permanence of burial.[5]

Another persuasive argument for removing cemeteries from cities was the belief that gases emanating from graves threatened public health. At Guilford, Timothy Dwight surmised that the "proximity of these sepulchral fields to human habitations is injurious to health." This theory was resurrected in the aftermath of the outbreak of yellow fever in 1822, when several prominent physicians pointed to urban graves as causing or contributing to the devastating epidemic. According to Dr. Francis D. Allen, for example, the "putrid exhalations arising from grave-yards, will not only feed and strengthen yellow fever when once introduced, but will generate disease equally malignant as yellow fever, and possessing at least some of its characteristics." Allen also reported that in October of 1822 a Doctor Roosa, alarmed at the threat to public health posed by the noxious gases escaping from graves, attempted to prevent such emanations by covering New York's Trinity Churchyard with fifty-two casks of quicklime. During this operation, Roosa noted, "the stench arising from thence was so excessive as to cause several of my laborers to *cascade* [vomit] freely." The following year Dr. Jacob Bigelow published a pamphlet outlining the dangers of contemporary burial practices, and in 1824 a committee of the New York City board of health translated and published Scipione Piatolli's *Essay on the Danger of Interment in Cities.* Although today it is easy to ridicule the belief that poisonous gases, or miasmas, were agents in spreading disease, many members of this generation believed that trees would "absorb deleterious gases," and they justifed the removal of cemeteries to landscaped areas away from cities as a means of protecting public health.[6]

The new attitude toward nature also contributed to the creation of rural cemeteries. It was a cardinal tenet of Romanticism that natural scenery had a positive impact on the mind. This belief was perhaps most cogently stated by Johann Georg von Zimmermann, an eighteenth-century Swiss physician and author. When separated from his family and suffering a deep melancholy, he found relief only by taking walks in a garden laid out in the English (or naturalistic) manner. Zimmermann concluded that scenes of serenity "always convey tranquility to the heart" and advised his readers to seek solitude in nature, where they could "forget all the pains and troubles of a wounded heart."[7]

Zimmermann's ideas found a receptive audience among certain types of readers in the United States. At least seven English-language editions of his book, *Solitude Considered,* were published between 1796 and 1840, several of them in America. The young Frederick Law Olmsted read it as early as 1831 and reread it, no doubt with greater understanding, in 1845. Charles Beveridge has recently pointed out that Zimmermann's ideas formed one of the cornerstones of Olmsted's theory of landscape design. *Solitude Considered* also struck a resonant chord with some of the Transcendentalists, who likewise deemed nature the most beneficial environment. In *Walden,* Henry David Thoreau echoed Zimmermann's sentiments: "There can be no very black melancholy," he wrote, "to him who lives in the midst of Nature and has his senses still." This belief, that landscape scenery assuaged grief and elevated the emotions, would become a regular theme among writers describing the influence of rural cemeteries. For example, in his compilation of essays and poems about Cambridge's Mount Auburn, naturalist Wilson Flagg included a chapter from *Solitude Considered* and quoted Zimmermann's passage: "Who has not in the moment of convalescence, in the hour of melancholy, or when separation or death has deprived one of the intercourse of friends, sought relief in the salutary shades of the country."[8]

The quality of the landscape was important as well: historian Stanley French has argued that Grove Street Cemetery (1796), located beyond what were then the corporate limits of New Haven, was really the first rural cemetery. But while Grove Street guaranteed the perpetual occupancy of the dead, and while its distance from the built area of the city minimized the danger that "miasmas" from graves might affect nearby residents, its six-acre plot was laid out in a compact gridiron. Obviously, scenic qualities proved more important than location, public health, or permanence, for Grove Street inspired no imitators. Only when cemeteries cast aside their urban heritage, when they abandoned traditional urban form and took on aspects of the country, did they indeed become "rural."[9]

Recognition of these factors—the disrepair of existing churchyards, the belief that urban cemeteries endangered public health, the insatiable demand for city land that often resulted in the desecration of older cemeteries, and acknowledgment of the psychological impact of scenery—led to the decision to remove cemeteries from their traditional urban context and to relocate them in the country. But apprehensions over changing the mode and location of burial were formidable. Jacob Bigelow, an organizer of Mount Auburn Cemetery, acknowledged the strong popular attachment to the "inveterate custom" of churchyard interment. Establishment of the rural cemetery was difficult, he later recalled, because "the subject was new, the public were lukewarm, and, in many cases, the prejudices and apprehensions of the community were strongly opposed to the removal of the dead from the populous cities and villages to the solitude of a distant wood." John Jay Smith, a promoter of Laurel Hill Cemetery in Philadelphia, had "to contend with some prejudice & with the feelings of those interested in the sale of Church grounds."[10]

Nevertheless, cities were growing and changing, and despite this resistance some cultural leaders chose to naturalize what had been one of the most urban of land uses. Boston became the first American city to overcome the tradition of churchyard burial by appealing to the new attitude toward nature. In 1831 its citizens established a rural cemetery, Mount Auburn, in neighboring Cambridge. The history of Mount Auburn begins with the redoubtable Jacob Bigelow. Best remembered as Rumford Professor of Medicine at Harvard, where he battled such contemporary "healing" practices as bloodletting and the prescription of heroic doses of purgatives, Bigelow was also a noted botanist and author of *Florula Bostoniensis* (1814), which remained for years the standard manual of New England botany. His concerns as a physician and civic leader naturally extended to matters of public health, and especially to preventing the transmission of disease. After the yellow fever epidemic of 1822, for example, he published *Remarks on the Dangers and Duties of Sepulture; Or, Security for the Living with Respect for the Dead* (1823). Bigelow's career thus embraced the two purposes eventually united in the Mount Auburn scheme – the rural cemetery as a means of protecting public health and as the location of an experimental botanical garden. [11]

In 1825 Bigelow invited several friends to his Cambridge home "to consider the expediency of instituting an extra-urban ornamental cemetery in the neighborhood of Boston." At this meeting Bigelow submitted his plan for a cemetery "composed of family burial plots, separated and interspersed with trees, shrubs, and flowers, in a wood or landscape garden." Although the men attending the meeting expressed approval of this goal, and even appointed a committee to select a suitable location, this apparently led only to further discussion and delay. Fulfillment of Bigelow's plan had to await the formation of the Massachusetts Horticultural Society in 1829. Several leaders of this new organization readily comprehended the importance of Bigelow's proposed rural cemetery, and the physician realized that he could best overcome objections to rural burial with the "co-operation of a young, active, and popular society." At the society's second annual festival, Zebedee Cook, Jr., noted that the "improvement and embellishment of grounds devoted to public uses, is deserving of especial consideration." More specifically, he suggested that the society undertake the "establishment of a public cemetery, similar in its design to that of Père la Chaise in the environs of Paris, to be located in the suburbs" of Boston. [12]

The Massachusetts Horticultural Society adopted the idea of a rural cemetery and agreed to unite it with an experimental garden, thereby adding the purpose of education to the original goals of the cemetery's promoters. In combining garden and cemetery, members hoped that the "whole would ultimately offer such an example of landscape gardening as would be creditable to the Society, and assist

Changing Conceptions of Urban Form

in improving the taste of the public in this highest branch of horticulture." Bigelow, meanwhile, negotiated with George Brimmer, who agreed to sell to the society for use as a cemetery and garden the tract of land known as Sweet Auburn, a seventy-two-acre site overlooking the Charles River four miles from Boston. The horticultural society then received from the Massachusetts General Court an amendment to its original charter of incorporation, granting permission to establish a cemetery and guaranteeing the "perpetual occupancy of the dead." By August of 1831 the society had raised enough money through the sale of subscriptions for lots to complete the purchase of the property. Henry A. S. Dearborn, president of the horticultural society and a member of its garden and cemetery committee, then engaged civil engineer Alexander Wadsworth to prepare a topographical survey of the site, renamed Mount Auburn. With great ceremony, punctuated by an address by Joseph Story, Bostonians consecrated Mount Auburn Cemetery on September 24, 1831.[13]

Mount Auburn was a felicitous choice for the cemetery and garden. Even before its purchase by the horticultural society the site was noted for its "beautiful and romantic scenery." In his consecration address Justice Story praised the "vigorous growth of forest trees" and described the tract of land as "beautifully undulating in its surface, containing a number of bold eminences, steep declivities, and shadowy valleys." To this appealing landscape Dearborn and Wadsworth added the improvements of art. Drawing upon the tenets of eighteenth-century aesthetic theory, they avoided straight lines and placed the avenues and paths to conform to the area's natural topography (fig. 5). The arrangement provided easy access to all lots, limited the cost of preparing the land for use, and achieved, in Story's estimation, "the picturesque effect of landscape gardening." Along the walks the designers placed grave plots averaging some three hundred feet in area. Bigelow enhanced the sylvan appeal of Mount Auburn by naming the paths and avenues after well-known trees and plants. He then designed an Egyptian-style gateway, based upon examples at Denderah and Karnac, which bore the inscription "The Dead Shall Be Risen." The overall effect of Mount Auburn conveyed what Olmsted considered the cardinal precept of cemetery design, "the respect paid by the community of the living to the community of the dead."[14]

In 1831, as work on the cemetery continued, Dearborn directed part of his energies to the creation of the adjoining experimental botanical garden. This was an area of thirty-two acres, adjacent to the cemetery but separated from it by a long watercourse. In addition to the requisite nurseries, gardens, floral beds, and greenhouses, Dearborn proposed converting the ponds into "picturesque sheets of water" and planting "clumps and belts" around their borders. The ex-

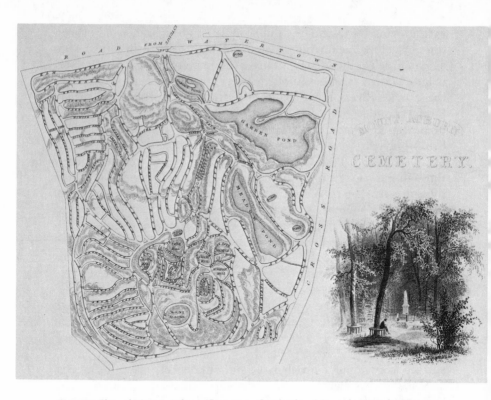

Figure 5. Plan of Mount Auburn Cemetery, Cambridge, Massachusetts, by Henry A. S. Dearborn and Alexander Wadsworth, 1831. Engraving by James Smillie, 1854. (Courtesy, Prints and Photographs Division, Library of Congress, Washington, D.C.)

perimental garden existed until 1835, when the horticultural society and cemetery became separate corporations and it was annexed to the cemetery.[15]

From its inception Mount Auburn Cemetery was a resounding success aesthetically, financially, and as a cultural institution. Two thousand people attended the consecration ceremony, and soon after its opening the cemetery attracted so many visitors that the roads to Mount Auburn were "lined with coaches." So great was this stream of visitors that the horticultural society felt compelled to regulate access to the cemetery. Although all pedestrians continued to be admitted freely, no person on horseback could enter the grounds, nor any coaches save those of lot proprietors. Sunday crowds became so large that only proprietors and their families and guests were admitted on that day. Because of its popularity, Downing called Mount Auburn the "Athens of New-England," a site favored by pilgrims from other cities. The cemetery's beauty also inspired hundreds of poems, descriptive essays, illustrated guides, and large, handsome giftbooks.[16]

Perhaps most important, Mount Auburn's success encouraged

leaders in other cities to create their own rural cemeteries. "No sooner was attention generally roused to the charms of this first American cemetery," Downing noted, "than the idea took the public mind by storm." Thus, in a conscious attempt to apply the lessons of Mount Auburn, Philadelphian John Jay Smith proposed the formation of Laurel Hill Cemetery in 1835. At his urging, a group of friends incorporated as a cemetery company (to prevent the grounds "from ever being cut up by streets or roads") and in 1836 purchased Joseph Sims's thirty-two-acre estate, Laurel Hill, located on the eastern bank of the Schuylkill River a short distance from the city. Like that of Mount Auburn, the site was renowned for its natural beauty. The proprietors of Laurel Hill chose to determine the cemetery's design by a public competition, which John Notman won over fellow architects William Strickland and Thomas U. Walter. Notman's plan (fig. 6) follows the precepts of landscape gardening in the natural style, though its central feature is a stylized circular drive with interior spaces divided into sections by intersecting paths. The most striking combination of scenery and art was the terrace, "shaped like an amphitheatre" on the slope adjacent to the Schuylkill, which was used as the site of large tombs and mausoleums. Smith, an amateur horticulturist who visited Laurel Hill daily, assumed responsibility for specific details of planting, and he attempted to create an arboretumlike effect by including examples of all the trees and shrubs that would flourish in the middle Atlantic states. Comparing Laurel Hill with Mount Auburn, Smith concluded that "both are calculated to strike the imagination & make it in love with *nature*."[17]

At Laurel Hill, Smith attempted to unite the works of man and of nature, to create a *"tout ensemble"* of scenery, landscape design, architecture, and sculpture. His success is recorded in the reactions of contemporary visitors. Philadelphia diarist Sidney George Fisher often drove through the cemetery "to enjoy the beautiful view." In 1838 he predicted, "When the improvements are completed, there will be few prettier places." Essayist N. P. Willis judged Laurel Hill the most attractive cemetery in America; and R. A. Smith, author of a popular guidebook to the cemetery, sugested that in "rural beauty, and picturesque appearance, it is perhaps unrivalled by any similar place of the same extent in the world." Downing found the cemetery to be a *"charming pleasure-ground"* and reported that almost thirty thousand people visited Laurel Hill between April and December of 1848.[18]

With the establishment of Green-Wood Cemetery (fig. 7) in Brooklyn, New Yorkers completed the grand triumverate of America's first and most influential rural cemeteries. In 1838 the state legislature granted to the cemetery company a charter of incorporation, and real estate promoters David B. Douglas and Henry E. Pierrepont recom-

Figure 6.
Plan of Laurel Hill Cemetery, Philadelphia,
Pennsylvania, by John Notman, 1836.
Lithograph by E. J. Pinkerton for the *Guide
to Laurel Hill Cemetery* (Philadelphia, 1844).
(Courtesy, Collections of The Athenaeum of
Philadelphia.)

mended the purchase of a two-hundred-acre site in Brooklyn.
Located on Gowanus Heights, overlooking New York harbor and the
two cities standing on opposite banks of the East River, Green-Wood
possessed a view more spectacular than either of its two predecessors. Douglas laid out the paths and roads and planted trees and
shrubs in a "broad and simple style" that Downing praised as "grand,
dignified, and park-like." Green-Wood surpassed Mount Auburn, he
believed, not only in size but "in the diversity of surface, and especially in the grandeur of the views." Fredrika Bremer described the
cemetery as "a young Père la Chaise, but on a more gigantic scale as
to situation and plan. One drives as if in an extensive English park,
amid hill and dale." The proprietors of Green-Wood added one innovation to cemetery administration by permitting the purchase of large

Changing Conceptions of Urban Form

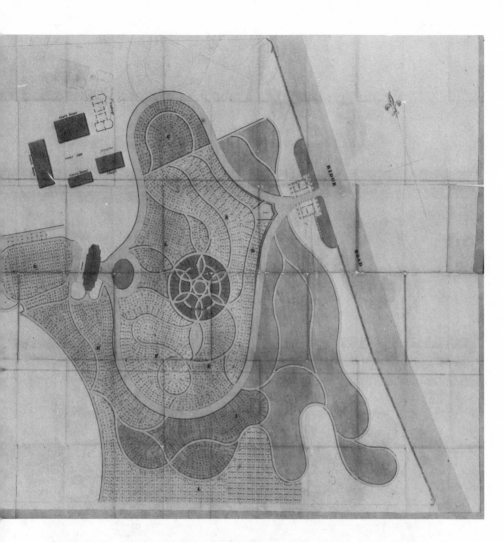

plots of land by individual churches or fraternal organizations, thereby enabling whole congregations to be buried together rather than scattered throughout the cemetery.[19]

From these three northeastern cities the idea of creating rural cemeteries spread throughout the nation. Numerous other cities, towns, and villages laid out similar places of interment, and, following the precedent of the first three, usually selected names suggestive of sylvan beauty and repose. By 1849 Downing could declare, "There is scarcely a city of note in the whole country that has not its rural cemetery."[20]

These numerous rural cemeteries convey vividly to modern historians a rich understanding of the cultural values widely held a century

Figure 7. Plan of Green-Wood Cemetery, Brooklyn, New York, by David B. Douglas, 1839. Lithograph by John Bachman, 1852. (Courtesy, Prints and Photographs Division, Library of Congress, Washington, D.C.)

ago. The cemeteries' landscape design and sepulchral architecture illustrate the aesthetic ideals of the Victorian era. Their popularity and that of the widely circulated giftbooks, pocket companions, and consolation pieces they inspired, indicates a new psychology of death and its meaning for survivors. Perhaps most important, the use of these spaces for contemplative recreation indicates the beginning of a reconciliation of country and city in nineteenth-century America.

As the first large spaces laid out in what then was termed the modern or natural style, rural cemeteries took advantage of changing tastes and popularized a style of landscape design compatible with the idea that domesticated "country" was the optimal alternative to the rectangularity of the city. This less formal treatment of landscape—which undoubtedly originated in the Far East but which came to fullest expression in England as a reaction to the prevailing emphasis on geometrical forms in the garden—was perhaps the major aesthetic development of the eighteenth century. So many historical studies have delineated this transformation in taste, the shift from classic to romantic, that it needs little elaboration here. One of the most important tenets of late eighteenth-century theory was the belief that the goal of art was to stimulate a mental impression in the observer. In his thirteenth discourse Sir Joshua Reynolds advised painters that the purpose of art was "to produce a pleasing effect upon the mind." More adamant was Archibald Alison, who, in his seminal treatise *An Essay on the Nature and Principles of Taste*, published in 1790, claimed that art possessed no intrinsic qualities. Objects, he reasoned, were to be considered beautiful or not because of the associations they evoked in the mind of the spectator.[21]

This new emphasis on aesthetic associations changed the nature of art perception. Heretofore the observer had admired forms of pure beauty, works of art that conformed to abstract criteria of order, symmetry, and proportion. Associationism, however, valued those characteristics and qualities in art that induced a mental response, a response based on emotional as well as intellectual premises. This combination of romanticism and rationalism found its most complete expression in rural cemeteries.

The cemeteries' gateways and sepulchral monuments attempted to induce contemplation, to stimulate the observer through appeals to associations with alien cultures and domestic concerns, and herein lay their didacticism. Represented in the entrances and monuments are the major architectural styles of the antebellum period. Of these perhaps the most significant in terms of rural cemeteries was the revival of interest in Egyptian forms. Although at first a twentieth-century reader might find the use of the Egyptian style puzzling, its strong associational qualities appealed to many Americans a century ago. In what was probably the first important American contribution

Changing Conceptions of Urban Form

to architectural history, Mrs. L. C. Tuthill explained that the revived interest in things Egyptian was due to their strength and durability as well as their appeal to sublimity and historical associations. Egypt was thought to be the oldest civilization, and nineteenth-century Americans admired its well-known respect for the dead. Thus Jacob Bigelow's design for an Egyptian-style gateway at Mount Auburn, as well as the placement of obelisks and small pyramids on the individual plots, would reassure families and visitors that the dead interred within the cemetery would long be revered.[22]

Even before the establishment of Mount Auburn, Maximilian Godefroy had incorporated Egyptian details in his 1814 plan for the gateway to Baltimore's Western Burying Ground and had placed a pyramid within the cemetery. But following Mount Auburn's example numerous cemetery companies adopted the Egyptian style for their entrances. Boston's Old Granary, New Haven's Grove Street, and Philadelphia's Mikveh Israel and Odd Fellows cemeteries are a few of the many that asserted the permanence of burial by the use of Egyptian ornament. This ornamentation was made suitable for Christian burial by stripping away pagan associations and adding biblical inscriptions.[23]

The great expense and attention lavished on monumental decoration and the popularity of cemeteries as places for contemplation suggest the degree to which the landscape of the dead was didactic. Philippe Ariès has pointed out that the new attitude toward death which emerged during the seventeenth and eighteenth centuries emphasized human mortality. Erwin Panofsky's research has explored the roots of this phenomenon in European paintings of the same centuries. For example, on the canvas *Et in Arcadia Ego* (c. 1630) Nicolas Poussin depicts four pensive Arcadians at a sepulchre, engaged in calm discussion. According to Panofsky their conversation represents not a "dramatic encounter with death" but a "contemplative absorption in the idea of mortality." In eighteenth-century England Sir Joshua Reynolds incorporated this theme in his own paintings. In a double portrait of Mrs. Bouverie and Mrs. Crewe, for example, Reynolds included figures of the tragic Muses and added the inscription "Et in Arcadia Ego." Panofsky convincingly demonstrates that to contemporaries this cryptic phrase clearly meant "Even in Arcadia, I, Death, hold sway." The popularity of rural cemeteries must be understood within this context of death as a subject of contemplation, a reminder of human mortality.[24]

Edmund Burke added another context to this interpretation. Contemplating the death of a loved one could actually be pleasant, he believed, because in such a pensive state we recall the happiest moments of life or the finest manifestations of character. Such an attitude toward death gave rise to emotions so mixed as to border on

Figure 8. "View from Mount Auburn," depicting the passive or contemplative reflections of a cemetery visit. Engraving by James Smillie for *Mount Auburn Illustrated* (New York, 1847). (Courtesy, John Crosby Freeman.)

vicarious joy: "In grief, the *pleasure* is still uppermost; and the affliction we suffer has no resemblance to absolute pain, which is odious, and which we endeavor to shake off as soon as possible."[25]

Mount Auburn's historian, Wilson Flagg, thus reasoned that visits to cemeteries could evoke that "agreeable emotion" he termed "melancholy pleasure." The pain and grief inflicted by the death of a friend or relative, he argued, "seldom endures a great while" and is soon replaced by "a quiet state of mind." The many expressions of approbation for Mount Auburn appear to indicate that it fulfilled its didactic role by provoking pensive reflections (fig. 8). In promoting exactly the sort of land use exemplified in Mount Auburn Cemetery, Zebedee Cook echoed the sentiments of Zimmermann's *Solitude Considered*, stating that at the grave "the heart is chastened, and the soul is subdued, and the affections purified and exalted." After visiting Mount Auburn a writer in the *New-England Magazine* concluded that "every thing within is indicative of repose, and invites to contemplation." The cemetery's landscape evoked not the bitterness of recent grief, George Ticknor Curtis pointed out, but elevating and soothing recollections. By robbing death of its terrors, the natural beauty of Mount Auburn helped to reduce the "passionate expressions of afflic-

Changing Conceptions of Urban Form

tion" and instead acted to induce a pensive state. Wilson Flagg believed that visitors came to Mount Auburn not to be saddened but "to think more earnestly of the higher purposes of life, of its transient duration."[26]

Contemporaries even thought that cemeteries acted to heal the wounded heart. Visits to cemeteries provided solace to at least one fictional character afflicted with unrequited love. When Mary Ashburton rejected Paul Flemming's attentions, the protagonist of Longfellow's *Hyperion* suffered a wound "too deep ever to heal." Yet upon visiting the village churchyard at St. Gilgen he at last found comfort: "A quiet calm stole over him. The fever of his heart was allayed. He had a moment's rest from pain; and went back to his chamber in peace." Flemming was at a loss to explain this "holy calm," this "long-desired tranquility," though he sensed that his visit to the cemetery was a cause. Longfellow, however, had anticipated Flemming's experience by pointing out "how peaceful is the dwelling place of those who inhabit the green hamlets and populous cities of the dead."[27]

Cemeteries were also thought to exercise an important moral influence over their visitors. Wilson Flagg included in his history of Mount Auburn a chapter entitled "The Moral Influence of Graves," and George Ticknor Curtis emphasized the "moral influence" of a visit to the cemetery. At the consecration of the Albany, New York, rural cemetery, civic leader D. D. Barnard predicted that the burial ground would become a "great moral Teacher"; and the rules of the Laurel Hill company praised the "salutary effects of ornate and well preserved cemeteries, on the moral taste and general sentiments of all classes." A writer in the *Yale Literary Magazine* recognized the "moral effect" of a cemetery, and especially one located "in the vicinity of a mammon-serving and tumultuous city." As Downing concluded, rural cemeteries possessed "the double wealth of rural and moral associations."[28]

Finally, because of their proximity to cities, rural cemeteries stood as pastoral counterpoints to the urban environment. Most obviously, the curvilinearity of the natural landscape contrasted with the straight lines of the gridiron city. Thomas Bender's *Toward an Urban Vision* points out that the imagery of Joseph Story's consecration address placed Mount Auburn's "wildness" in opposition to the city of Boston. Other speakers and writers echoed this assessment. The proprietors of Brooklyn's Green-Wood Cemetery placed its naturalistic appeal "in contrast with the *glare, set form, fixed rule,* and *fashion* of the city." Nathaniel Parker Willis described New York's Cypress Hills Cemetery as "at just the sufficient remove from the city, to be near and yet secluded, remote enough for sacred stillness, and yet ease of access." He recommended a visit to the cemetery "to those of our friends who need and like, now and then, to shut the city and its associations out of their thoughts." Wilson Flagg saw Mount Auburn affording visitors the opportunity to "ponder on those themes which are neglected by the multitude, during the hurry of business or in the idle whirl of pleasure." Thus, at the cemetery the visitor could leave behind some of the cares of urban life, revel in the natural beauty of the scenery, and learn the moral lessons of the landscape and its monuments. The rural cemetery functioned as a kind of suburban park.[29]

Although today many of these extra-urban burying grounds have been engulfed by sprawling cities and are so crowded with graves that they retain little of their original beauty, the rural cemeteries created in nineteenth-century America left an enduring legacy. In 1840 Downing judged the nation's rural cemeteries superior in design to the grounds of most country seats and believed them "likely to affect in a very considerable degree the general taste for laying out and embellishing grounds." Indeed, visitors to the cemeteries experienced their "first acquaintance" with the "beauty of landscape gardening in the natural style" and returned "to apply the taste thus acquired to the improvement of their own grounds."[30]

The popularity of rural cemeteries contributed significantly to the realization that large expanses of natural beauty were essential means of protecting the health and vitality of an urban population. In 1833 — a year after the first cholera epidemic swept through the United States and two years after the establishment of Mount Auburn — Baltimore clergyman Stephen Duncan Walker urged the creation of open spaces within that city as places for healthful recreation. Undoubtedly influenced by the success of Mount Auburn, Walker advocated the establishment of a rural cemetery as the most efficacious way of acquiring a "public walk." To an English audience Downing reported that America's rural cemeteries were "the first really elegant public gardens or promenades formed in this country," and so people used them. In the absence of similar recreational areas in the neighborhood of cities, many visitors came to the cemetery not in search of solitude but to escape the confines of the urban environment. Despite what a writer in Scribner's Monthly later called a "certain incongruity between a graveyard and a place of recreation," Americans went to rural cemeteries "to get fresh air, and a sight of grass and trees and flowers."[31]

The crowds of visitors attracted to the beauty of the rural cemeteries soon created an unexpected problem. Downing was alarmed that a "gala-day air of *recreation*" marred the contemplative intent. In 1848 he observed, "People seem to go there to enjoy themselves, and not to indulge in any serious recollections or regrets." Olmsted, who throughout his distinguished career as a landscape architect declined most cemetery commissions, shared Downing's sentiment. In his opinion the cemetery, which should have been a place of "rest, silence, seclusion, and peace," had instead become a "constant resort of mere pleasure seekers, travellers, promenaders, and loungers." Downing and Olmsted did agree, however, that the success of rural cemeteries reinforced the public recognition of the importance of naturalistic parks as part of the new urban landscape. Eight years before the commencement of construction at New York's Central Park, Downing wrote, "In the absence of great public parks, such as we must surely one day have in America, our rural cemeteries are doing a great deal to enlarge and educate the popular taste in rural embellishment." Moreover, he noted, the crowds that visited the cemeteries were "plain enough" evidence of "how much our citizens, of all classes, would enjoy public parks on a similar scale." Olmsted concurred, pointing out that the use of cemeteries for recreational purposes "indicates, as much as any thing else, the need that exists in every town and village for a proper pleasure ground."[32]

For Downing the success of rural cemeteries provided a model for the creation of public parks. Presumably because he had little faith in governmental action, Downing proposed that interested citizens incorporate as a joint stock company, purchase a suitable tract of land in the nearby suburbs, and lay out a public garden. He suggested charging a small admission fee to defray the cost of maintenance. Such a garden would soon become a "great promenade," the most interesting and attractive feature of the city. "If the road to Mount Auburn is now lined with coaches, continually carrying the inhabitants of Boston by thousands and tens of thousands," he reasoned, "is it not likely that such a garden, full of the most varied instruction, amusement, and recreation, would be ten times more visited?"[33]

Downing's suggestion that the cemetery model be pursued by private corporations as a means of meeting public needs proved unnecessary because municipal governments acted to provide such recreational facilities. Nevertheless, as the ideology of the public park evolved in the antebellum years, it would draw upon the lessons of rural cemeteries. Parks would differ from cemeteries in a number of ways, however. Most obviously, the park would provide the scenic attractions of the cemetery, but "without the graves and without the funeral processions." Thus the Brooklyn *Eagle* objected in 1859 when advocates of a large park in the Ridgewood section of the city proposed incorporating neighboring rural cemeteries as part of the landscape. The newspaper argued that "people hard pressed by the toils of manual labor, the cares and anxieties of business, or the sorrows that fall in greater or lesser degree to most people, would hardly choose...the gloomy associations of a cemetery." The park would serve purposes different from those of the cemetery; its landscape treatment would also be different.[34]

The transition from cemetery to park would mark a shift from the didactic to the naturalistic landscape and from a somewhat private to an intentionally public space. The debate over what a park should be would force nineteenth-century Americans to further refine the new conception of urban form and culture. The park would come to be a recreational institution appropriate to American republicanism, one located not in the suburbs but in the city and available not only to the wealthy and middle class but to all citizens, a natural landscape standing within and in sharp contrast to the rectangularity of the urban environment. The park—the country within the city—would be, in Calvert Vaux's words, "the big art work of the Republic."[35]

PART TWO

The Evolution of the Urban Park

CHAPTER IV

THE IDEOLOGY OF THE PUBLIC PARK

How rapidly is civilization treading on the footsteps of nature!
— JAMES FENIMORE COOPER

By the middle decades of the nineteenth century the movement to create public parks within cities was gaining momentum throughout much of the Western world. The American park movement would differ from contemporary European developments, however, because of a greater urgency of need. Whereas in the Old World there were extensive royal parks that had been or could be opened for public use, no such tradition existed in the United States. The dramatic growth of America's cities, in absolute numbers of residents and in size and complexity, made it imperative that a nation founded on the primacy of agrarian values create such open spaces to protect public health and provide suitable areas for recreation. In the United States these parks would also have to be democratic institutions that would be compatible with republicanism. The emerging park ideology in America owed much to the popularity of rural cemeteries, but the differences between ornamental graveyards and recreational facilities necessitated a reformulation of the use of natural scenery—from a didacticism that promoted contemplation of moral subjects to a landscape that, in its very rusticity, would stand as an antidote to conditions of life within cities. Thus the public park would evolve as part of the continuing redefinition of urban form and culture in nineteenth-century America. In the hands of the nation's cultural leaders it would promote the reconciliation of country and city by creating large expanses of natural beauty within the urban environment.

Both in Europe and in America the ideology of the public park began with a recognition of the importance of open spaces to the health and vitality of the urban population. In the aftermath of the first major cholera epidemic, in 1832, many English reformers attributed the spread of disease to congestion and squalor. More precisely, they believed that miasmas created or carried by impure air were the principal cause of the epidemic. Thus, from the standpoint of public health, an important function of the park was to purify the disease-ridden atmosphere, to ensure the free circulation of fresh breezes that would eliminate miasmas. In 1833 the Select Committee on Public Walks, which had been created in response to the outbreak of cholera, informed Parliament of the need for recreational spaces in urban areas. Its report explained that conditions in large cities were especially unhealthy for workers, who were "often shut up in heated Factories." The Select Committee then urged Parliament to enact a law requiring every town in the kingdom to establish a public walk or park as a means of effecting needed sanitary improvement.[1]

Even before the cholera epidemic some observers had pointed out the importance of parks to public health. As early as 1803 landscape gardener John Claudius Loudon had claimed that London's squares were "of greatest consequence to the health of its inhabitants" because they promoted "the free circulation of air." But in the years following the Select Committee's report, parks came to be considered essential to the health of the urban population. In 1835 a correspondent in the *Gardener's Magazine* echoed Loudon, praising the "utility" of London's squares for "their admitting of a more free circulation of air." Blackwood's *Edinburgh Magazine* published in 1839 an essay describing public parks as the "lungs of London," the breathing places of the metropolis, while the *Westminster Review* pointed out the importance of open spaces "for air and exercise, as a necessary sanitary provision for the inhabitants of large towns." In 1852 Charles H. J. Smith used the lung metaphor in a systematic study outlining the benefits of public parks, hailing them as places where the "pale mechanic and the exhausted factory operative might inhale the freshening breeze and some portion of recovered health."[2]

Americans who visited Europe also recognized the sanitary purposes of parks. A "friend" of the Boston Common found "much aptness as well as truth" in the statement that the "parks of London are the lungs of that city" and noted that, much as parks "contribute to the beauty of a city, they are no less necessary to its salubrity." Architect Howard Daniels shared this understanding of the role of parks, as did Thomas B. Fox, who described them as "almost the only breathing-places in large cities." This perception of the park persisted into the 1870s: in his crusade to establish a Chicago park the physician and sanitary reformer John H. Rauch asserted that "parks have been aptly termed 'the lungs of a city.'"[3]

New York responded to the 1832 cholera epidemic by planning what eventually would become the Croton Aqueduct system, and Philadelphia's physicians advocated locating a park along the Schuylkill River to protect their city's water supply. But after a second virulent cholera epidemic swept the United States in 1849, sanitary reformers turned to the need for open spaces in the crowded cities. Almost every municipality had already set aside some public squares,

The Evolution of the Urban Park

of course. William Penn's 1682 plan for Philadelphia included five squares, which its founder hoped would contribute to the aspect of a green country town. Savannah had similar spaces, and Charleston a waterfront promenade. Boston had its Common, and New York's Battery Park, which originally had served as a fortification, was that city's favorite promenade.[4]

After the second appearance of cholera, however, these spaces were deemed inadequate. The newly formed American Medical Association published in 1849 a sanitary survey of the nation's cities, modeled upon Edwin Chadwick's *Report on the Sanitary Condition of the Labouring Population of Great Britain* (1842). The association's Committee on Public Hygiene made numerous inquiries "directed to the effect produced on the inhabitants by residence in large towns." Predictably, that body found in the crowded cities conditions that caused the "destruction of human life." In order to mitigate the dangers to public health present in cities, several physicians advocated that the urban environment take on aspects of the country through the creation of public parks. The function of trees and parks within cities, one medical expert reported, was to "absorb deleterious gases, and receive or prevent the reflected heat from brick houses, which is so oppressive to those who cannot otherwise escape their influence." Parks would "assist in likening a city to the country," a place thought to be superior in promoting good health. John H. Griscom, who prepared the sanitary survey of public health in New York, praised that city's squares as "remarkable for their beauty," but noted to his chagrin that they were "by no means so numerous as they should be in so large a city." It was in recognition of crowded urban conditions, as well as the absence of open spaces that might otherwise have operated as the city's "lungs," that the American Medical Association's Committee on Public Hygiene advocated the creation of parks: "The necessity for public squares, tastefully ornamented and planted with trees, cannot be too strongly urged upon public attention, as one of the most powerful correctives to the vitiated air within the reach of the inhabitants of a populous place."[5]

During the next decade, as sanitary reformers reiterated the need for open spaces within cities, other advocates of parks adopted the public health argument. A. J. Downing, for example, praised the "sanitary value and importance of these breathing places for large cities." Philadelphian Charles S. Keyser claimed that parks were "intimately allied, in a broad though absolute view, to the comfort, health, the lives of our citizens." The nineteenth-century correlation between public health and the development of parks cannot be overstated. In his address inaugurating Baltimore's Druid Hill Park, Mayor Thomas B. Swann quoted the English landscape gardener Edward Kemp: "It is only by the occurrence of modern epidemics, producing that attention to sanitary matters...that the necessity for good Parks has been duly recognized, and the insufficiency of those already existing properly felt."[6]

In addition to this concern for public health, proponents of park development lamented the absence of spacious recreational facilities within America's cities. The existing public squares were too limited in extent to serve the needs of an increasing population. Downing noted in 1851, "Deluded New-York has, until lately, contented itself with the little door-yards of space—mere grassplats of verdure, which form the squares of the city, in the mistaken idea that they are parks." Instead, he asserted, "What have been called parks in New-York are not even apologies for the things: they are only squares, or paddocks." In advocating the creation of a large public park in Phila-delphia, Charles Keyser equated the city's squares with "little squirrel cages," which were totally inadequate for recreational needs. More-over, if in the early years of the nineteenth century it was only a short walk from the center of the city to outlying fields, the spatial expan-sion of urban areas made imperative the development of public parks: the march of the gridiron was relentless, and once city blocks covered the surrounding country there would be no respite from compulsory crowding. When people could no longer escape the city by walking to the country, and when suburban development threatened to destroy popular retreats such as Hoboken's Elysian Fields, advocates of parks urged the creation of large expanses of rural beauty within the urban environment.[7]

What made existing city parks seem especially inadequate was the startling rate of urban growth and a belated recognition of the extent of urban squalor. To many contemporaries it seemed that the founding fathers' well-known fear of a large, dependent working class was becoming a reality. New York's infamous Five Points was only the best known of many impoverished and crime-ridden city neighborhoods. As thousands of residents crowded into such areas, they lost all contact with the agrarian existence that was thought to foster republican virtue. William Ellery Channing was one spokes-man who feared for a civilization in which so many people "are cut off from nature's common bounties, and want those cheering influences of the elements which even savages enjoy." Moreover, conditions in the squalid tenements—cold and damp in winter, enervatingly hot in summer, and poorly ventilated at all times—presented a serious threat to health. Not only did epidemics fester in these areas, but each year thousands perished "for want of God's freest, most lavish gifts." According to another observer, the confinement of cities was causing the development of a race of urban denizens who were only *"physical apologies for men."*[8]

Joining the sanitary reformers in urging the creation of public parks in the United States were the numerous Americans who visited Europe in the antebellum years. Indeed, Europe's parks became a cultural lodestone for American travelers. In "The Young American" (1844) Emerson wrote, "There is no feature of the old countries that strikes an American with more agreeable surprise than the beautiful gardens of Europe." Olmsted wrote in 1850, "Probably there is no object of art that Americans of cultivated taste more generally long to see in Europe, than an English park." Stephen Duncan Walker ranked European parks among "those things that strike the traveller with most interest," and clergyman J. O. Choules reported in 1852, "No one comes to London without being told by every one to go and see the parks."[9]

In the pages of travel accounts and other writings, the lavish praise bestowed on European parks had as a corollary an explicit criticism of America's failure to set aside comparable spaces. Novelist Catharine Maria Sedgwick, for example, found it impossible to "enter the London parks without regretting the folly (call it not cupidity) of our people, who, when they had a whole continent at their disposal, have left such narrow spaces for what has so well been called the lungs of a city." These "lovely green parks," she wrote, offered the worker a temporary escape from "his smoky place of daily toil." Emerson believed that public gardens could be "easily imitated here," and author Caroline Kirkland added, "Nothing we saw in London made our own dear city of New York seem so poor in comparison as these parks." For her it was the "tired workman" and his family who constituted "the class for whom it is worth while to make parks." Arguing that Americans must be dissatisfied with the absence of large open spaces within cities, Kirkland concluded: "After seeing these oases in the wilderness of streets, one can never be content with the scanty patches of verdure. . .that [in New York] form the only places of afternoon recreation for the weary, the sad, the invalid, the playful."[10]

William Cullen Bryant, poet and editor of the New York *Evening Post*, visited London in 1844 and found the parks there to be essential to the "public health and happiness of the people." Glancing westward he mused that urban growth made it a "cause of regret that in laying out New York, no preparation was made, while it was yet practicable, for a range of parks and public gardens along the central part of the island." He advised New York's leaders to set aside some available lands immediately, as "the advancing population of the city is sweeping over them and covering them from our reach."[11]

Horace Greeley, editor of the *New-York Daily Tribune*, who traveled to England in 1851 to report on the Crystal Palace exhibition, also praised the influence of London's parks and offered prescriptions for creating them in American cities. "The *Parks*, *Squares*, and *Public*

Gardens of London," he wrote, "beat us clean out of sight." After comparing New York's cramped squares with London's vast open spaces, he regretfully conceded, "Our city ought to have made provision, twenty years ago, for a series of Parks and Gardens extending quite across the island somewhere between Thirtieth and Fiftieth streets." Although the city's growth had already covered up much of that area, Greeley advised that "all that can be should be done immediately to secure breathing-space and grounds for healthful recreation to the Millions who will ultimately inhabit New York."[12]

Another American, Henry P. Tappan, described London's parks as offering "rural sights and sounds in the midst of the city itself." From Hyde Park he observed that "the city beyond is hidden from your view, and a country scene lies before you apparently without limits." However crowded its streets, neighborhoods, and commercial and public spaces, Tappan noted, London's parks and squares gave the city "the beauty and freshness of the country." Public parks, he realized, effectively mitigated the clash of country and city. In such areas, the population exchanges the "pent air of streets and alleys, for wide avenues under overhanging trees, winding footpaths through forest scenes and along the banks of flowing streams, and rural seats and arbors." If New York could not afford parks as extensive as London's, Tappan advised the creation of numerous smaller ones in Manhattan, while locating larger grounds in the city's immediate suburbs. With adequate foresight, he predicted, the city might yet possess "an acropolis, and gardens with trees and fountains – nature and art wedded in every form of beauty."[13]

Visits to European parks touched a sensitive nerve among American travelers. Although most of these parks were originally restricted for use by royalty, by the 1840s and 1850s they were open for the enjoyment of all classes of people. Those who trumpeted the advantages of republican government over Old World aristocracy had to admit that European provisions for public recreation were more successful than anything undertaken in America. English observer Francis J. Grund found one "deficiency" in the United States to be "particularly oppressive to the labouring classes," namely, "the almost total absence of public gardens or pleasure-grounds in the large cities." Lewis F. Allen termed it a "disgrace" that America's "cities and large towns show[ed] no specimens of extended park and pleasure-grounds for the multitude." Downing numbered parks among those European institutions that had "raised the people in *social* civilization and social culture to a far higher level" than had yet been attained in "republican America." The challenge to national self-esteem was explicit: if monarchical Europe could provide parks for the people, so too must the United States. Could not "our sovereign *people*," Downing inquired, also "make and support these great and healthy sources of pleasure and refinement for themselves in America?"[14]

Moreover, American travelers discovered that although in the Old World governments were monarchical and societies thought to be more stratified than in the New, parks helped to create a more democratic social order. In failing to provide opportunities for public recreation, Downing explained, American society had set up barriers of class and caste: "We owe it to ourselves and our republican professions," he declared, "to set about establishing a larger and more fraternal spirit in our social life." Much as they would create healthier cities, so would parks bring together all classes of people in the common enjoyment of nature. Stephen Duncan Walker was one American who praised the park as "a commonwealth, a kind of democracy, where the poor, the rich, the mechanic, the merchant and the man of letters, mingle on a footing of perfect equality." Downing called parks the "pleasant drawing-rooms" of European cities, places where the people "gain health, good spirits, social enjoyment, and a frank and cordial bearing towards their neighbors." Indeed, parks fostered a *"social freedom*, and an easy and agreeable intercourse of all classes" that Downing believed struck an American "with surprise and delight." In the German parks, he reported, "all classes assemble under the shade of the same trees, – the nobility, (even the king is often seen among them,) the wealthy citizens, the shopkeepers, and the artisans, etc." There was "true democracy" in the European parks, he concluded, something "worth imitating in our more professedly democratic country."[15]

Another attraction of the European parks Downing termed their *"social* influence." Parks would not just bring all classes of society together for recreation, but would act as agents of moral improvement. S. D. Walker described the park as a place

> where the rough corners of character become smoothed by the attractions of genteel intercourse, by the communications that such places afford; multiple influences insensibly steal over the heart of the most pure and desirable character, and while the sight is gratified by an exhibition of what is beautiful in nature and art, the taste improves, the mind becomes buoyant, the manners chastened by viewing what is pleasing, refined, cultivated and appreciable in the more active graces of life.

Downing advanced the claims of the park as an instrument of moral improvement through a theory of social reform he called "popular refinement." The keystone of this theory was the "elevating influences of the beautiful in nature and art." For Downing the common school provided only the rudimentary beginnings of education, and he advocated supplementing it with public parks and gardens, libraries, art museums and galleries. "By these means, you would soften and humanize the rude, educate and enlighten the ignorant, and give continual enjoyment to the educated." If the United States were to fulfill its national destiny, Downing reasoned, "this broad ground of popular refinement *must* be taken up" and implemented; if the nation were to "banish the plague-spots of democracy," all must enjoy the "refining influences of intellectual and moral culture." Thus Downing urged his compatriots:

> Open wide, therefore, the doors of your libraries and picture galleries, all ye true republicans! Build halls where knowledge shall be freely diffused among men, and not shut up within the narrow walls of narrower institutions. Plant spacious parks in your cities, and unloose their gates as wide as the gates of morning to the whole people.

Such a comprehensive program of moral and intellectual improvement, Downing believed, would result "in elevating the national character."[16]

The failure to achieve a truly republican society in America also distressed Frederick Law Olmsted. He believed that education should include more than "miserable common schools." If the United States were to achieve a "democratic condition of society," it must create institutions that would "more directly *assist* the poor and degraded to elevate themselves." To this end he urged Charles Loring Brace, "Go ahead with the Children's Aid [Society], and get up parks, gardens, music, dancing schools, reunions which will be so attractive as to force into contact the good & bad, the gentlemanly and the rowdy." For Olmsted, as for Downing, parks were an essential part of a reformist program that would provide for the poor "an education to refinement and taste and the mental & moral capital of gentlemen."[17]

Acknowledgment of worsening urban conditions and of the importance of open spaces in fostering public health and recreation, as well as a concern for the nation's self-esteem as a republic and its intellectual and moral improvement, led Americans of various regions and occupations to advocate the establishment of public parks in their cities. Underlying and uniting these diverse concerns was the continuing redefinition of urban form and culture in what nineteenth-century Americans considered "Nature's Nation." Thus the reformulated agrarianism, an appreciation of the psychological and social benefits of natural scenery, and the need to address the realities of urban growth and change combined in the attempt to create a new urban form by bringing the country into the city.

The park, then, embodied a new urban symbolism—the curvilinearity of the natural landscape—and stood in sharp contrast to the straight lines and rigid angles of the gridiron, a pastoral counterpoint to the urban environment. "The object of a park," wrote landscape architect H. W. S. Cleveland, "is to secure to the dwellers in cities the opportunity of enjoying the contemplation of such objects of natural beauty as the growth of the city must otherwise destroy." It should, therefore, incorporate scenery that would present "the strongest possible contrast to the streets and blocks around it." According to another observer, the park "should present the greatest possible contrast to the artificiality of the city, with its straight and closely built up streets." The *Scientific American* urged that the park "combine the rural with the artificial in cities," while the *Magazine of Horticulture* asserted that parks must "afford the means of rural enjoyment" for the industrial population. Henry David Thoreau advocated that each community set aside "a park, or rather a primitive forest" as a place that would "keep the New World *new*, [and] preserve all the advantages of living in the country." Such a place, Downing advised, should "have broad reaches of park and pleasure-grounds, with a real feeling of the breadth and beauty of green fields, the perfume and freshness of nature." If it were necessary that Americans live in cities, large public parks could provide, for those "whose means do not permit them to receive the benefits of the country," an aspect of rural beauty within the urban environment.[18]

But however much proponents agreed on the inadequacy of existing urban squares and on the necessity for larger, more naturalistic parks, there was little consensus on how best to approximate the country within the city. Walt Whitman, then editor of the *Eagle*, spearheaded the creation of a park in a working-class neighborhood of Brooklyn in 1847. But the site, Fort Greene, was chosen largely because it was so hilly that the cost of grading the land and laying out rectangular streets would have been prohibitive, and its constricted size precluded the diversity of scenery of "the country." As a result Fort Greene was really more of an enlarged city square than a naturalistic landscape. The same can be said of A. J. Downing's plan for the Boston Public Garden, which he prepared at about the same time. If John Bachmann's lithograph is indicative of Downing's design, both the Common and the Public Garden were essentially urban spaces— less escapes from the relentless cityscape than extensions of it.[19]

Downing's 1851 design for the public grounds at Washington, D.C., however, marks the confluence of sanitary, recreational, scenic, and reformist ideas and the first application of the maturing theory of public parks. As an expression of the evolving redefinition of urban form and culture in nineteenth-century America, Downing shaped, for the first large city park, a carefully contrived landscape that sought, however imperfectly, to achieve a reconciliation of man and nature. Although left incomplete after his death in 1852, Downing's treatment of the Washington Mall gave unity and momentum to the idea that public parks were essential to the health and vitality of an urban population.

The area Downing was commissioned to lay out was included in L'Enfant's original design for the federal city. The public ground, designated by the letter *H* on the plan (fig. 1), was an *L*-shaped area connecting the Capitol and the President's House. L'Enfant had intended that the Mall, a "grand avenue" four hundred feet wide and almost a mile long, serve as the aesthetic focus of the city. The capital grew haphazardly in the aftermath of L'Enfant's dismissal in 1792, and much of his plan was ignored. The condition of the public ground, the centerpiece of his design, was especially unfortunate. Instead of becoming the grand avenue L'Enfant envisioned, the Mall was settled by squatters, who soon exercised their sovereignty by cutting down its trees. In 1870 a journalist recalled that before Downing's improvements the Mall was

> a large common...presenting a surface of yellow or white clay, cut into by deep gullies, and without trees except one or two scraggy and dying sycamores. The streets were mud roads, along which an omnibus scrambled once a day, to the steamboat wharf, and foot travel paced its muddy or dusty way over the bleak, unhospitable common in zig-zag meanderings.

The low grounds near the partially constructed Washington Monument and surrounding the President's House became a malarial swamp during parts of the year and constituted a serious threat to the health of the executive and his family.[20]

The chartering and building of the Smithsonian Institution, in the 1840s, provided impetus for improving the Mall. The Smithsonian's Board of Regents immediately recognized the importance of making the grounds of the new national seat of learning as attractive as possible. Thus, while awarding contracts for construction of the building, the Regents also appropriated one thousand dollars for the purchase, transplanting, and fencing of trees on its nine-acre site at the southern end of the Mall. In 1847 the Smithsonian's first secretary, Joseph Henry, petitioned Congress to landscape the entire Mall, but the legislature voted only enough money to plant hedges around the new building.[21]

Three years later Henry and Washington financier W. W. Corcoran convinced President Millard Fillmore to undertake a more ambitious program for improving the Mall. (Fillmore's interest may have stemmed more from a concern for public health than aesthetics: his predecessor, Zachary Taylor, had become ill at a patriotic ceremony at the Washington Monument on July 4, 1850, and had died of typhoid fever several days later.) Assured of the new president's support, Henry and Corcoran met with Mayor Walter Lenox and Commissioner of Public Buildings Ignatius Mudd. The result of the session Henry recorded in his "locked book" diary:

> After some conversation it was at length concluded to send for some competent landscape gardener, to give a general plan of the improvement to be made, and on the suggestion of the Mayor, it was resolved to request the President to direct that Mr. Downing, of Newbourg [sic], be requested to examine the grounds and report a plan of improvement.

The next day Henry, Lenox, and Mudd presented their proposal to Fillmore, who then directed the Commissioner of Public Buildings to invite Downing to undertake landscaping the Mall. Recognizing the opportunity to translate theory into practice, Downing readily embraced the task.[22]

When Downing arrived in Washington on November 25, 1850, he and Henry called on the president, who "entered with much interest into the plans." Then, according to Henry, Downing "examined all the ground between the Capitol and the [Potomac] River," which he found "admirably adapted to make a landscape garden and drive." Downing spent much of the next two months drafting and completing a plan of development, which he presented to the Regents of the Smithsonian on February 27, 1851. The Regents approved Downing's scheme and sent it to Fillmore, who likewise assented. Downing was awarded an annual salary of twenty-five hundred dollars for supervising the improvements.[23]

Downing's plan (fig. 9) was an attempt to make the Mall into an "extended landscape garden, to be traversed in different directions by gravelled walks and carriage drives, and planted with specimens, properly labelled, of all the varieties of trees and shrubs which will flourish in this climate." The text accompanying his plan outlines a threefold purpose: "To form a national Park, which should be an ornament to the Capital of the United States"; to "give an example of the natural style of Landscape Gardening which may have an influence on the general taste of the Country"; and to "form a public museum of living trees and shrubs." The third of Downing's purposes is clearly educational, and the first and second are extensions of his belief in the principle of reform through imitation. If Washington had a great urban park, Downing reasoned, other cities would recognize the importance of open spaces and immediately establish their own. A park laid out according to his specifications, Downing believed, "would exercise as much influence on the public taste as Mount Auburn Cemetery," which had inspired the creation of rural cemeteries in numerous other cities. The Washington park would become a "Public School of Instruction in every thing that relates to the tasteful arrangement of parks and grounds."[24]

There are six significant features to Downing's plan for the Mall. The first, the President's Park and Parade Ground, was located directly behind the executive mansion. Downing proposed "to keep the large area of this ground open, as a place for parade or military reviews, as well as public festivities or celebrations," and to encircle the space with a carriage drive and rows of elms. He also suggested the construction of a "large and handsome Archway of marble" at the end of Pennsylvania Avenue, which would serve as the principal entrance to the public grounds. The second aspect of Downing's plan,

The Evolution of the Urban Park

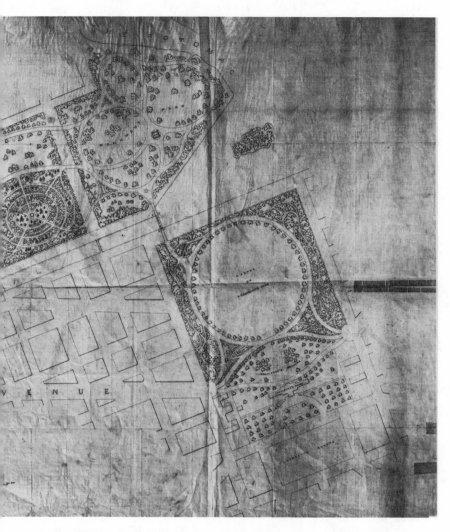

Figure 9. Plan showing the proposed method of laying out the public grounds at
Washington, by A. J. Downing, 1851. (Courtesy, Geography and Maps Division,
Library of Congress, Washington, D.C.)

Monument Park, was a meadowlike garden of American trees surrounding the still-incomplete obelisk honoring the memory of
George Washington. Between the president's house and Monument
Park flowed the Tiber Canal, and to carry pedestrian and carriage
traffic across it Downing designed a wire suspension bridge (fig. 10).
The third element of the plan was the Evergreen Garden, which
Downing suggested should include a museum of every species of
evergreen that would thrive in Washington. He described this garden
as especially valuable because the city was most crowded during the

winter and early spring, when Congress was in session. For the fourth area, Smithsonian Park or Pleasure Grounds, he designed an "arrangement of choice trees in the natural style," as thick clusters of evergreens would enhance the building's irregular outlines. East of the Smithsonian, Downing located the Mall's fifth feature, Fountain Park, with its fountain, curvilinear carriage drives, and man-made lake. He then proposed placing the three greenhouses of the nation's Botanical Garden at the foot of Capitol Hill, and offered advice on plantings for this area. Downing ran the carriage drive to the eastern end of the Mall, where a large gateway opposite the entrance to the Capitol grounds marked the termination of his plan. Almost five miles of curvilinear drives and pedestrian paths led the visitor through the park. Because of the demands of crosstown traffic, three city streets extended through the Mall, but Downing proposed lining

The Evolution of the Urban Park

Figure 10.
"Washington, D.C., The Projected Improvements." Lithograph by B. F. Smith, 1852. (Courtesy, Prints and Photographs Division, Library of Congress, Washington, D.C.)

them with thick plantations to screen out the bustle of the city and protect, as best he could, the integrity of the park. The result, he believed, would "injure the general effect of the grounds as little as possible."

In the spring of 1851 Downing began the grading, drainage, and clearing of the grounds surrounding the Smithsonian. Because of his numerous other commissions, and because the early stages of construction involved "only the roughest operations of ground labor," Downing spent only a part of each month in the capital. To compensate for prolonged absences he devised a "rigid system of daily overseeing." Nevertheless, Downing's absentee supervision provoked the ire of William Easby, the new Commissioner of Public Buildings. Easby evidently told Fillmore that the last time Downing was in Washington he remained only long enough to draw his pay. Downing thought Easby was "ambitious to *manage* everything relating to Washington—and among other matters *myself*." Downing considered his role in the capital an artistic one, and he informed Henry, "If I am interfered with or trammeled by any petty commissioner I will throw up the matter at once—as I am wholly independent of both it and the President." At the urging of Henry and Corcoran, however, Downing journeyed to Washington, where he met with Fillmore "to settle the matter as to who has the jurisdiction of the grounds." As a result of this conference the president extended Downing's authority to include all the public spaces in the city.[25]

Several months later, Easby again challenged Downing's position, this time because of the high cost of projects at the eastern end of the Mall. Then, in the summer of 1852, while debate over appropriations continued, Downing died in a tragic fire aboard the Hudson River steamboat *Henry Clay*. The momentum behind the Washington improvements died with him. During the congressional debates, one legislator claimed that the task of transforming the Mall into a landscaped park probably never would have been undertaken had Downing refused the appointment. But following his death Downing's plans were in large part altered or ignored, and the Mall was developed in parcels rather than according to a comprehensive plan.[26]

Even as work in Washington foundered, the goal of creating large expanses of natural beauty within congested cities was advancing. Because his writings embraced sanitary, scenic, recreational, and reformist ideas, Downing was the most articulate early spokesman for the emerging theory of urban park space in nineteenth-century America. In his estimation the park must serve as the country within the city. Underlying his design for the Washington Mall was Downing's desire to create a landscape of "curved lines and natural groups of trees" that would provide relief from and contrast to the "straight lines and broad Avenues" of the urban environment. Though it might be "needful in civilized life for men to live in cities," he pointed out, there was no reason why Americans must be "voluntarily and ignorantly living in a state of complete forgetfulness of nature." Downing had accepted the commission to landscape the Mall only because of a "sincere desire of giving one good example of a *real* park in the United States," and he hoped that this first successful urban park in America would encourage other cities to preserve or create their own spaces for health and recreation.[27]

After Downing's death other spokesmen advocated that parks serve as the country within the city. *Crayon* editor William J. Stillman, for example, demanded that they include the "wholesome, graceful and delicious verdancy of umbragious foliage and grassy breadths." Parks, he asserted, must have an "extent sufficient to enable us to simulate that paradise of poor city-reared children, 'the country.' " Charles S. Keyser advocated the creation of a Philadelphia park that would afford a "change of scene away from the bustle of the town," a space that would be the "one green spot in the heart of the city." But perhaps it was George William Curtis, one of Downing's first biographers, who best summarized the purposes of the public park:

> A Park is not for those who can go to the country, but for those who can not. It is a civic Newport, and Berkshire, and White Hills. It is fresh air for those who can not go to the seaside; and green leaves, and silence, and the singing of birds, for those who can not fly to the mountains. It is a fountain of health for the whole city.[28]

Only a year after Downing's death in 1852, New York City adopted his suggestion of a centrally located park. Significantly, the two men who in 1858 captured the first premium in the competition for designs and who translated that plan into pastoral acres were Calvert Vaux, Downing's architectural partner, and Frederick Law Olmsted, the young friend whose first writings on public parks Downing had published in the *Horticulturist*. Both men shared Downing's ideal of creating within the city "broad reaches of park and pleasure-grounds, with a real feeling of the breadth and beauty of green fields," and together they worked to refine and implement his conception of the new urban landscape.[29]

Downing's contribution to the shaping of the ideology of the park movement was important, and no one appreciated it more than Olmsted and Vaux. Thus, in the spring of 1860 they circulated a proposal to erect a memorial to Downing in Central Park. "We think it fitting," they wrote, "that it should ere long contain some appropriate acknowledgment of the public indebtedness to the labors of the late A. J. Downing, of which we feel the Park itself is one of the direct results." The bust they hoped to place in the Ramble area was never erected, but Olmsted and Vaux later collaborated on the design of Andrew Jackson Downing Memorial Park in Newburgh, New York.[30]

However important, Downing's conception of the new urban landscape remained incomplete at the time of his death and wanting in scope. He never had the opportunity to carry out a program of park development, nor did he come to see the suburb not as an escape from the city but as part of the process of creating a new, more openly built urban environment. Olmsted realized this, and later confessed that he found Downing's plans for buildings and grounds "far less excellent with reference to their ostensible ends, than they were with reference to the purpose of stimulating the exercise of judgment and taste in the audience addressed." He appreciated Downing's contribution to the evolving ideology of the public park and attributed to Downing's influence his own recognition of the role of art and taste in civilizing American society, but there agreement ended. Thus in 1882 Olmsted described the grounds of the Smithsonian Institution as "the last and only important public work of Downing, who was not only a master of the art, but distinctly a man of genius, of whom his country should always be proud." He urged that the surviving parts of Downing's design receive "special and reverent attention, as representing the only essay, strictly speaking, yet made by our government in landscape gardening."[31]

With this cryptic phrase Olmsted indicated the principal difference between his work and that of Downing. Some twenty-five years after he began the task of superintending the construction of Central Park he described the Washington improvements as a kind of period piece in the development of "gardening," which clearly was not the same thing as park-making. In this he may have been referring to specific aspects of Downing's design—to Monument Park, for example, with its display of individual specimens of plants in the "gardenesque" style Olmsted thought inappropriate in a park, or perhaps to the geometrical formality of the Evergreen Garden. Olmsted may also have been referring to the streets crossing the Mall, which prevented the realization of broad stretches of landscape effect. In any event, Olmsted thought of Downing's Washington project as a promenade and compared it with the pedestrian mall at Central Park. But the promenade in Central Park was part of a much larger ensemble, one that also included large areas of sweeping pastoral scenery. In short, Olmsted learned from Downing's work that the purposes of a park were different from those of a garden: whereas a garden might be decorative and artificial, the park must be a natural or at least seemingly natural landscape, the antithesis of the confining conditions of the urban gridiron. The park must be the country within the city.

CHAPTER V

THE NATURALISTIC LANDSCAPE: CENTRAL PARK

... this many sided, fluent thoroughly American high art work...
— CALVERT VAUX

At the time of Downing's death in 1852 the ideology of the park movement was a powerful yet somewhat incomplete force in the evolving redefinition of American urban form and culture. To be sure, many of the nation's cultural spokesmen believed that parks were necessary correctives to the congestion of the city, but they hardly agreed on precisely what form nature should take in the expanding urban environment. Downing's Washington Mall had demonstrated one possibility, but it was left unfinished, and his "extended landscape garden" was didactic and still conceptually only a partial solution to the absence of open spaces within cities. In the late 1850s, however, the nation's principal metropolis, New York, began the construction of Central Park. Its designers, Frederick Law Olmsted and Calvert Vaux, would further refine the role of parks as part of the new urban landscape.[1]

Central Park is a naturalistic landscape, especially as compared to earlier city squares and to Downing's Washington design. Its 843 acres hold out to residents "the beauty of the fields, the prairie, of the pastures and the still waters." Central Park appears so natural, in fact, as to belie the immensity of its achievement. Upon visiting the park in 1859 the journalist Horace Greeley expressed surprise and delight that the designers had made so few alterations in the landscape.[2]

Nothing, of course, could have been further from the truth. When New York acquired the site in 1856, the land was barren and desolate, covered with squatters' shacks, swampy lowlands, and the massive outcroppings of Manhattan's rocky foundation. Egbert L. Viele, a civil engineer who prepared the first topographical survey of the area, described it in 1857 as a "pestilential spot, where rank vegetation and miasmatic odors taint every breath of air." Olmsted found the future park "filthy, squalid and disgusting," as it contained not trees and grass but wretched hovels and "heaps of cinders, brick-bats, potsherds, and other rubbish." Chosen because its central location was less desirable than the waterfront for commercial purposes and because its rough topography made the site prohibitively expensive to grade into the city's rectangular street system, the park's lands "did not have a single natural advantage." Indeed, noted one contemporary, "landscape gardening was never set quite such a puzzling problem" as the task of transforming these acres into a scene of seemingly natural beauty. Under Olmsted's supervision an army of laborers blasted tons of rock, moved thousands of cartloads of earth, installed a comprehensive underground drainage system, shaped swampy morasses into lakes and ponds, planted turf, trees, and shrubs—created, in every sense of the word, the park. It is thus a subtle irony, and a testament to the vision of its designers, that, like the city that surrounds it, Central Park is totally a man-made environment. As such it stands as one of the most innovative and enduring responses to urbanization undertaken in nineteenth-century America.[3]

During the 1850s the parks movement in New York City gained widespread support. Especially after 1845, with the city's recovery from the Panic of 1837, New York experienced a decade of prosperity perhaps unmatched in its history. Following the completion of the Croton Aqueduct, Manhattan's fabled march uptown accelerated. It was the advance guard in a building boom that transformed the city by translating streets once laid out only on paper into massive piles of brick and brownstone and by establishing the differentiation of commercial and residential spaces. As the wealthy congregated in the northern wards, once-choice residential areas in the southern end of the island became immigrant quarters or business and warehouse districts. The city's population doubled between 1845 and 1855, and the built area of Manhattan expanded at a similar rate. Faced with such dramatic growth, some of New York's cultural leaders began to rethink the elements of what a city should be, to explore the possibilities of restructuring the urban environment. [4]

Beginning in February of 1853 an anonymous writer for *Putnam's Monthly*, probably Clarence Cook, surveyed the physical changes the city was experiencing in a series of essays entitled "New-York Daguerrotyped." His purpose was to examine "the present state and prospects of New York, architecturally considered"; just as important was his implicit attempt to reform architectural design and building in the expanding city. These essays probed into virtually every aspect of the urban fabric: commercial and public buildings, benevolent institutions, churches, educational institutions, places of public amusement, and private residences. What headed the author's list of subjects—what made Manhattan's remarkable growth possible—was commerce, which established the city as the dominant metropolis of

Figure 11. "Liberty-street, in process of re-building, 1852," depicting the "tearing down and building up" of Manhattan Island. Engraving by J. W. Orr for *Putnam's Monthly*, February, 1853. (Courtesy, Shadek-Fackenthal Library, Franklin and Marshall College, Lancaster, Pennsylvania.)

the nation. Although he enthusiastically celebrated the engine of progress, the New York that "armed itself with bricks and mortar. . . and went energetically to work, tearing down and building up," Cook nevertheless lamented "the great business which spreads with such astonishing rapidity over the lower part of the city, prostrating and utterly obliterating every thing that is old and venerable, and leaving not a single land-mark" (fig. 11). He resisted the idea that Columbia College move uptown ("Shall there be nothing calm and quiet left in the seething mass of our business domain?") and urged an urban scale that was appropriate to human needs. Anything more than five or six stories was simply too tall.[5]

Cook's initial essay had praised the Commissioners Plan of 1811, which established the city's rectangular street system. But as new construction projects swept northward on Manhattan Island the gridiron became more and more intractable. Uptown development resulted in congestion, not only on the east-west streets that traditionally had served the wharves but on the great north-south avenues that became the new focus of communication among New York's various neighborhoods. Urban growth was producing a degree of congestion that impeded the flow of traffic even as new building increased the distance separating country and city. Thus, in his concluding piece Cook took a less positive view: "Carts and omnibuses are daily at a deadlock for half an hour together, and the pedestrian desirous of crossing, stands in the situation of the rustic in Horace, waiting upon the bank until the river has run by!" Moreover, expansion of the physical city threatened to confine residents within unrelieved walls of brick and brownstone. The few squares and other open spaces in the inhabited quarters of New York were hopelessly inadequate to meet the sanitary and recreational needs of an expanding urban population. At best these tiny oases of grass and flowers were urban in character — defined by the gridiron and on hot summer days as crowded and noisy as the surrounding streets.[6]

Cook envisioned a metropolis with room for both commercial and domestic purposes, and he lauded the development of handsome residential areas north of the commercial sectors. Most of all he was heartened by the 1853 law authorizing the creation of a large public park. Such a park, Cook predicted,

> will convert the central part of the island on which New-York is built into a pleasure ground, around which will spring up terraces, villas, and blocks of dwelling houses excelling in beauty and magnificence any we can now boast of in the New World, and giving new ideas of the beneficent principle of democracy, which permits the mind to expand to its utmost possibilities.

Together with museums and other cultural institutions, such a park would create in New York the *"national, liberal and cosmopolitan spirit* that is generated only, by *one acknowledged central city* of a great country." Thus to this writer the park was more than an escape from the city: it was an integral part of the transformation of urban space, an expression of urban optimism, and a means of raising the level of civilization in the city.[7]

Given the nature of political culture in New York during the 1850s, it was almost inevitable that the park would become the object of controversy. The acquisition of land for the park would require the expenditure of millions of dollars, and construction promised lucrative patronage opportunities. Moreover, any such action undertaken by a local government would have to be ratified by the legislature at

Albany and city-state relations were already severely strained. After much debate the city rejected the first park site, the Jones Wood area along the East River, and turned, with state approval, to acquiring the vast tract of land near the geographical center of Manhattan Island.[8]

On June 3, 1856, the first Central Park commissioners, Mayor Fernando Wood and Street Commissioner Joseph S. Taylor, adopted a plan of development prepared by Egbert L. Viele. The text accompanying Viele's design indicates a careful reading of the principal writings on parks, but the plan itself demonstrates an utter neglect of the cardinal precept of landscape art, namely, the need to adapt any design to what Alexander Pope called the "genius of the place." Most of the report discussed such matters as topography, drainage, geology, and botany; in the remainder Viele offered only a meager description of the plan and its implementation. Two main features were a circuit drive, which followed the rectangular outline of the park, and four transverse roads, which crossed the park on the surface and thus divided the landscape into five distinct sections. On the whole, Viele's plan merited Clarence Cook's characterization as "just such a matter-of-fact affair as is always produced by engineers (begging the pardon of the whole useful body), when they attempt anything in the way of ornamental design."[9]

Under Viele's direction the city began hiring laborers to implement the design, but in what Olmsted termed a "storm of reform" the Republican-dominated state legislature wrested control of the park from the Democratic city government and vested it in a newly created, state-appointed Board of Commissioners of the Central Park. In what must have been one of the earliest demonstrations of recurrent attempts to eliminate machine rule, the legislature changed the city's charter and abolished the municipal police force, replacing it with a metropolitan force whose chief was appointed by the governor — all in the hope of undermining the strength of the Democratic party.[10]

In August of 1857, in one of their first official acts, the new Central Park commissioners — a group of lawyers and businessmen rather than politicians — rejected Viele's design and announced a public competition for a plan. In this action the commissioners surely were repudiating Wood's appointee, but they were also asserting their policy of an open handling of the public's affairs (a policy that included a public exhibition of all entries after the commission reached its decision, as well as the printing of its minutes and documents). Then this "professedly nonpartisan" body determined that, because chief engineer Viele was a Democrat, the new superintendent of laborers to be appointed must be a Republican, though not a practicing politician. Olmsted, who had retired to a Connecticut inn to work on the manuscript for what eventually was published as *A Journey in the Back Country*, there met Charles Wyllys Elliott, one of the commis-

sioners of the park. Elliott urged Olmsted to apply for the superintendent's position and gave him a letter of recommendation to other
Republican commissioners. Olmsted hurried to New York, circulated
petitions on his behalf, and was named superintendent on September 11, 1857.[11]

In his first days of work at the park Olmsted discovered that party
service had been a much more important criterion than skill or
strength in those men employed. Each laborer, he wrote,

> undoubtedly supposed that he owed the fact of his preference over
> others, often much abler than himself to do a good day's work, to the
> fact that a member of the Common Council had asked his appoint-
> ment. He also knew that the request of his patron was made not
> because of his supposed special fitness to serve the city or the park,
> but because of service that he was expected to render at primary
> meetings and otherwise with a view to the approaching municipal
> election.

Himself a political appointee, Olmsted was the object of considerable
humor to the Democrats controlling park operations. When he first
appeared in Viele's office, intending a social call, the new superintendent was subjected to a rigorous hazing. Viele sent the unprepared
and overdressed Olmsted on a tour of the park, led by a young man
who, with evident amusement, marched him through "a number of
vile sloughs" of "black and unctious slime." For some time thereafter
Olmsted's appearance on the park provoked the laughter of men
among whom, he later recalled, "the idea that I might expect a day's
work from them for each day's due-bill was thought a good joke."[12]

Politics intervened again later in the autumn of 1857. The city
government withheld funding, forcing the Central Park commissioners to lay off most of the construction crew. But as the Panic of
1857 worsened, thousands of jobless workers seeking employment
descended upon the park, including one mob carrying a banner
inscribed Bread or Blood. Olmsted later recalled that to reach his
office one morning he had to

> penetrate a body of men estimated by some newspapers to be five
> thousand strong. Most of them were laborers, but a number of mem-
> bers of the legislature and aldermen were among them. As I worked
> my way through the crowd, no one recognizing me, I saw & heard a
> man then a candidate for reelection as a local magistrate addressing
> it from a wagon. He urged that those before him had a right to live;
> he assumed that they could live only through wages to be paid by the
> city; and to obtain these he advised that they should demand em-
> ployment of me. If I should be backward in yielding it — here he held
> up a rope and pointed to a tree, and the crowd cheered.

In order to placate the unemployed and provide jobs for as many workers as possible, in early November the city government allocated enough money to enable Olmsted to hire one thousand laborers, who worked at clearing the park and enclosing it with a wall.[13]

Despite innumerable difficulties, during his first months on the park Olmsted shaped the one-thousand-man labor force into "a capital discipline." Then, together with Calvert Vaux, Downing's former partner, he collaborated on an entry in the competition to determine the park's design. Vaux later recalled that, although Olmsted had no previous experience in public landscape design, as superintendent he could contribute to the plan "accurate observations in regard to the actual topography which was not clearly defined on the survey furnished to the competitors by the [Park] Board."[14]

A young English architect, Vaux had studied with Lewis N. Cottingham, best remembered as a proponent of the Gothic Revival, and had worked with George Truefitt, an architect with decidedly republican sympathies. Vaux immigrated to the United States in the fall of 1850, when he accepted Downing's offer that they form a partnership. After Downing's untimely death in 1852, Vaux continued to expand his architectural practice and, like his American mentor, became a publicist urging governmental support of the fine arts. Olmsted later asserted that Vaux was the "chosen co-operator of the greatest master in America of landscape gardening, and had been associated with him in the most important and best public work that had been done in the country." His architectural training, knowledge of European parks, commitment to republicanism, and experience as Downing's colleague complemented Olmsted's knowledge of the site. It was perhaps equally significant that Vaux had designed the home and bank of John A. C. Gray, the Republican vice-president of the Board of Commissioners of the Central Park. Throughout the winter and spring of 1858 Olmsted and Vaux worked at night devising and finishing a plan for the creation of the most important and influential public park in the United States. Their design, anonymously submitted under the descriptive title "Greensward" and the last of the thirty-three official entries, captured first prize.[15]

That the Central Park commissioners undertook a public competition to determine the design of the park is significant for several reasons. Not only was this the first such competition to determine a major public landscape design in the United States, but it also involved some of the most talented architects, landscape gardeners, and engineers then practicing in the nation. The commissioners also solicited the advice of authorities responsible for managing parks in England and France. Most important for historians, the texts of the competition entries and the surviving plans demonstrate what nineteenth-century Americans thought a public park should be.

Traditionally, parks had served as repositories for public buildings, monuments, statuary, and fountains. Certainly Andrew Jackson Downing envisioned the public park as a didactic landscape that would serve educational and associational functions. In "The New-York Park," his influential editorial advocating the creation of a large, centrally located public landscape in Manhattan, Downing asserted that the park would be an appropriate location for "noble works of art, the statues, monuments, and buildings commemorative at once of the great men of the nation, of the history of the age and country, and the genius of our highest artists." In addition, the park might contain "winter gardens of glass, like the great Crystal Palace," as well as zoological and horticultural gardens, and serve as the site for industrial fairs and international exhibitions. The competition requirements established by the Central Park commissioners reflected this conception of what a park should be. The commissioners mandated that all entries provide for such features as a hall for exhibitions and concerts, a prominent fountain, a parade ground, and an observatory.[16]

Like Downing and the Central Park commissioners, most of the designers who submitted entries in the competition valued the park primarily for its associational and educational purposes. A number of the plans proposed that the Crystal Palace, which had been constructed by an independent commission in 1853 but which had recently become city property, be dismantled and moved to the park to serve as the hall for exhibitions and concerts. Others suggested the construction of pavilions and temples, in virtually every conceivable architectural style, to house the halls and museums of geology, zoology, botany, and kindred sciences. Several plans advocated that the old (rectangular) Croton receiving reservoir be made the centerpiece of the park and recommended placing a promenade along its high retaining walls. Still others proposed to enhance the park by constructing a tall monument topped by a "figurative image of the Croton river pouring water on the city," or by littering the landscape with triumphal arches, arcades, statues, classical columns, suspension bridges, labyrinths, and the like. In what was undoubtedly the most bizarre plan submitted in the competition, Louis Masquerier recommended the construction of Downing's unexecuted plan for the Crystal Palace as the hall of concerts and the rejected Bogardus-Hoppin design for the same building as the museum. Masquerier also intended "to lay out the southern half of the park into a miniature representation of the continents of the earth," complete with oceans. In all these plans the works of man—triumphs of architecture, sculpture, and engineering—would dominate the natural landscape.[17]

By contrast, even in their first collaborative landscape design

Olmsted and Vaux attempted to subordinate the requirements of the competition to the achievement of large expanses of natural beauty that would stand as the antithesis of urban conditions. Indeed, the Greensward plan was conceived as a response to nineteenth-century New York's dramatic and sustained growth. Every decennial census after 1800 had confirmed that the city's population and physical size were increasing faster than anticipated, and the building boom of the late 1840s and early 1850s that Cook had examined promised accelerated growth. It was regrettable, Olmsted and Vaux informed the Central Park commissioners, that, "in planning public works for the city of New York, in no instance has adequate allowance been made for its increasing population and business." In the 1850s the park was located so far to the north in the city's "straggling suburbs" that the epithet central was a misnomer, yet Olmsted and Vaux had grasped the reality of urban growth. Shrewdly they recognized that "twenty years hence, the town will have enclosed the Central Park." Prophetically they predicted, "No longer an open suburb, our ground will have around it a continuous high wall of brick, stone, and marble." Practically they shaped their design to meet the requirements of a time "when New York will be built up, when all the grading and filling will be done, and when the picturesquely-varied, rocky formations of the Island will have been converted into foundations for rows of monotonous straight streets, and piles of erect, angular buildings."[18]

Thus the primary intent of the Greensward design (fig. 12) was to create an expanse of rural beauty within the urban environment, a consciously constructed piece of "the country" that would meet the psychological and recreational needs of residents of the city. Olmsted and Vaux realized that the park should be "something more than a mere exemption from urban conditions" and should instead "secure an antithesis of objects of vision to those of the streets and houses." In Olmsted's estimation the park should be a rural landscape within the town. If successfully designed, it would "present an aspect of spaciousness and tranquility, with variety and intricacy of arrangement, thereby affording the most agreeable contrast to the confinement, bustle, and monotonous street-division of the city." Above all, Olmsted reasoned, the park must "supply to the hundreds of thousands of tired workers, who have no opportunity to spend their summers in the country, a specimen of God's handiwork that shall be to them, inexpensively, what a month or two in the White Mountains or the Adirondacks is, at great cost, to those in easier circumstances." The park would be the country within the city—nature, improved by art, offering respite from the "compulsory art of the city."[19]

The Greensward design attempted to create within the man-made city an equally artificial but seemingly natural environment.

MAP OF THE CENTRAL PARK

Showing the progress of the Work up to January 1st 18

SCALE 60 FEET TO THE INCH

RESERVOIR

CROTON

86

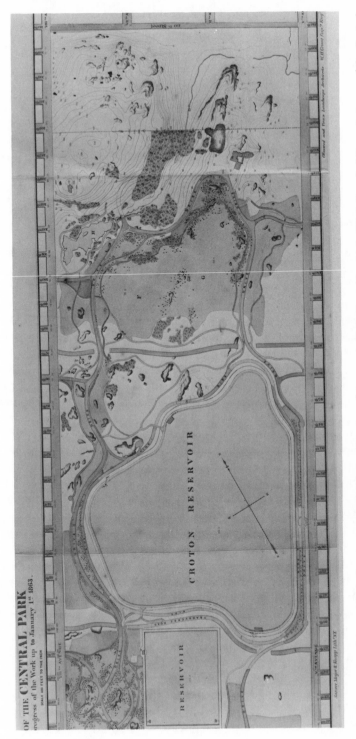

Figure 12. Map of Central Park showing construction completed as of January 1, 1862. From New York (City), Board of Commissioners of the Central Park, *Fifth Annual Report* (New York, 1862). (Author's collection.)

Olmsted and Vaux proposed planting a thick boundary of tall trees along the park's borders, thereby blocking a view of the buildings that eventually would surround it and shutting out the city from the pastoral landscape. Similarly did they suggest plantings to screen from sight the most conspicuous structure within the park, the high walls of the old Croton receiving reservoir, thus avoiding an awkward visual confrontation between the arts of engineering and landscape architecture. In Olmsted's conception of the park, nature would reign supreme.[20]

This same combination of characteristics—a realistic appraisal of the "imperative future needs of the city" and recognition of the importance of open spaces within the urban environment—is also evident in the Olmsted-Vaux proposal for sunken transverse roads. The terms of the competition had specified that at least four direct roads cross the park to accommodate the demands of commerce. Olmsted, especially, realized that as the city expanded to the north these roads would become "crowded thoroughfares, having nothing in common with the park proper" and would instead represent "every thing at variance with the agreeable sentiments which we should wish the park to inspire." Moreover, if placed at the surface such crosstown streets would divide the park into five discrete sections, no one of which would be large enough to contain broad reaches of scenery. Greensward was the only plan submitted in the competition that effectively resolved considerations of park and city by placing the transverse roads beneath the surface of the landscape. A "little judicious planting" in the area adjacent to these sunken thoroughfares and on the bridges carrying the drives and paths over them, Olmsted believed, could "entirely conceal both the roads and the vehicles moving in them, from the view of those walking or driving in the park" (fig. 13). Thus, the sunken transverse roads eliminated, or rather obscured, the necessary presence of a "turbid stream of coarse traffic," allowed the crosstown roads to be kept open at night when the rest of the park was closed, and preserved, at least visually, the unity of the design.[21]

In addition to its distinctive treatment of the transverse roads, what made the Greensward plan exceptional, what separated it from the thirty-two other entries submitted in the competition for designs, was the conscious attempt to exclude the city from the park and to subordinate all structures to the natural landscape. For example, instead of constructing a new building to serve as a museum and exhibition hall, Olmsted and Vaux recommended that the Arsenal, erected in 1851 as a state armory and already located near the southeastern corner of the park, fill those functions. The designers attempted to minimize the visual impact of the building by planting "in its vicinity forest-trees calculated to become handsome specimens of large size," which would, after a few years, "prevent the museum from attracting an undue share of attention in the general landscape." Olmsted and Vaux then effectively circumvented the commissioners' conception of the park as associational and educational by placing all important structures and formal elements mandated by the terms of the competition on the eastern side of the park, closest to Fifth Avenue. The area extending north from the Arsenal they considered the "dress ground," and there located the site for a music hall, the formal flower garden, the fountain, and the arboretum. By collecting these structures in one place, Olmsted and Vaux ensured that the rest of the park would be much more informal and minimized the extent to which the works of man would intrude on the seemingly natural landscape.[22]

Olmsted and Vaux considered the drives and paths at Fifth Avenue and 59th Street the principal entrance to the park. From there they directed traffic in curvilinear lines around the lower lake to the promenade, or Mall. A long (twelve-hundred-foot), elm-shaded avenue, the Mall extended diagonally northward through the lower park, ending at Bethesda Terrace. Although "averse on general principles to a symmetrical arrangement of trees," Olmsted and Vaux explained that the Mall's diagonal direction would lead visitors into the park's interior and "withdraw attention" from its boundaries. Moreover, they considered it essential that a metropolitan park contain a "grand promenade, level, spacious, and thoroughly shaded." In the Greensward design they used the Mall as a device by which to integrate a space for concerts, an arbor, and a prominent fountain—all located near the northeastern end of the avenue—within, but not intruding upon, the natural landscape.[23]

Olmsted and Vaux gave the Mall such attention because they considered it a central feature of the lower park, and they ascribed to it a visual importance comparable to that of a mansion within a private estate. The avenue also provided opportunity for that type of recreation Olmsted termed gregarious—for walks, or promenades, with rustic seats carefully placed to afford occasions for social intercourse. But despite the Mall's formality, the designers arranged the surrounding landscape "in connection with it," carefully placing trees and shrubbery so that the avenue would be invisible except when looking directly down it.[24]

Similarly did Olmsted and Vaux consciously shape the landscape to be seen from Bethesda Terrace, the architectonic structure at the northern end of the Mall that provided for the separation of traffic. They made this a focal point for the lower park not only because of its location adjacent to the central lake but also because at the terrace the hills to either side blocked all view of the city and the reservoir was "planted out." From this vantage, Olmsted explained, the "whole

Figure 13.
View of Transverse Road
Number 2 (at 79th Street),
Central Park. From *The
Central Park: Photographed by
W. H. Guild, Jr., with Descrip-
tions and a Historical Sketch, by
Fred. B. Perkins* (New York,
1864). (Courtesy, The Avery
Architectural and Fine Arts
Library, Columbia University,
New York City.)

Figure 14.
View of Rustic Stone Arch,
The Ramble, Central Park.
From W. H. Guild and Fred.
B. Perkins, *The Central Park.*
(Courtesy, The Avery
Architectural and Fine Arts
Library, Columbia University,
New York City.)

The Evolution of the Urban Park

breadth of the Park will be brought into this landscape." For the view from the terrace, Olmsted and Vaux devised a tripartite compositional arrangement composed of a foreground "enriched with architectural decorations and a fountain," a middle distance of "rocks with evergreens and dark shrubs interspersed among them, reflected in the pond," and a distance "extended into intricate obscurity by carefully planting shrubs of lighter and more indistinct foliage among and above the gray rocks of the back ground."[25]

This carefully composed arrangement was called the Ramble (fig. 14). Olmsted and Vaux employed its rough hillside to block out the view of the retaining wall of the Croton receiving reservoir. The Ramble, as the designers conceived it, would be uneven in terrain and covered with masses of rocks and lush foliage. Although Olmsted later asserted that "very rugged ground, abrupt eminences, and what is technically called picturesque in distinction from merely beautiful or simply pleasing scenery, is not the most desirable for a town park," he and Vaux determined to manage this thirty-acre site according to "its form and the character of its present growth." They proposed clearing away some of the stone and "various indifferent plants," replacing them with an abundance of varieties of shrubs and evergreens. Because of its location and irregular topography, only a single carriage drive crossed the Ramble. As Olmsted and Vaux implemented the Greensward design, they eliminated this roadway, and the Ramble was instead "entirely laid out with secluded walks and shrubbery" and ornamented with rustic bridges and seats. Some years after its opening, when the plants had matured, one visitor described the Ramble as "the most attractive and satisfactory part of the park." Here was a scene of rural beauty "very unlike what one would expect to find in a great city," for in the Ramble the "art of concealing Art was never better illustrated."[26]

Throughout the rest of the lower park Olmsted and Vaux emphasized pastoral scenery and attempted to make the landscape a self-contained entity. Vistas looked not toward the city but inward, across meadows and groups of trees, a series of carefully contrived scenes offering a tranquil alternative to the confusion of urban sights and sounds. In Greensward the designers set aside three adjacent areas in the lower park to achieve the impression of spaciousness and rusticity. One, the Central Plateau, was a swampy, rocky, thirty-three-acre tract that they transformed by blasting and filling into a broad, sweeping lawn, of gently undulating surface, which resembled a "great country green." As this area was surrounded by woods, they explained, "Views of an open and pastoral character are thus obtained, for a quarter of a mile in either direction, terminating in a forest obscurity."[27]

Olmsted and Vaux arranged the elements of the landscape to

enhance the impression of spaciousness within the park. From the entrance at Eighth Avenue and 59th Street, for example, the visitor approached three large expanses of turf, sprawling over the sunken transverse roads and seemingly endless in extent, which terminated visually at Vista Rock, the highest point in the Ramble. "Here is a suggestion of freedom and repose," they later wrote, "which must in itself be refreshing and tranquilizing to the visitor coming from the confinement and bustle of the crowded street."[28]

Along the western side of the park Olmsted and Vaux located a winter drive, a mile and a half long and thickly planted with evergreens and a few deciduous trees. Throughout the area they placed "open glades of grass" in order to achieve the scenic effect of "a richly wooded country, in which the single trees and copses have had plenty of space for developing their distinctive characteristics to advantage." The creation of a winter drive ensured that the park's landscape would remain interesting even when the deciduous trees were bare.[29]

In the upper park, the area above the reservoirs, Olmsted and Vaux combined "rudely picturesque" and meadowlike scenery. The topography there was "bold and sweeping," as the slopes had "great breadth in almost every aspect in which they may be contemplated." Because this type of scenery was "in most decided contrast to the confined and formal lines of the city," the designers explained that symmetrical plantings, architectural elements, and roads should not intrude upon the landscape. Instead they proposed to enhance, but not alter fundamentally, the existing scenery. They also made provision in the upper park for an extended meadow, a rugged ravine and watercourse, and an arboretum, which they located in the northeastern corner. But because of the contemplated extension of the park from 106th to 110th Street, most of the upper area remained undeveloped until after the Civil War.[30]

At Central Park, Olmsted and Vaux attempted to create an alternative urban environment, one that would provide relief from the "devouring eagerness and intellectual strife of town life." But unlike most landscape architects then practicing in Europe and America, Olmsted rejected the vague outlines of the public health rationale for parks, as well as the longstanding notion that country was implicitly superior to city, and considered a naturalistic recreational ground an essential element of the modern metropolis. To meet the needs of residents he devised a comprehensive theory of landscape design. The task of the park maker was not merely to put down a few roads and let nature do the work, or to plant beds of flowers, but to consciously shape the park to produce scenery that would promote psychological as well as general physical health. As Charles Beveridge has pointed out, underlying all of Olmsted's public designs was his "desire to use landscape art to meet deep human needs."[31]

Indeed, the single most important aspect of Olmsted's theory of landscape design was a concern for creating pastoral scenery, and whenever possible in Central Park he and Vaux planted broad expanses of lawn to achieve "the antithesis of the confined spaces of the town." Olmsted believed that this type of park scenery would have an unconscious influence upon the mind of the visitor. The contemplation of such a sweeping lawn would induce in visitors an *"unbending* of the faculties," thereby providing healthful relief from the pressures of urban life. This understanding of scenery's impact on the mind led Olmsted to see the park as a place affording opportunities for *"receptive"* or passive recreation—where the observation of landscape would "cause us to receive mental pleasure without conscious exertion."[32]

On the other hand, Olmsted classified games requiring mental skill or athletic effort as exertive recreation. Although the terms of the competition for designs specified the inclusion of at least three playgrounds and a military parade, Olmsted clearly believed that such activities would interfere with the quiet contemplation of scenery. As early as 1858 he circumscribed the use of the park for athletics: "Sports, games and parades, in which comparatively few can take part, will only be admissible in cases where they may be supposed to contribute indirectly to the pleasure of a majority of those visiting the park." Years later, in a letter to architect Henry Van Brunt, Olmsted reiterated what he considered the purpose of pastoral scenery within the urban environment:

> My notion is that whatever grounds a great city may need for other public purposes, for parades, for athletic sports, for fireworks, for museums of art or science, it also needs a large ground scientifically and artistically prepared to provide such a poetic and tranquilizing influence on its people as comes through a pleasant contemplation of natural *scenery,* especially sequestered and limitless natural scenery.

Above all, Olmsted reasoned, the park must preserve within the urban environment a rural enclave, free from the tyranny of the inexorable gridiron, a place where the sights and sounds of nature might soothe the harried resident of the city.[33]

The Greensward plan was a creative response to New York's dramatic growth in the years after 1845. In contrast to the straight lines and sharp angles of the expanding city, its paths were curvilinear, its landscape a series of scenes of seemingly natural beauty. Moreover, through boundary plantings, the transverse roads, and the complete separation of traffic they later implemented within the park, Olmsted and Vaux minimized the degree to which the city would intrude upon the man-made landscape. But in the largest sense the designers shaped a naturalistic park that would approximate the scenic beauty of the country within the city. Central Park thus stands as perhaps the most important landmark in the emergence of an American tradition of landscape design and urban planning.

The Greensward plan attempted to create an alternative environment to that of the urban gridiron, but to its creators it was also an instrument of social and moral progress. Olmsted and Vaux believed that the park was a republican institution that would combat the forces of barbarism that existed not only in the slaveholding South and on the frontier but in America's cities as well. In an undated manuscript fragment Olmsted cautioned:

> We are too apt to regard the great towns in which so many new-comers are held as old towns—old settled towns, but we have no-where on the western frontier a population newer to its locality and so little socially rooted or in which it is possible for a man to live so isolatedly from humanizing influences and with such constant practice of heart-hardening and taste smothering habits as that to be found in our great Eastern cities.

As early as the summer of 1858 Olmsted explained the role of public parks in refining and civilizing American society. Writing to journalist Parke Godwin in August of that year he called Central Park "a democratic development of the highest significance & on the strength of which, in my opinion, much of the progress of art & esthetic culture in this country is dependent."[34]

Unfortunately, not everyone shared this optimism. In what Olmsted called the "fallacy of cowardly conservatism" the *New York Herald* predicted, "The great Central Park. . .will be nothing but a huge beer-garden for the lowest denizens of the city." Olmsted readily admitted that New Yorkers, unfamiliar with the luxury of a large park within their midst, "will need to be trained in the proper use of it, to be restrained in the abuse of it." To this end he successfully urged the Central Park commissioners to create a force of keepers, under his personal supervision, modeled after the metropolitan police who patrolled London's extensive West End parks. Olmsted shaped the keepers into a highly effective educational and order-maintaining force, and their impact on the park's visitors was admirable. One writer told of encountering in the park one of the city's most notorious saloonkeepers, who had come there one Sunday to visit his former customers, who found the park a more attractive place than the bar. Olmsted noted that the park exercised "a distinctly harmonizing and refining influence over the most unfortunate and lawless classes of the city—an influence favorable to courtesy, self-control, and temperance." For amid the beauty of "natural" scenery, and with the aid of an effective constabulary, order prevailed in this most dem-

The Evolution of the Urban Park

ocratic of institutions. In terms that must have pleased Olmsted, Henry W. Bellows described what he considered Central Park's most important contribution to city life: "To teach and induce habits of orderly, tranquil, contemplative, or social amusements, moderate exercises and recreation, soothing to the nerves, has been the most needed 'mission' for New York. We think we see daily evidence that the Park accomplishes not a little this way."[35]

Bellows, like Olmsted, considered the park both a great work of art and an experiment in republican institutions, and in this he reiterated several of the arguments Downing had presented almost a decade earlier. But if Downing could only encourage Americans to build for themselves the parks of a European monarchy, Bellows looked upon Central Park and proclaimed it "a royal work, undertaken and achieved by the Democracy." Here, indeed, was suitable testimony to the wisdom of a republican society, "the most striking evidence of the sovereignty of the people yet afforded in the history of free institutions—the best answer yet given to the doubts and fears which have frowned on the theory of self-government."[36]

Most people undoubtedly would have greeted the creation of any park enthusiastically, but, even after the adoption of Greensward, debate over the appropriate design of the urban public landscape persisted. Olmsted was appointed Architect-in-Chief and Superintendent of Central Park, to be sure; but on May 18, 1858—the very day of that designation—Commissioners Robert J. Dillon and August Belmont offered a series of seventeen amendments that threatened to subvert the integrity of the Greensward plan. Dillon, the principal dissenter, rejected the naturalistic landscape Olmsted and Vaux had designed and instead argued that the park should be more formal. He proposed that a "grand Cathedral avenue" sixty feet wide lead pedestrians from 59th Street to the central lake, where a wire suspension bridge would carry the promenade across the water. The avenue would continue atop the walls of the Croton receiving reservoir, as a number of the competitors had suggested, and thereby make as the centerpiece of the park the structure Olmsted and Vaux planned to block from sight. From the reservoirs the avenue would extend northward, across another suspension bridge, to the terminus of the park. Dillon's proposals would have transformed the park into a handsomely landscaped extension of the urban environment rather than an alternative to the straight lines and formality of the city.[37]

Olmsted successfully argued against the adoption of most of Dillon's amendments, but this was only the first of many assaults on Greensward and its designers. Usually these attempts to undermine the plan were politically motivated, as city Democrats anxious to abolish the state-appointed commission and to gain control of the park charged that the high cost of land acquisition and construction was evidence of corruption. At other times Olmstèd had to battle the fiscal parsimony of Andrew H. Green, the park's comptroller, who refused to allocate funds for certain necessary operations. But the most fundamental challenge to Greensward was the traditional belief that the park should be an associational landscape, an outdoor public museum and omnibus educational institution.[38]

This alternative to Olmsted and Vaux's conception is implicit in Richard Morris Hunt's designs for monumental gateways to Central Park. In 1863 the Central Park commissioners had initiated another competition, this one to determine appropriate designs for the principal entrances to the park. But on September 2 of that year, at the urging of Olmsted and Vaux, the commissioners declined to adopt any of the entries submitted. Then, following the resignation of Olmsted and Vaux, who found that Green's dominance on the board made their position untenable, the commissioners engaged Hunt to modify his designs. On April 19, 1864, the park board adopted those plans. During the next two years, when they were exhibited at the National Academy of Design and evaluated in the press, Hunt's plans for the gateways became the focal point of a debate over what should be the role and function of a park in the modern metropolis.[39]

Hunt's designs, according to one of his supporters, would be the *"facade,"* the "frame" of the park. They would, he predicted, "ultimately secure for the principal entrances to the Central Park structures which would be [in] every way worthy of the magnificence of this great public improvement and of the metropolis to which it belongs; satisfying the pride and educating the taste of our citizens." Hunt, through this spokesman, asserted that as the city grew the landscape would become "more of a garden and less of a park." He rejected as impossible what he thought was the intention of the Olmsted-Vaux design, the creation of scenes of "rusticity" within the city. It would be absurd, Hunt explained, "to cheat ourselves into the belief that this is always to be a sylvan retreat fit for shepherds and their flocks." Instead, he argued,

> in the future, when this shall be the resort of two millions of people, when the roar of traffic through the transverse roads shall drown the singing of the birds—when the restaurants and summer houses, and music halls, and conservatories, and winter gardens and museums shall be greatly multiplied—when statues and busts, and monuments and columns shall crowd the avenues, the Central Park will become one great open air gallery of Art, instead of being, as some dreamers fancy it, a silent stretch of rural landscape caught up and inclosed within the raging tumult of a vast metropolis.

For Hunt the park would be the appropriate repository for the artistic expression of "great national ideas," the location of public museums, and a home for historical and social organizations.[40]

Hunt's design for the grand entrance at Fifth Avenue and 59th Street demonstrates how fundamentally different was his conception of the park from that of Olmsted and Vaux. Visitors entering the park at this gate would have to pass through a massive paved plaza, ornamented with a decorative fountain. The gates to the park's drives and paths would be demarcated by large marble pedestals (fig. 15) embellished with sculptural groups representing the "arts of peace." But the central element of Hunt's plan for this entrance was a semicircular pedestrian terrace, 100 feet wide and flanked by curving staircases that extended from the plaza to the lake below. This "grand monumental feature" included a classical column fifty feet tall, "surmounted by the Indian and Sailor, supporting the Arms of New York." At the base of the steps was "a spacious basin of water, containing figures representing the East and North [Hudson] rivers, with the figure of Hendrick Hudson between them on the bow of an antique vessel." But, significantly, the plaza not only created views of the park from the street; it also opened up views from the park to the city beyond (fig. 16) – and would have compromised the self-contained naturalistic landscape Olmsted and Vaux had shaped so carefully.[41]

When Hunt's plans for the gateways were exhibited at the National Academy of Design, Vaux, no longer associated with the park, orchestrated a journalistic campaign criticizing the proposals. In a letter to Clarence Cook, who later wrote a scathing indictment of Hunt's entrances, Vaux outlined what he and Olmsted considered the relationship of park and city:

> We contend and have always contended that but little architectural decoration should be made at the entrances beyond a generous treatment of the constructive facts – believing that the first need of the visitor when he leaves the city sidewalk is a perfectly free & unencumbered draught of "Park." The success we have aimed for is to make the change from city to country instantaneous and complete and in accordance with our theory that the change cannot be too abrupt.

Indeed, at Central Park, as in their later designs, Olmsted and Vaux had carefully planted tall trees on the park's periphery to screen out all views of the city, and they introduced the Mall, the only formal element in the lower park, to "withdraw attention" from its boundaries. Olmsted and Vaux reasserted the importance of a proper treatment of boundary plantations in 1872, when attempting to redress the vandalism inflicted upon the park during Boss Tweed's administration: "No one, looking into a closely-grown wood, can be certain that at a

Figure 15. Central Park. Entrance at corner of Fifth Avenue and 59th Street, by Richard Morris Hunt, 1863. From [R. M. Hunt], *Designs for the Gateways of the Southern Entrances to the Central Park...* (New York, 1866). (Courtesy, Library of Congress, Washington, D.C.)

short distance back there are not glades, or streams, or that a more open disposition of trees does not prevail." Such handling of the park's perimeter would enable visitors to leave behind the sights and sounds of the city, to escape, if only temporarily, the noise and congestion of the urban environment for the silence and seclusion of the country. Clarence Cook, writing at Vaux's prompting to dispute the artistic merit of Hunt's entrances, informed his readers that

> We want to forget the city utterly while we are in the Park, and we want to get into it as soon as possible; we don't want to lounge about the gates, but we want to find ourselves, without unnecessary delay, among trees and grass and flowers. And the makers of the Park have felt this as strongly as we have felt it, and have given us as little stone and as little architecture as was possible to get along with.

Figure 16. Central Park. Rear view of terrace near the entrance at corner of Fifth Avenue and 59th Street, by Richard Morris Hunt, 1863. From [R. M. Hunt], *Designs for the Gateways of the Southern Entrances to the Central Park...* (New York, 1866). (Courtesy, Library of Congress, Washington, D.C.)

That is, the park must not be an extension of the city but its antithesis, a series of carefully contrived scenes that would provide to citizens the opportunity for daily contact with the beauties of nature.[42]

But perhaps most significantly, Vaux found Hunt's designs for the entrances to Central Park more European than American, more appropriate to monarchy than to a republic. In a letter to Cook he asserted, "the park typifies what we have been fighting for, and the gates typify what we have been fighting against—it is Nap[oleon]. III in disguise all over." Vaux, like Olmsted, believed that the people of a republic needed pleasure grounds characterized not by Haussmann's imperial trappings but by the simplicity of nature. Only such a naturalistic park would complement the rectangularity of the city; only such a public landscape would be the appropriate expression of the urban optimism and civic awareness of New York's most enlightened cultural leaders in the 1850s and 1860s.[43]

Although the creators of Central Park managed to keep the gateway designs on the drawing board in the 1860s, Hunt's proposals reasserted the traditional conception of a public park as an associational and educational landscape, an extension of rather than an alternative to traditional urban form. Nevertheless, even as hundreds of new building projects took shape in the wards surrounding the park, accelerating uptown development and enriching the city's tax base, the spectre of Hunt's massive plazas and monumental architectural gates threatened to supplant the new definition of urban form Olmsted and Vaux first cogently presented in Greensward. There would be other challenges, but none proved more persistent and, at a later time, more compelling than the belief that the park should educate the public through didacticism rather than through the unconscious influence of natural scenery.

CHAPTER VI

CITIES AND PARKS:
THE LESSONS OF CENTRAL PARK

A Park is but one of many public improvements that serve to give character to a City.
— FREDERICK LAW OLMSTED and CALVERT VAUX

On March 7, 1855, a writer in the Ruskinian journal the *Crayon* suggested that the absence of large city parks in America proved that the "public taste is slumbering for some great new idea to awaken it to veritable life." Thus, while New York acquired the acreage and began developing a naturalistic landscape near the center of Manhattan Island, proponents of parks in other cities watched carefully. Philadelphian John Jay Smith, who reviewed the 1858 competition for designs, predicted, "When once a good specimen [of park] is seen, our people will excel in the formation of pleasure grounds, and we shall have them attached to every city and town where there is a particle of good taste or public spirit." As New York's park attracted increasing crowds even in its incomplete state, the phenomenon A. J. Downing termed *"Parkomania"* swept the nation. The *Scientific American* called Central Park "an enterprise which we advise every city in the country to imitate," and the editor of the *Horticulturist* reported in 1859 that parks were becoming "the great features in all cities of any importance." "The great Central Park," this writer concluded, "has given the initiative, and awakened inquiry and conviction of their importance." By the spring of 1861, when he published an essay on the subject in *The New American Cyclopaedia*, Olmsted could report that Philadelphia, Baltimore, Brooklyn, Hartford, and Detroit had begun the process of park development.[1]

In fast-growing cities throughout the United States leaders who recognized the "civilizing and humanizing influence" of Central Park adopted the vocabulary of sanitary science and recreational and reformist ideas to urge the creation of spacious rural enclaves within the urban environment. "Men cannot labor without relaxation," declared Baltimore mayor Thomas B. Swann, "and the heated atmosphere of a city is not favorable to physical growth and development."

In 1860 he ascribed to the "broader and more enlarged views of experienced sanitarians and philanthropists" recognition of the inadequacies of existing city squares. Similarly did Charles S. Keyser advocate supplementing Philadelphia's "little squirrel cages" with a large urban park that would provide "opportunities for rest and amusement which give fresh vigor to the bodies and minds of the people." As rhetoric gave way to practice, however, the designs chosen by various cities revealed different conceptions of what an urban public park should be.[2]

Less than a year after Olmsted and Vaux captured first premium in the 1858 Central Park competition for designs, Philadelphia's City Councils adopted a plan for the enlargement of Fairmount Park. The original park had been laid out in 1812, when the city moved its water pumping station to a five-acre tract on the banks of the Schuylkill River. Fairmount Gardens, which surrounded the neoclassical structures of the waterworks, became so popular as a place of resort that by 1828 the original site had been expanded to twenty-four acres. On his visit to the city, Charles Dickens reported that the waterworks were "no less ornamental than useful, being tastefully laid out as a public garden, and kept in the best and neatest order." In the 1848 survey of sanitary conditions in the nation's cities undertaken by the American Medical Association, physician Isaac Parrish noted that Philadelphia "has wisely appropriated the grounds at Fairmount to public use, and has ornamented them with a degree of taste and elegance highly creditable to the city." According to Parrish, the park served as the "resort of thousands of the inhabitants, and is admirably adapted for general recreation."[3]

Concern for public health was hardly limited to setting aside recreational areas. Even before Parrish's sanitary investigation some Philadelphians had recognized that a much larger Fairmount Park would be necessary to preserve the purity of the city's water supply. Thus, when merchant Thomas P. Cope suggested in 1843 that the city purchase the adjacent Lemon Hill estate as an addition to the park, Philadelphia's College of Physicians endorsed the acquisition as a sanitary measure that would protect the river. Eight years later John Price Wetherill, a prominent manufacturer, revived the idea of an expanded Fairmount, and Frederick Graff prepared an unexecuted design for landscaping the nearby estates Sedgley and Lemon Hill. From its inception, one of the essential purposes of Fairmount Park was to ensure the availability of a supply of pure water for the city.[4]

This unity of sanitary and recreational purposes motivated the enlargement of the landscaped area surrounding the waterworks. Charles S. Keyser, one of the most influential proponents of a greater Fairmount, reasoned that a more extensive park would "preserve the water [supply] from contamination, and secure at the same time in the most eligible spot near the city, a pleasure-ground commensurate with the demands of its crowded population." In February of 1854, a year after New York City received from the state legislature a grant of power to acquire land for a park, Pennsylvania's legislature enacted a law mandating the "duty of the [Philadelphia] City Councils to obtain, by dedication or purchase, within the limits of the said city, an adequate number of squares or other areas of ground, convenient of access to all its inhabitants, and to lay out and maintain such squares and areas of ground as open public places, for the health and enjoyment of the people forever." On September 28, 1855, Philadelphia's mayor approved an ordinance of the City Councils declaring Lemon Hill "hereby devoted and dedicated to public use as and for a park."[5]

A part of the former estate of Revolutionary War financier Robert Morris, Lemon Hill was located to the west of the city on the banks of the Schuylkill. Even with this addition, however, Fairmount remained comparatively small. Nevertheless, by arousing the "public spirit and liberality" of the people, who would then contribute to its further extension, Keyser believed that Lemon Hill might become the nucleus of a much larger park. Two years later he and Thomas P. Cope headed a citizens' committee that purchased William Cramond's estate, Sedgley, adjacent to Lemon Hill, and donated that land to the city for use as a park. Together these two "fine old villa grounds" added seventy-nine acres to the garden.[6]

While initiating proceedings to acquire land on the opposite bank of the Schuylkill as an additional measure of protection for the water supply, the city solicited designs for the improvement of the park. On March 3, 1859, after a "considerable competition"—itself a testament to the influence of Central Park—the councils adopted a plan of development prepared by "rural architect" James C. Sidney and his partner Andrew Adams (fig. 17). Unlike Central Park, where Olmsted and Vaux employed landscape art to transform an unattractive site into one of seemingly natural beauty, the additions to Fairmount Gardens were already notable for their scenery. According to Olmsted, the estates possessed numerous fine trees and "many very valuable advantages in position, character of soil, and beauty of natural surface." Sidney and Adams recognized that a minimum of alteration was required: "Natural features of the ground are, happily, so park-like already, that little more art is necessary than to complete what is already so perfect in outline." As a result they proposed to "utilize that which nature has already made beautiful, rather than to introduce showy, complicated, formal and necessarily expensive features."[7]

As had Olmsted and Vaux, Sidney and Adams pointed out that the purpose of a park was to "present the greatest possible contrast to

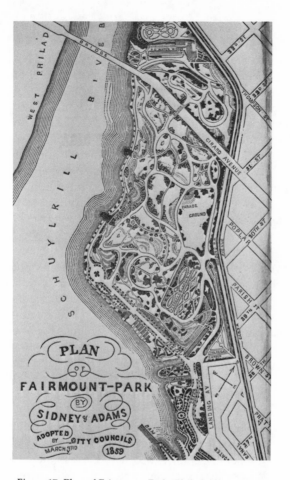

Figure 17. Plan of Fairmount Park, Philadelphia, Pennsylvania, by James C. Sidney and Andrew Adams, 1859. From Philadelphia, Councils, Committee on City Property, *Description of Plan for the Improvement of Fairmount Park, by Sidney and Adams* (Philadelphia, 1859). (Courtesy, Library of Congress, Washington, D.C.)

the artificiality of the city." To realize this goal they suggested "planting a thick screen of deciduous trees on the outside boundaries of the Park," those nearest the city. By such an arrangement Sidney and Adams hoped to "shut out as much as possible the view from within the Park, of buildings now existing or likely to be put up around its borders." The same concern motivated them to place thick plantings along Girard Avenue, to obscure the city street that crossed the park and that otherwise would divide it into two sections. As Olmsted and Vaux had done with the transverse roads at Central Park, Sidney and Adams suggested placing the grade of Girard Avenue below the surface. "We propose to slope the sides of the avenue," they wrote, "and plant them thickly with bushy deciduous and evergreen trees,

The Evolution of the Urban Park

so as to shut out entirely the view from the Park to the street below." To ensure the uninterrupted flow of traffic the designers adopted, in part, the principle of separation of ways that Olmsted and Vaux had introduced at Central Park; they arranged the two drives leading to the northernmost reaches of the park to cross Girard Avenue not at street level but above and below the surface. "Once in the park," they reasoned, "one should not be reminded of the city."[8]

At Fairmount, Sidney and Adams had an opportunity Olmsted and Vaux did not in Central Park—a waterfront location. The city had recently announced its intention to acquire additional park land on the west bank of the Schuylkill, and the designers seized this potential advantage by framing handsomely landscaped views of the water. Along the east bank, for example, they located a "Grand Avenue," ninety-six feet wide, with two pedestrian paths separated from the drive by grass borders. For almost a half-mile this avenue became a promenade that terminated at a circle near the westernmost point in the park. Such treatment of the riverfront was desirable not only for scenic reasons but because it created the impression of greater spaciousness within the park.[9]

Nevertheless, despite the advantages of the riverfront and these first additions to Fairmount Park, the area was still too small to accommodate large expanses of pastoral scenery, too small to provide adequate escape from the confines of the urban environment. Sidney and Adams even proposed cutting down a number of existing trees to attain a feeling of greater breadth within the landscape, but because of the limited extent of the grounds, their plan for Fairmount necessarily had more of a gardenlike quality than the expansiveness of a park. An additional flaw of the plan was that footpaths crossed carriage drives at grade, which consigned the pedestrian to the same concerns about traffic that existed outside the park. But perhaps the most important impediment was that Philadelphia failed to acquire at once all the land that would become Fairmount Park, which prevented Sidney and Adams from conceiving of the park as a totality, which Olmsted and Vaux considered essential. "The Park throughout is a single work of art," they wrote in defense of Greensward, "and as such, subject to the primary law of every work of art, namely, that it shall be framed upon a single, noble motive, to which the design of all its parts, in some more or less subtle way, shall be confluent and helpful."[10]

Sidney and Adams won the competition for designs in early 1859, but few of the improvements they advocated were implemented. The outbreak of civil war undoubtedly caused this. When Sidney George Fisher visited Fairmount in 1861 he observed: "Not much work appears to have been done at the park, except to make some winding drives. A few clumps of trees, most of them evergreens, have been planted, but seem neglected. No work is going on there now, the city finances not being very flourishing during the war."[11]

Less than two years after Appomattox the Pennsylvania state legislature granted Philadelphia title to the land on the west bank of the Schuylkill and directed that it "be laid out and maintained forever, as an open public place and park, for the health and enjoyment of the people of the said city, and the preservation of the water supply." The same law vested in a sixteen-member commission the power to acquire and improve the land. This body solicited of Olmsted, Vaux & Company and the Boston landscape architect Robert Morris Copeland suggestions for determining adjustments to the park's boundaries. As a result of their recommendations, on March 4, 1868, the City Councils announced the intention to "appropriate the shores of the Wissahickon creek," which drained into the Schuylkill, and to add that land to the park. An additional act of the legislature, approved on April 14, 1868, empowered Philadelphia to raise money for the purchase and improvement of the land through the sale of bonds. Noting that the development of Central Park had resulted in dramatic increments in the value of adjoining property, the Commissioners of Fairmount Park predicted that the "tax income, from the increased assessments of properties surrounding the Park, will soon equal the interest upon our permanent investment, and ultimately extinguish its cost."[12]

While taking steps to acquire the additional land, the commissioners appointed a committee to study plans for improvement. Its report reiterated the importance of the park as a buffer to protect the Schuylkill and the Wissahickon. By preventing the location of dwellings and factories on their banks, the park would "provide against the pollution of the water." In addition to this sanitary precaution, the committee pointed out the importance of "clean air and ample grounds" for recreation to the health of residents and the anticipated effect of the park in advancing the "refinement of their taste."[13]

By 1870 the land included in Fairmount Park totaled 2,648 acres. Because it presented great variations in topography and scenery—fields of a sweeping pastoral character, forests, river views, and rugged gorges along the Wissahickon—the site finally acquired for the park was well adapted for recreational purposes. "Nature herself has so adorned" the park, claimed the Committee on Plans and Improvements, "that little remains for art to do, except skilfully, with cautious good taste, to open such paths as may best develop the natural beauties of the ground."[14]

Determining who could best add those artistic touches by which natural beauty would be enhanced proved difficult. R. M. Copeland offered his services as landscape architect, as did the firm of Olmsted, Vaux & Company. Copeland informed Olmsted that he would accept employment at the park "on terms consistent with our views of professional rights, but on no other basis." Evidently the commissioners found his "demands" in conflict with their own responsibility to the public. Philadelphians deemed his plan unacceptable, Copeland wrote, "mainly because if granted the Commission would be superceded by me—and besides my price was extravagant."[15]

Upon rejecting Copeland's services the commissioners entrusted the preliminary work of surveying and grading the land to engineer John C. Cresson. Because the park's boundaries were not yet finally determined, and because as late as 1870 the process of land acquisition was incomplete, the commissioners determined that "no system of improvement which at once embraces the whole and each of these parts can be finally adopted." But the commissioners hoped to make certain areas of the west park accessible to the public even before preparation of a comprehensive plan. Cresson then directed his assistant, architect Hermann J. Schwarzmann, to begin the "work of laying out and constructing the Provisional Drives and adjacent walks" of the west park.[16]

On July 8, 1871, the commissioners requested Olmsted and Vaux to "submit, with the least possible delay, a plan for the improvement of the Old Park," the area Sidney and Adams had designed twelve years earlier. In the draft report he prepared on behalf of the firm, Olmsted defined three types of activities generally associated with parks: "general simple recreation," or the enjoyment of scenery; athletic events, or "special open air exercises"; and general education afforded by museums and zoological or botanical gardens. Olmsted dismissed the latter two and argued that the primary purpose of a park was "to provide for counteracting the special evils which result from the confinement of life in cities." In his estimation, the crowds, "multitudinous walls," and energy of cities had a harmful impact on residents. Olmsted believed that park scenery could have a psychologically therapeutic effect if it led visitors "away from the mental contemplation of objects associated with the conditions which have produced previous strain or fatigue." Thus, the park's landscape should "supply a place where people can assemble, rest, drive or ride with such change of scene and suggestion to the mind as shall as much as possible reverse that which is commonly established by the ordinary things of the town."[17]

Olmsted, Vaux & Company probably submitted their preliminary report on the Old Park in late July or early August of 1871. This was a "study in outline embodying a series of initial propositions." But the firm announced that it could not prepare a finished plan until it received an accurate topographical survey and information on approaches to the park from the city. More than a year elapsed before the commissioners announced their readiness to begin work and inquired about the plan's status. Olmsted then explained that the firm was unable to produce a complete design without knowing the Old Park's relationship to "other parts of the Park and to the general plan of the city." Only with a comprehensive plan of development could the park be a unified work of art and a corrective to conditions of life in the city.[18]

Neither Olmsted nor Vaux could devote sufficient attention to the Philadelphia park at that time, however, undoubtedly because of the dissolution of their partnership in October of 1872. As a result, the commissioners awarded the task of landscaping the park to H. J. Schwarzmann, who had been directing preliminary operations. Then, on July 4, 1873, after more than two years of negotiations, the commissioners transferred 450 acres of Fairmount west of the Schuylkill to the United States Centennial Commission, and that part of the park was developed as the site of the 1876 international exhibition. Designation as the site of the centennial gala meant that Fairmount continued to be planned and developed in a piecemeal fashion. Even worse, several of the buildings—most notably Schwarzmann's Memorial Hall, the art gallery of the exhibition—were permanent structures whose intended use was unrelated to park purposes. The Fairmount Park Art Association organized to collect statuary to adorn the landscape, and the commissioners accepted the donation by Robert H. Gratz of two colossal bronze statues for display in the park. Thus the centennial inspired the reassertion of the traditional associational and educational purposes of the park. Philadelphia learned the lessons of Central Park only incompletely.[19]

In his 1849 report on sanitary conditions in Baltimore, physician James Wynne lamented that, with the exception of a few small fountains and their grounds, the city was "destitute of public squares." Nor did civic leaders "appreciate the advantages incident to their establishment in a large and increasing town." Alarmed by the absence of open spaces in Baltimore, Wynne advocated that the city "make provision for their creation and maintenance, on a scale commensurate to the wants of its inhabitants."[20]

A decade after Wynne's report, Mayor Thomas B. Swann and his party newspaper, the *Baltimore American*, undertook a series of actions that would culminate in the purchase of Lloyd Rogers's estate, Druid Hill, for use as a public park. On March 3, 1859, the *American's* lead editorial asserted that there was "no subject connected with the growth and prosperity of our city, upon which all classes of the community are more nearly unanimous, than they are with reference to the necessity for a Park." In this and subsequent editorials the newspaper cited the recreational needs of the city's children and other public health arguments to urge the creation of a park. To make the issue more dramatic the *American* suggested that the City Council "look at the weekly reports of deaths, and see what a monstrous proportion of these little ones are sent to the grave prematurely, from causes which might be obviated by the pure, fresh air of a city park, and by free exercise in its shady avenues." Supporters of the proposed park compiled a lengthy list of signatures petitioning the city government to establish a "suitable place of Public Resort" for the residents of Baltimore.[21]

Although the park proposal enjoyed strong popular support, opponents expressed doubt that the city could afford the expense of purchasing and improving a large tract of land. In the hope of promoting continued economic growth and prosperity by tapping the agricultural resources of the surrounding hinterland, the city government had purchased stock in the Baltimore and Ohio Railroad. Because the city was already carrying this large debt, even Mayor Swann admitted that Baltimore "was in no condition to impose additional taxes upon her people." The *American* also expressed caution: impressed by the success of Central Park, the newspaper predicted that the "cost of the entire park would be materially reduced by taking into consideration the probable enhanced value of the city property contiguous to its borders," but added that it might be years before inflated real estate prices and the taxes collected on newly developed properties adjacent to the park could pay interest on and amortize the debt.[22]

While debate on the park question continued the City Council was studying a bill that would enfranchise streetcar lines. Employing the pseudonym "Public Good," a writer in the *American* insisted that the "city should become a partner in the large [financial] benefit to accrue from this great enterprise." Estimating that a fare of four cents "would pay all expenses for working the roads and leave a high rate of interest for capital," this writer advised charging a five-cent fare. Then, he reasoned, "one cent in each fare might be applied to the city treasury as a very just and proper source of revenue." Swann recognized that such a measure could be joined to the park proposal and recommended that funds derived from the city streetcar lines "be applied toward the purchase of a public park." Thus, he later recalled, "when the ordinance creating these passenger railways was presented for my approval, I deemed it my duty to insist, as a condition of the franchise, that one-fifth of the gross receipts should go into the treasury as a fund for this purpose." Following Swann's suggestion, on July 19, 1860, the City Council enacted a bill "to provide for a public Park or Parks." This law mandated the creation of a "Public Park Stock" (similar to the Central Park Improvement Fund) of thirty-year term, to be used for the purchase and improvement of an appropriate site. Moreover, it determined that the "revenue derived and to be derived by the Mayor and City Council of Baltimore from the City Passenger Railways, be and the same is hereby pledged and set apart—for the payment of interest on the Certificates of Stock to be issued under this Ordinance."[23]

The income from the city passenger railways, usually called the "park tax" or "park cent," proved to be an effective means of financing public open spaces. During the first nine months of 1863, for example, the transit companies paid the city $35,624.81. Revenue so exceeded expectations that the city was able to finance subsequent bond issues and purchase additional land for parks, all while continuing improvements on Druid Hill Park. According to Swann, this method of funding allowed the citizens of Baltimore to "ride as cheaply as those of any other city, and the bonus secured *goes into their hands for their sole and exclusive benefit.*" Because of the park tax, the mayor stated, "In delivering into the hands of the people this princely acquisition, this noble patrimony for those who come after us, we bring no bill of cost, and ask no provision for its support and maintenance in the future."[24]

In the law establishing the park tax the City Council also appointed a five-member commission to administer park affairs. After examining several potential sites, on October 1, 1860, this group purchased Lloyd Rogers's 517-acre estate for use as a park. Within three weeks the citizens of Baltimore gathered at Druid Hill to inaugurate the park. At the ceremony the Reverend George D. Cummins called the park "another blessing added to our list of mercies this day" and invited the poor to "find in its shady groves rest and solace from exhausting toil." Mayor Swann praised the park as a "transition from the busy and crowded streets" of the city, a place where the "toil-worn laborer rejoices in the prospect of his newly acquired heritage."[25]

The commission assigned the improvement of the park to architect and landscape gardener Howard Daniels. The designer of more than fifteen rural cemeteries, Daniels had worked with Eugene A. Baumann at the New Jersey suburb of Llewellyn Park. He had also visited European parks and described his impressions in a series of articles published in the *Horticulturist* and in C. M. Hovey's *Magazine of Horticulture*. Most important, Daniels had captured fourth premium in the Central Park competition for designs, and the difference between that earlier proposal and his plan for Druid Hill demonstrates the extent to which Daniels had grasped the lessons of Central Park.[26]

In his fourth-place entry in the 1858 competition, signed "Manhattan" and numbered twenty-six, Daniels took the position that the park should be an associational and educational landscape. "As a park is an artificial work," he declared, "art should every where be avowed and recognized." He proposed to develop the area below 76th Street between Sixth and Seventh avenues as a formal garden: "By treating it geometrically, a new and grand feature, with an entirely different character, is introduced, still leaving ample breadth on either side to be treated or improved in the natural style." The unifying element in the park, as Daniels envisioned it, would be a central avenue, lined with rows of tulip poplars and lindens, extending from colonnaded terraces at 59th Street northward to the reservoir. This formal avenue he saw as "the grand feature of the park," and suggested that it would "make the deepest and most lasting impression on the beholder." Daniels also proposed to ornament the rectangular receiving reservoir with architectural terraces and ornate flower gardens and to create Italian, French, English, and Dutch flower gardens throughout the park. He also recommended the use of gardenesque beds as well as more naturalistic scenes. In order to serve associational and educational purposes Daniels advocated constructing in the park Egyptian, Grecian, and Roman temples and a "Walhalla" to house twenty statues and some one hundred life-size busts. He designated an additional forty-eight sites for statues and five for monuments and obelisks elsewhere in the landscape. Daniels, like Downing before him, thought of New York's park in European terms—as a monumental civic space that would awe and instruct visitors rather than as a soothing oasis of rural beauty.[27]

Few such structures, however, would intrude upon the landscape at Druid Hill. Daniels admitted that in this case his task as a landscape gardener, like that of Sidney and Adams at Philadelphia, was to convert an existing estate for use as a public facility. Like Fairmount, the Baltimore estate was "already, for the most part, in condition for the uses of a Public Park." In his inaugural address, Swann assured his listeners that the estate "comes to you embellished by the hand of nature." Daniels described the site as "beautifully diversified by gentle hills of varied forms, connected by flattened ridges into groups, or irregular ranges, forming grand foregrounds, and broken and intricate middle-grounds and distances." The landscape gardener proposed to enhance the gently flowing lines of the topography and to preserve most of the "large, healthy, and *park-like* trees" on the estate. "Little else appears to be required," wrote horticulturist C. M. Hovey, "than laying out roads and walks, clearing openings, and thinning out the trees, which already cover a large portion of the Park." Daniels concurred and described as his task "to open a vista here, fill out a group there, and plant out an offensive object in another direction." With minimal expenditure, he predicted, "Baltimore may in a year or so have a park that will not be equalled in the world."[28]

Daniels and the laborers under his direction commenced work at Druid Hill on October 3, 1860, by preparing the park for the inau-

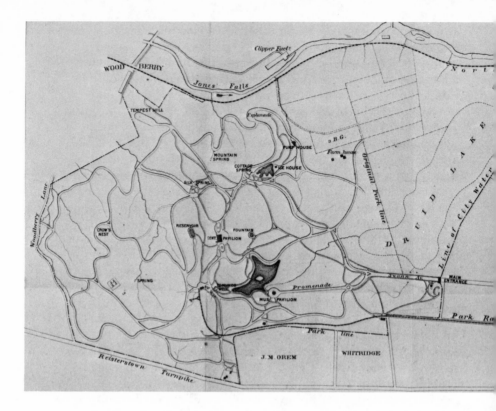

gural ceremonies. They attended first to the "widening and repairing of the old farm roads already existing upon the place, and their formation into a circuit of pleasant drives." The most important drive was the four-mile roadway near the park's boundary. Daniels arranged this drive to follow "graceful curves and easy grades" and so placed it that the visitor would enjoy "glimpses of distant landscape views of rare and varied loveliness." The park commission reported that "while in some parts the Drive presents the loveliest features of the champaign country, in others there are to be found the wild scenery and the magnificent forest trees of the Alleghenies." Throughout the park Daniels placed other winding roads and pedestrian paths. Only for the promenade did the designer forsake curvilinear arrangement; like the Grand Avenue that Sidney and Adams had proposed for the addition to Fairmount Park, this pedestrian mall terminated at a circle surrounding an ornamental structure (fig. 18).[29]

Druid Hill Park was especially noteworthy for its trees. C. M. Hovey felt that because the estate was "already highly embellished with trees and shrubbery" it presented a natural situation far superior to New York's Central Park, and Daniels believed that the woods at Druid Hill were the equal of those in any other public park in the world. Because of their "capacity for producing agreeable effects in

The Evolution of the Urban Park

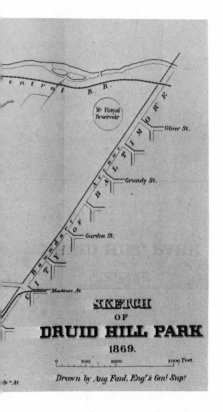

SKETCH
OF
DRUID HILL PARK
1869.

0   500   1000   2000 Feet.

Drawn by Aug. Faul. Eng.! & Gen! Sup!

Figure 18.
Plan of Druid Hill Park, Baltimore, Maryland, 1861.
Drawing by Aug. Faul after plan by Howard
Daniels. From Baltimore, Park Commission, *Ninth
Annual Report* (Baltimore, 1869). (Courtesy, Library
of Congress, Washington, D.C.)

the landscape of the Park," he considered trees the most essential
aspect of scenery. "Umbragious woods and groves," Daniels wrote,
"constitute the chief element or source of enjoyment in American
Parks." Unfortunately, in the years prior to its purchase by the city,
Druid Hill had been inadequately maintained. In parts of the park
"noble" trees had been "greatly injured by the numerous smaller
ones" which had grown around them. The sparseness of their lower
branches led Daniels reluctantly to advise a "thinning out of the less
vigorous growth, in order that the more valuable trees may have
scope for robust development."[30]

Daniels suggested that the southern part of the park, the area
closest to the city, "receive the most careful attention, and highest cultivated finish." There he placed a twenty-five acre lake and large
expanses of lawn to create the kind of scenery Olmsted termed pastoral. But if in some areas of the park Daniels employed landscape art
to consciously shape the antithesis of the confinement of the urban
environment, in others he left what nature had created. "The northern section now covered with old and sturdy woods presenting many
magnificent forest scenes," he advised, "should be left untouched in
all the grandeur and luxuriance of its primitive growth."[31]

As construction continued Daniels turned to the necessity of policing the park. Like Olmsted, who at Central Park employed a force of keepers to maintain order and to educate visitors in the uses of the park, Daniels suggested that Baltimore's commissioners hire an "efficient, uniformed police, composed of intelligent, obliging and energetic men." In addition to "maintaining a proper respect for the rules of the Park and the requirements of decorum," the designer hoped that such a force would also "disseminate correct ideas as to the duty of the public to guard and protect its own property." Respectful use of the park was a "matter of education," and Daniels placed responsibility for the maintenance of order on the "influence of the better class of citizens," who by "example and precept" would teach "the thoughtless and careless the duty of enjoying the Park without abusing it."[32]

Daniels never completely learned the lessons of Central Park—he urged the construction of a terrace and massive entrances, which the city could not afford—but the differences between his 1858 plan for New York and that for Druid Hill are striking, and must ultimately reflect the influence of Greensward. Work on the Baltimore park would continue for years, but soon after its opening Druid Hill became the "resort of thousands." David Murray, who in 1863 advocated the creation of a public park in Albany, New York, praised the grounds at Druid Hill as being of "more than ordinary extent and elegance." A publicist for the Providence, Rhode Island, park found Druid Hill "one of the finest public grounds in the country," possessing "all the essential features of a magnificent park, such as lawns, forest, wilderness, lakes, glens, and meadows." In Mayor Swann's estimation Druid Hill was the pastoral resort of Baltimore's "swarming multitudes," a scene of rural beauty where they might escape "the noise of the hammer and the smoke of the furnace and the workshop."[33]

As early as 1815 some civic leaders had recognized Brooklyn's future as a place of residence for New York City's workers, and in 1823 land speculator Hezekiah Pierrepont advertised the sale of lots on Brooklyn Heights, an especially desirable location, he explained, because it combined "all the advantages of the country with most of the conveniences of the city." Three years later Pierrepont proposed the creation of a promenade along the heights, but his plan anticipated public demand by a number of years. Brooklyn was still a village. Open spaces dotted the maps and the streetscape, and it was only a short walk from the center of population to the countryside beyond the built area of the city.[34]

Within a generation all that would change. In the early years of the nineteenth century engravers traveled to Brooklyn to exploit the pastoral foreground as a contrast to the bustle of Manhattan, but in the 1830s and 1840s country gave way to city. During these years Brooklyn's civic leaders undertook to enhance its appeal as a place of residence for Manhattan's workers—most notably by advocating, in an 1839 commission report on laying out streets, the creation of eleven new public squares, and by establishing Fort Greene Park eight years later. But as the city's population soared (from 24,310 in 1835 to 266,661 in 1860), as its physical size expanded through annexation with Williamsburg and Bushwick and through growth, and as New York began the process of developing Central Park, Brooklyn's fore-sighted citizens recognized the inadequacy of their public spaces. "The great need of Brooklyn," editorialized the *Star* in the spring of 1858, "is public parks." Later that year its editor, Edwin Spooner, argued that a "park of larger dimensions than Washington [Fort Greene], beautiful as that is, is very desirable, and will be found essential when this city has a population of half a million, as it will in another quarter of a century." Such a park was especially important to Brooklyn, which owed much of its prosperity to its image as a middle-class suburb of Manhattan. Central Park was already stimulating uptown development across the river, and Brooklyn's leaders must have feared that, without a similar attraction, the clerics of the famed "city of churches" might look out one Sunday morning and find pews vacated by those who found New York more appealing.[35]

Henry R. Stiles, minister and historian, attributed the parks movement in Brooklyn to "improved public taste," which had brought about a "new era" and a new appreciation of public recreational facili-ties. But even Stiles, one of his city's biggest boosters, admitted that the "success of New York's Central Park suggested a similar under-taking to Brooklyn." Thus, on April 18, 1859, the New York state legis-lature appointed a commission to lay out parks in Brooklyn. The legislature charged the commission to determine park lands "in view of the present condition and future growth and wants of the city." But when the commission recommended the creation of four large parks in the city the legislature balked. Sensitive to opponents of parks, wary of giving the Democratic-controlled city too much power, and already hearing tales of fraud at Central Park, the Albany body approved only the site at Prospect Heights and an East New York parade ground. The April 17, 1860, enabling legislation also named a new commission, headed by James S.T. Stranahan, to purchase and improve these lands.[36]

The site of Mount Prospect Park was an irregular area bounded by nine different streets and bisected by Flatbush Avenue. As at Central Park the space set aside in Brooklyn included the distributional reser-voir of the city's water system—a concession to public health concerns—and was located beyond the built area of the city so that the cost of land acquisition would not be prohibitive. To prepare a suitable plan of improvement the commissioners employed civil and topo-graphical engineer Egbert L. Viele, who had submitted a preliminary design of Central Park in 1857 and who two years later had presented to the South Brooklyn Association a proposal for the development of a park at Prospect Heights.[37]

In an 1861 report to the Brooklyn Park Commission Viele defined the park as a "rural resort, where the people of all classes, escaping from the glare, and glitter, and turmoil of the city, might find relief for the mind, and physical relaxation." He praised the area selected for the park as a "succession of beautifully wooded hills and broad green meadows, interrupted here and there by a natural pond or water." Because of its attractiveness, Viele assured the commissioners that the site would "require but little from art to fit it for all the purposes of health and recreation, to which it is devoted." To enhance the naturalistic appeal he proposed to "conceal every appearance of art," to "disguise the real boundary," and by judicious planting to obtain the "greatest possible extent of view."[38]

Despite this statement of intent, Viele was unable to overcome the difficulties of the site and turn them to advantage. This was especially true of his treatment of Flatbush Avenue, which divided the park into two irregular sections (fig. 19). Viele admitted that this street "might be regarded as a serious blight to the beauty of the park," but he pro-posed to make it a "striking feature of the general design of improve-ment." Unlike the transverse roads Olmsted and Vaux had brilliantly placed beneath the surface at Central Park, Flatbush Avenue was already a major traffic artery, and Viele calculated that the cost of changing its grade would be prohibitive. Instead he suggested plant-ing a double row of trees on either side of the thoroughfare, which would "hide from view the disagreeable accompaniments of a traffic road." Flatbush Avenue would then "form a fine municipal prome-nade," opening vistas to the city at the north and to the ocean at the south. By treating Flatbush Avenue in this way, Viele may have been trying to make the best of an unfortunate situation. More likely he was demonstrating bad judgment: Viele had, after all, submitted a preliminary plan a year earlier—which probably determined the lands that were acquired—and if his performance in the case of Central Park is indicative, Viele's preliminary plans were his final ones.[39]

Outbreak of civil war disrupted the improvement of Prospect Park as it did public works in other cities. Viele, an 1847 graduate of the United States Military Academy, resigned to become captain of engineers in the Union cause. Stranahan, president of the park com-mission, lamented that 1861 was "not a propitious year," for park development or for anything else: "The commerce of the nation sus-pended; the industry of the nation checked; the hearts of the people crushed by a wicked attempt to destroy the benign government under which they lived and prospered, all public improvements became necessarily paralyzed." For the duration of hostilities, Stranahan pledged, the commission would perform "no active service connected with the contemplated improvement of the Park grounds."[40]

Although the park commissioners were unable to continue development of the grounds during the war years, in Viele's absence Stranahan did on a number of occasions solicit the advice of Calvert Vaux on details of the park's design. In September of 1864, Stranahan informed Vaux that although Viele had been paid for his plan and report, the engineer "made no very favorable impression" on the Brooklyn commissioners. That Stranahan was dissatisfied with Viele's plan indicates how much his own attitude toward urban parks had changed and how well he had learned the lessons demonstrated in Central Park. In 1847 he had opposed the creation of the park on the site of Fort Greene, and twelve years later he was chairman of the South Brooklyn Association, the very group that had proposed Viele's plan for a park on Prospect Heights. Only five years later Stranahan realized that Viele's plan did not measure up to what an urban public park should be. With this enlarged vision of civic culture, this more comprehensive understanding of the role of parks in creating a new urban landscape, Stranahan turned for advice to Vaux, codesigner of the nation's first great municipal park.[41]

In January of 1865, Stranahan and Vaux toured the Prospect Park site and discussed possible alterations in its boundaries. Vaux suggested a major reorientation of the park by acquiring additional lands to the south and west of the original site (fig. 20). Although this low-lying area was thought to be unsuited for residential use, Vaux shrewdly recognized its potential as a lake. To finance the purchase of this tract and a smaller one at the intersection of Vanderbilt and Flatbush avenues for the park's principal entrance, he proposed that the commission sell all its property east of Flatbush Avenue except the reservoir site. Flatbush would then become the northeastern boundary and carry traffic south from the built area of the city without dividing the park. Vaux's imaginative scheme at once eliminated the major defect of Viele's plan, ensured the aesthetic unity of the park, and incorporated more diversified scenery. Olmsted judged the plan excellent and predicted that if adopted it would "form a much simpler and grander and more convenient kind of Park."[42]

In February 1865, Vaux submitted a preliminary report on the rearrangement of the boundaries for the park on Prospect Heights. Anticipating a major commission, Vaux invited Olmsted to return from California, where he was managing a gold mine at Mariposa, to collaborate on a design for Prospect Park. "I am a very incomplete Landscape Architect," he confessed in his letter, "and you are off at

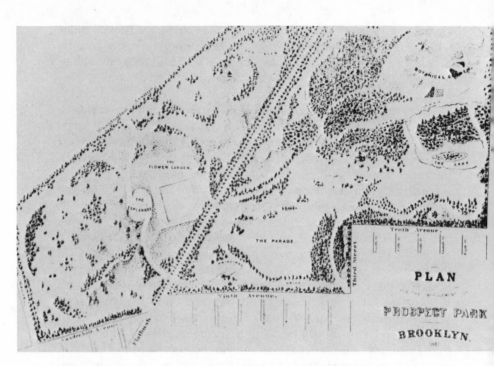

Figure 19. Plan of Prospect Park, Brooklyn, New York, by Egbert L. Viele, 1861. From Brooklyn, Park Commission, *First Annual Report* (Brooklyn, New York, 1861). (Courtesy, Library of Congress, Washington, D.C.)

the other end of the world depriving the public of your proper services." Vaux encouraged Olmsted to return east to renew their work; the fate of the parks movement, he reminded Olmsted, "is of vital importance to the progress of the Republic." But because the state legislature had established the park's original boundaries, Stranahan first had to go back to Albany to gain approval of the major changes Vaux suggested. When the legislature enacted this supplementary bill in May of 1865, Vaux informed Olmsted, "We may have some fun together yet." On May 29 the Brooklyn Park Commission appointed Olmsted, Vaux & Company landscape architects.[43]

When Olmsted rejoined Vaux later that year, they undertook a final review of the park's boundaries. Their report, submitted on January 24, 1866, began with a justification of Vaux's proposed alterations. They reiterated the necessity of abandoning the land east of Flatbush Avenue because the road would bring city traffic into the park and limit the designers' ability to create the landscape effects they thought city dwellers needed. Moreover, the city's distributional reservoir effectively divided the eastern half of the park into two parts, neither of which would be large enough for "park purposes." Even with the expenditure of large sums of money, Olmsted and Vaux

The Evolution of the Urban Park

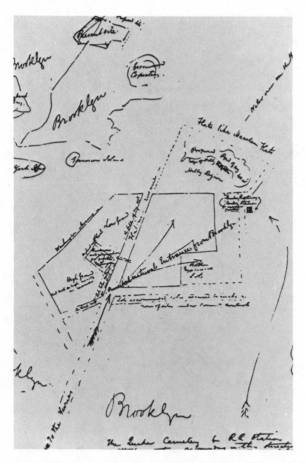

Figure 20. Proposed redrawing of the boundaries of Prospect Park, by Calvert Vaux, 1865. Note additions indicated by dashed line. From a letter by Vaux to Frederick Law Olmsted, January 9, 1865, Frederick Law Olmsted Papers, Manuscript Division, Library of Congress, Washington, D.C.

concluded, the land east of Flatbush Avenue "would always present a cramped, contracted and unsatisfactory appearance." In order to realize broad expanses of natural scenery, Brooklyn's park would have to take a different shape, with new boundaries that made it possible for visitors to escape the confines of the urban environment.[44]

What made the Olmsted-Vaux plan superior to the work of Viele and other engineers and landscape designers then working in the United States was their understanding of the park's relationship to urban growth. They realized that Brooklyn was an integral part of metropolitan New York. Because they anticipated that the city would continue to grow, Olmsted and Vaux recognized that in the future the park would serve as the primary or sole recreational facility for a large

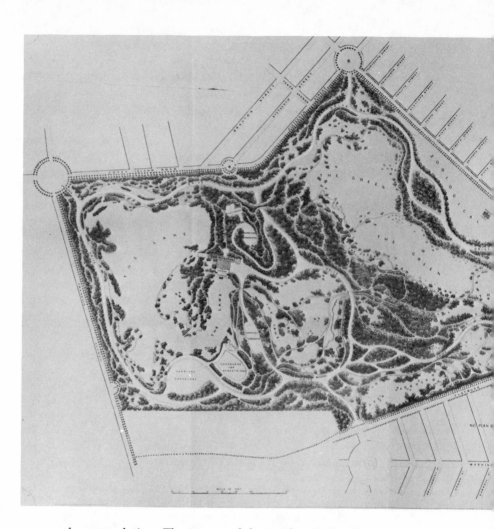

urban population. They asserted that such a city park must convey to the visitor a *"sense of enlarged freedom,"* a temporary escape from the "cramped, confined and controlling circumstances of the streets of the town." In the park, Olmsted and Vaux attempted to create not an associational landscape—one filled with museums and statuary—but a seemingly rural enclave that would induce an *"unbending of the faculties,"* a process of recuperation from the strains of urban life.[45]

Olmsted and Vaux defined two purposes of a city park. Most important was the contemplation of "scenery offering the most agreeable contrast to that of the rest of the town." They also recognized that the park must provide opportunity for people of all classes to meet on an equal basis "for the single purpose of enjoyment." Olmsted and Vaux admitted that these purposes were not quite compatible. Enjoyment of scenery required the absence of, or at least the "subordina-

The Evolution of the Urban Park

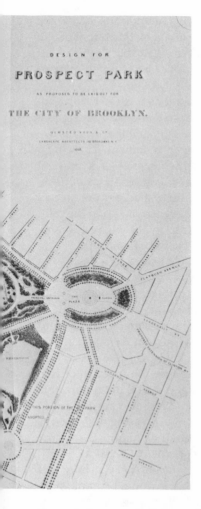

Figure 21.
Plan of Prospect Park, by Olmsted, Vaux & Company, 1866–67. (Courtesy, National Park Service, Frederick Law Olmsted National Historic Site, Brookline, Massachusetts.)

tion of human influences"; congregations of people demanded concessions to the "human presence." By compromise, by a "careful adjustment of parts," they attempted to achieve harmony, to create a "rural, natural, tranquilizing and poetic character, in the scenery," while providing facilities for crowds larger than would be likely to gather at any other place in the city. Only such a consciously contrived park could fulfill the individual's need for solitude in nature and for participation in communal activities. [46]

In their plan for Prospect Park (fig. 21), Olmsted and Vaux proposed creating a verdant boundary that would "shut out of view that which would be inharmonious with and counteractive to our design." The shape of the park was essential for this; its irregular outline provided a greater sense of seclusion from the city than the designers had been able to achieve at Central Park, which was defined by the gridiron. Olmsted and Vaux also constructed mounds along the park's perimeter, and planted those high banks with evergreens, to shut out the sights and sounds of the city. Within the park a visitor left behind the urban environment and confronted a seemingly natural landscape.[47]

The Prospect Park site afforded the designers greater opportunities than had the New York park, and Olmsted and Vaux used them to fullest advantage. For the interior—one not divided by massive reservoirs—they devised a tripartite spatial arrangement. The Green (later renamed the Long Meadow) presented scenes of a pastoral character, which they defined as consisting of "combinations of trees, standing singly or in groups, and casting their shadows over broad stretches of turf, or repeating their beauty by reflection upon the calm surface of pools." This type of scenery was "in the highest degree tranquilizing and grateful, as expressed by the Hebrew poet: 'He maketh me to lie down in green pastures; He leadeth me beside the still waters.'" Because pastoral scenery was spacious and peaceful, Olmsted and Vaux considered it the most important requirement of a large urban park. By acquiring the land to the south and west of the original site, as Vaux had suggested, the designers were able to give the three hundred-foot-wide Long Meadow a dramatic sweep visually endless in extent. The result was an impression of space so extensive that "the observer may not see all the boundaries of free sunlight before him at a glance" (fig. 22), a man-made but naturalistic alternative to the cramped, congested city. "Here is a suggestion of freedom and repose," the designers wrote in expressing their intent, "which must in itself be refreshing and tranquilizing to the visitor coming from the confinement and bustle of crowded streets."[48]

The second major area within the park, the Ravine, was hilly and heavily wooded. The designers admitted that it would be impossible to create a wilderness within the city, but, they asserted, "we may have rugged ravines shaded with trees, and made picturesque with shrubs, the forms and arrangement of which remind us of mountain scenery." To achieve this effect Olmsted and Vaux emphasized the rockiness of the topography and created a watercourse, which began at pools adjacent to the Long Meadow and meandered through the Ravine to the Lullwater. They then added rustic seats and shelters for visitors. Similar in intent to the Ramble at Central Park, the Ravine offered pedestrians pleasant, shaded groves and as total an escape from the city as was possible in an urban park.[49]

Together with a sweeping greensward and groves, Olmsted and Vaux considered a sheet of water one of the three principal elements of park scenery. Thus, on the low ground at the southern end of the park they placed an irregularly shaped lake. The Lake was not only an indispensable aspect of scenery but the natural receptacle for the

The Evolution of the Urban Park

Figure 22. Prospect Park, the Long Meadow, c. 1890. (Courtesy, National Park Service, Frederick Law Olmsted National Historic Site, Brookline, Massachusetts.)

park's drainage system. It also provided facilities for fishing and boating in the summer, and for that increasingly popular winter sport, ice skating, during the time of the year people usually had stayed indoors. Along the shores of the Lake, Olmsted and Vaux placed sites for the two major architectural features for large groups of visitors, the Refectory and Concert Grove, and constructed rustic bridges and shelters.[50]

Throughout the park Olmsted and Vaux located drives, walks, and bridle paths. They arranged the main entrance so that carriages would follow the drive to the southeast, which led "more directly into the heart of the park." The main drive served as a circuit and embraced the three types of scenery (turf, trees, and water) the designers considered essential to an urban park. Along its length the drive presented views "agreeable and harmonious" to the eye. From this circuit a second drive crossed the park's interior and carried visitors to the Lookout, with its shaded seats and spectacular views of the surrounding scenery. Although the proximity of the Lake to the southern boundary prevented them from achieving a complete separation of ways, Olmsted and Vaux arranged the traffic system so that pedestrians could "ramble over the whole extent of the property with as much apparent freedom as if the whole park had been intended solely for their enjoyment."[51]

Olmsted and Vaux were unable to shape Prospect Park completely according to their designs, but they did create in Brooklyn a "formidable rival to the Central Park." Olmsted admitted that Prospect Park included a "considerable amount of old wood, and for this reason, and because of better soil, climate, and early horticultural management, it has a finer rural and more mature character than the New York park." Landscape architect Robert Morris Copeland also found the Brooklyn park "much finer than the Central" and predicted that it would prove "much more satisfactory to all competent judges in the future." But perhaps the best measure of the Olmsted-Vaux achievement at Prospect Park was the appraisal of Charles Sprague Sargent, director of Harvard's Arnold Arboretum, who in 1888 came to defense of their conception of an urban park.

> Prospect Park, in the City of Brooklyn, is one of the great artistic creations of modern times. It is the best expression of the powers of masters in the art of landscape-making, who, more fortunate here than elsewhere in features of natural beauty, and especially in a native growth of majestic trees, were able to produce an urban park unsurpassed in any part of the world in the breadth and repose of its rural beauty.[52]

In restructuring the boundaries and designing and superintending the construction of Prospect Park, Olmsted and Vaux demonstrated how much they had learned from their experience at Central Park. Moreover, in Brooklyn they confronted two design issues that clarified what they thought an urban park should be: the location of a parade ground and the propriety of structures within the park. The parade was not originally part of Prospect Park. Indeed, the legislative act creating Brooklyn's parks specified that the parade be built in East New York. Olmsted and Vaux believed that military displays were incongruous with park purposes: at Central Park they had transformed the parade ground into "a great country green or open common"–and so it remained, even during the Civil War. Nevertheless, at Prospect Park they advised the commissioners to acquire the "ground immediately beyond Franklin avenue" for a parade. Availability of such an area would obviate use of the park's meadows by the militia and offer a less disruptive location for the kinds of athletic activities Olmsted found antithetical to the silent contemplation of natural scenery. The selection of this site for the parade would also prevent construction on the low-lying area near the Lake, where tall buildings would have been impossible to screen from park visitors.[53]

At Prospect Park, Olmsted and Vaux were also able to forestall use of the park as an associational and educational landscape by reserving two adjacent areas for those purposes. Undoubtedly chastened by the near success of Richard Morris Hunt's proposed monumental gateways to Central Park, Olmsted and Vaux realized that the open ground of a park would always appear appropriate for other public uses. Thus at Prospect Park they set aside spaces for a museum and a botanical garden near, but not intruding upon, the naturalistic landscape. Above all, they attempted to prevent the construction of buildings "which are not strictly auxiliary to park purposes, within its boundaries." If the park were to be the rural oasis of a busy metropolis, the landscape must remain inviolate.[54]

But undoubtedly the greatest lesson of Central Park was that by itself the park was inadequate to the task of refining and civilizing America's cities. Thus, even as construction in Brooklyn continued, Olmsted and Vaux studied the park's relationship to the urban environment as a totality and found it wanting. They recognized the need to extend the benefits of parks to all areas of the city, and in planning parkways and comprehensive park systems they contributed even further to the realization of the new urban landscape.

CHAPTER VII

PARKS, PARKWAYS, AND
PARK SYSTEMS

Your scheme should be comprehensively conceived.
— *FREDERICK LAW OLMSTED and CALVERT VAUX*

The naturalistic landscape presented relief from the rectangularity of the urban gridiron, but by itself the park could not redefine city form, and it had serious limitations as the instrument of social progress and civilization that Olmsted had hoped it would be. Central Park, for example, was so far from the populated areas of Manhattan that it was virtually inaccessible to those who lived in tenements miles to the south. Downing and other cultural leaders had advocated that New York's park provide recreational opportunities for people in the course of their daily lives, but the inadequacy—and to the poor, the cost—of transportation to the northern reaches of the city precluded Central Park's serving this function. Indeed, Olmsted conceded in 1870 that "for practical every-day purposes to the great mass of the people, the Park might as well be a hundred miles away." Only years after its construction would the park merit the epithet "central."[1]

The differences between their preliminary (1866) and final (1868) reports on Prospect Park demonstrate how rapidly Olmsted and Vaux recognized the limitations of a single park, regardless of size and quality of design, and how radical were their prescriptions for a new urban form. In the preliminary report, which ended with a consideration of routes connecting the park to Brooklyn's suburbs, Olmsted and Vaux suggested the creation of a "shaded pleasure drive" extending west from the circular entrance at the park's southern end. This road would have a "picturesque character" and would wind over rolling countryside, between groups of trees and shrubs, and terminate at the ocean. The designers advised that this or another road sweep through the outskirts of the city and approach the East River. There a bridge or ferry might transport vehicles to Manhattan and, by another shaded drive, bring them to Central Park. "Such an arrangement," Olmsted and Vaux explained, "would enable a carriage to be driven on the half of a summer's day, through the most interesting parts both of the cities of Brooklyn and New York, through their most attractive and characteristic suburbs, and through both their great parks." The drive would become a "grand municipal promenade," as fine a pleasure road as existed in any city in the world.[2]

In this preliminary report Olmsted and Vaux first articulated the need to extend the benefits of parks throughout the city, but their proposed treatment was still not a solution. A carriage drive, however noteworthy in design, could not possibly redress the high levels of congestion that already existed in large parts of many cities, nor would it significantly benefit those residents who most needed some temporary escape from the oppressiveness of the urban environment. In short, the proposed drive would have presented a series of handsome views, but only to those people who could afford to keep or hire a carriage—the wealthy.

Two years later, however, Olmsted and Vaux elaborated on this earlier suggestion and again attempted to look beyond the boundaries of the park and consider its place within the present and future metropolis. Their pretext was the Brooklyn Park Commission's recognition of the inadequacy of approaches to Prospect Park. But, whereas their 1866 report had only sketched the rudimentary outlines of a single "grand municipal promenade," in 1868 Olmsted and Vaux took a broader view. Studying the relationship of cities and parks in the historical context of urban growth, they realized that a street arrangement other than the gridiron could help promote a higher quality of urban life. Their analysis of the evolution of street plans, from huddled medieval cities to contemporary metropolises, marked a major turning point in the rural-urban dichotomy because the designers were able to welcome, instead of dread, the "accelerated enlargement of metropolitan towns." Such growth was no longer threatening, Olmsted and Vaux explained, because in terms of public health, social order, and educational and cultural institutions, "the larger each town has grown, the greater, on an average, has been the gain." During the nineteenth century, public health reforms and the delivery of urban services caused a decline in epidemic diseases and devastating fires. Two other developments that had improved city life, they explained, were the "abandonment of the old-fashioned compact way of building towns, and the gradual adoption of a custom of laying them out with much larger spaces open to the sun-light and fresh air." They illustrated this beneficial change by comparing the wretched conditions in Liverpool with those of the much larger metropolis of London, which, because of its great public parks, was a healthier place to live. London's parks served as the proverbial lungs of the city, purifying the air of deleterious gases and affording opportunities for healthful recreation.[3]

Olmsted and Vaux then explained that a large park should be

only one element of a comprehensive city plan. Improvements in public transportation systems promoted urban expansion, and made possible the separation of workplace and residence, but also increased the distance city dwellers had to travel to reach the country. The differentiation of business and domestic life stimulated additional demands for urban recreational facilities, as well as for new residential areas on the periphery of cities. Anticipating continued urban growth, Olmsted and Vaux proposed an alternative to the gridiron. They urged the creation of a "series of ways designed with express reference to the pleasure with which they may be used for walking, riding, and driving of carriages; for rest, recreation, refreshment, and social intercourse." This new stage in the history of street development, the parkway system, Olmsted and Vaux defined as "a general scheme of routes of approach to and extensions from the Park, through the suburbs, in which the sanitary[,] recreative[,] and domestic requirements of that portion of the people of the city living at the greatest distance from the Park should be especially provided for." If complemented by an extensive system of such drives the park would no longer be a welcome though distant retreat from the town but an integral component of the city.[4]

Olmsted and Vaux proposed that Brooklyn's parkways be 260 feet wide, with a central roadway, service roads, and pedestrian paths separated by plots of grass and six rows of trees (fig. 23). Such a street system would provide for the complete separation of commercial and recreational traffic, create shaded walks and tree-lined avenues, increase the desirability of neighboring lots as sites for middle-class houses, and act as a barrier to the spread of fire. Like the Parisian boulevards then being constructed by Baron Haussmann, Olmsted and Vaux's parkways were a conscious attempt to enhance the attractiveness of the city. Significantly, however, these parkways would be constructed on a residential rather than imperial scale.[5]

Olmsted and Vaux established the routes for two major parkways in Brooklyn—Ocean and Eastern—and soon after beginning work at Prospect Park they assumed control of all the squares and public spaces in the city. But they were unable to plan comprehensively for the metropolis of the future: a shortage of funds curtailed all park operations from November 1869 until July of the following year; then the economic panic of 1873 halted construction for the remainder of the decade. Because of these financial conditions Olmsted and Vaux terminated their relationship with the Brooklyn Park Commission in 1873. The park was then only partially complete and their comprehensive system of public spaces and parkways only a blueprint for a different urban form.[6]

During the summer of 1868 Olmsted and Vaux had an opportunity to implement precisely the kind of comprehensive system of parks and

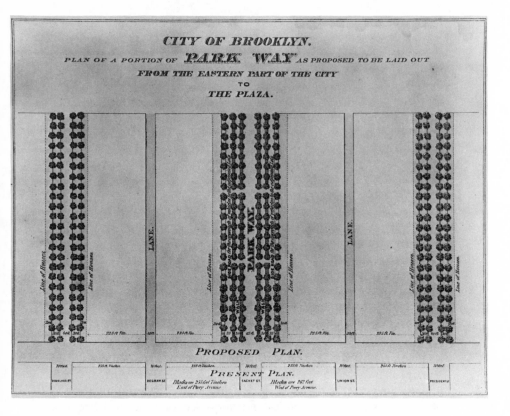

PROPOSED PLAN.

PRESENT PLAN.

Figure 23. Plan of a parkway for Brooklyn, New York, by Olmsted, Vaux & Company, 1868. (Courtesy, The Brooklyn Historical Society, Brooklyn, New York.)

parkways they first sketched in Brooklyn. In August Olmsted addressed a public meeting in Buffalo, chaired by former president Millard Fillmore, and explained the necessity for and purposes of public recreational grounds. While in Buffalo he examined three potential park sites and was thus able, for the first time in his career, to determine what land would be chosen for park use. On October 1, after considerable study, the firm of Olmsted, Vaux & Company submitted their preliminary report—significantly, one that outlined the development not of a single park but of a comprehensive system of parks and parkways. As Charles Beveridge has pointed out, Olmsted's plan for Buffalo marked the "first demonstration of the form he hoped the expanding American city would take."[7]

In their report Olmsted and Vaux explained that the object of a park was to establish conditions that would "exert the most healthful recreative action upon the people who are expected to resort to it." An urban park, they explained should be "of a character diverse from the ordinary conditions" of life in the city. A park must be appropriately located, occupying a site "in which natural conditions, as opposed to town conditions, shall have every possible advantage"; it must also contain desirable topographical features and space enough to permit the realization of large expanses of pastoral scenery. Almost by definition, the only undeveloped land conforming to these prerequisites would be located some distance from the built area of the city, and Olmsted and Vaux urged that parklike spaces be purchased in anticipation of urban growth.[8]

The principal feature of the Buffalo system was "The Park" (later renamed Delaware Park), a tract of some 350 acres located to the north of the city, near Forest Lawn Cemetery. Olmsted and Vaux described the large, meadowlike area of this site as "a series of open fields which are graced by a number of remarkably fine umbrageous trees, such as are never found except under unusually favorable conditions of soil and climate." Here was land that already resembled a park, and Olmsted and Vaux recommended that it be purchased immediately and transformed into the physical antithesis of traditional urban form. For the western part of the park they proposed damming Scajaquada Creek to form a 46-acre lake, which would provide for increasingly popular summer and winter sports and incorporate scenic effects different from those of the meadow and groves. Unfortunately, Delaware Avenue separated the two sections of the park; but as they had done with the transverse roads at Central Park, Olmsted and Vaux placed this street below grade and used thick plantings to block it from view, so that the sight and sound of traffic would interfere as little as possible with the sense of tranquility the visitor experienced while in the naturalistic landscape. They also made provision for the complete separation of vehicular and pedestrian ways inside the park.[9]

Based on their experiences in New York and Brooklyn, Olmsted and Vaux admitted that a large park should not be the only open public space within a city. The naturalistic landscape provided for "recreation of a decided character, involving an absence of some hours from ordinary pursuits," but as a result it could not meet the needs of most workers, except on Sundays or holidays, or of residents of distant neighborhoods. Thus, Olmsted and Vaux urged Buffalo's leaders to think of the park "simply as the more important member of a general, largely provident, forehanded, comprehensive arrangement for securing refreshment, recreation and health to the people." The city also needed smaller, more accessible parks "to which many can resort for a short stroll, airing and diversion, and where they can at once enjoy a decided change of scene from that which is associated with their regular occupation."[10]

To provide these other recreational opportunities Olmsted and Vaux recommended the acquisition of two additional sites for park use: the Front, a 32-acre tract adjacent to the Niagara River, and the

Parade, a 56-acre space near the eastern periphery of the city. The Front was a "comparatively elevated" ground, and Olmsted and Vaux predicted that, if developed as a park, it would provide spectacular scenic views of Lake Erie and the river and would possess a "character of magnificence admirably adapted to be associated with stately ceremonies, the entertainment of public guests and other occasions of civic display." They located at the Front a playground, a carriage concourse, an amphitheatre, and a large architectural terrace for musical events. The site of the proposed Parade was the highest ground in the city and had the additional asset of being "nearer to the more densely populated parts of the city than any other site having distinctive natural advantages." Olmsted and Vaux planned the Parade to include a level ground for military displays, a grove with the most modern play facilities for children, and Vaux's refectory, a large structure that would afford a place for "gregarious" recreation. Thus their plan for the three initial parks in the Buffalo system built upon the designs of Central and Prospect parks. Olmsted and Vaux provided for the differentiation of recreational spaces, using the Front and Parade as locations for functions that, while essential in a city, would be antithetical to the tranquility of a naturalistic landscape (fig. 24).[11]

Olmsted and Vaux also prepared plans for a system of parkways. Designed to be the principal approaches to the park, these 200-foot-wide, tree-lined roads united the three parks and extended into the built area of the city. These boulevards would be "adapted exclusively for pleasure travel" and, as they contained "turf, trees, shrubs and flowers," would be "more park-like than town-like." Perhaps most importantly, these roads would extend to distant parts of the city the benefits of parks; they would be pleasure grounds "suitable for a short stroll, for a playground for children and an airing ground for invalids."[12]

Based on this preliminary report, Buffalo acquired the three sites for park development and, in May of 1869, entrusted their design to the firm of Olmsted, Vaux & Company. Construction began the following year and was superintended by civil engineer George K. Radford. As the parks and parkways took shape, owners of land on the northern and eastern borders of the principal park commissioned Olmsted and Radford to plan a residential subdivision. At least since his visit to Birkenhead, a suburb of Liverpool, during his walking tour of England in 1850, Olmsted had recognized the stimulus that a park could give to urban development; the rapid rise in property values and the accelerated construction of handsome houses in areas proximate to Central and Prospect parks had reinforced that belief. But the commission to lay out streets in "Parkside" was Olmsted's first opportunity to plan an urban residential neighborhood that would complement the naturalistic landscape of a park. With Radford he platted

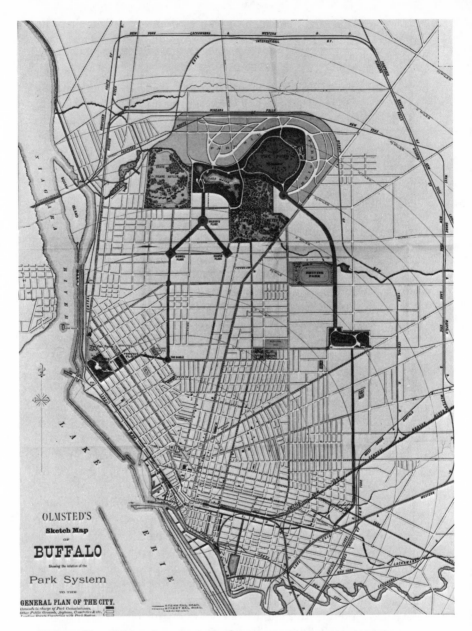

Figure 24. Plan of the park system for Buffalo, New York, by Olmsted, Vaux & Company, 1868. 1876 map showing parks and parkways in relationship to the city plan. (Courtesy, Center for Landscape Studies, Dumbarton Oaks, Trustees for Harvard University, Washington, D.C.)

curving, tree-lined streets, and divided the area into lots large enough for handsome homes and their grounds.[13]

Olmsted's association with the city of Buffalo continued intermittently for another thirty years. During most of that time his associate William McMillan superintended the parks, working assiduously to ensure the integrity of Olmsted's projects. Olmsted and his firm also designed other parks and squares in the city, including a system of parks and parkways in the southern end of town and the grounds of the New York State Asylum for the Insane, as well as a number of private residences. Thus, at Buffalo Olmsted had the opportunity to design a comprehensive park system and to watch it develop and evolve according to his principles of urban form. With the superimposition of his designs on Joseph Ellicott's original radial street plan, Olmsted believed, Buffalo was "the best planned city, as to its streets, public places and grounds, in the United States."[14]

If Buffalo represents the first superb example of comprehensive park planning in the United States, Chicago exemplifies the persistence of political intervention and the continuing debate over whether the park should be a naturalistic or an educational and associational landscape. Chicago had set aside six small open spaces in the years between 1839 and 1864, but after the Civil War the city's leaders recognized that the existing recreational spaces were inadequate and moved energetically to provide their city with a comprehensive system of parks and parkways. In 1867, attorney E. B. McCagg sponsored a bill that sought to establish an extensive recreational area in the Hyde Park neighborhood; although the bill passed in the state legislature it failed to carry in popular referendum. Less than two years later the legislature approved the acquisition of three large parks, to the north, west, and south of the city, and Chicago's voters ratified creation of the western and southern parks in February of 1869.[15]

As the park question attracted increasing popular attention, landscape architect H.W.S. Cleveland attempted to focus the debate on issues of design. This transplanted New Englander warned Chicagoans not to copy existing park plans. Instead, he argued, "every city should adapt the style of arrangement of her public grounds to the peculiar characteristics of her condition and topographical features." Cleveland believed that Chicago would be foolish to follow the examples of eastern parks, because its flat topography was totally unsuited to that style of design: "nature has denied us many of the features which have been commonly considered indispensable to the full development of her charms," he noted, "and art can only supply their want to a limited extent." Despite its title, Cleveland devoted most of his pamphlet entitled *The Public Grounds of Chicago: How to Give Them Character and Expression* to a discussion of the extensive boulevard system mandated in the park legislation. Because of the flatness of the land, he maintained, such parkways might become "utterly devoid of character," and curvilinearity merely for the sake of picturesque effect would be foolhardy. To enhance the attractiveness of these grand avenues he recommended the union of botany and landscape art:

> Let the avenue form in its whole extent, an arboretum, comprising every variety of tree and shrub which will thrive in this climate, each family occupying a distinct section, of greater or less extent, according to its importance, in which all the skill of the gardener's art may be displayed, but in which all the artistic effect shall be produced by the use of varieties of the single family to which the portion is appropriated.

The resulting drive would serve educational purposes and at the same time provide enough diversity of surroundings to alleviate the monotonous flatness of the prairie.[16]

Cleveland undoubtedly hoped that the publication of his pamphlet would result in a commission to develop the Chicago parks, but none was forthcoming. The legislative acts establishing the park system appointed two separate commissions, neither of which selected Cleveland to plan these spaces. The commission charged with developing the south park solicited designs from the New York firm of Olmsted, Vaux & Company, while the men responsible for parks in the western part of the city selected local architect William LeBaron Jenney to lay out those grounds.[17]

The 1,000-acre south park (fig. 25) was actually two distinct pieces of ground with vastly different landscape qualities. It consisted of an upper division (now Washington Park) of barren prairie and a lower division (now Jackson Park) of swampy lowlands adjacent to Lake Michigan. A parkway, the Midway Plaisance, joined the two areas. The western system embraced three separate spaces, Humboldt, Central (now Garfield), and Douglas parks, which were connected by boulevards. Taken together, the lands appropriated for park use afforded Chicago an unparalleled opportunity to provide adequate recreational grounds for its fast-growing population. But because two separate commissions were developing the parks, the result would be a series of discrete recreational grounds rather than the comprehensive, integrated park system Olmsted and Vaux were then implementing in Buffalo.[18]

In designing the south park Olmsted and Vaux determined to use to best advantage the landscape features of each division. For the tidal swamps adjacent to Lake Michigan in the lower park this required ingenuity not only in conception but also in engineering. They devised a scheme to drain the morass and, in its lowlying areas, exca-

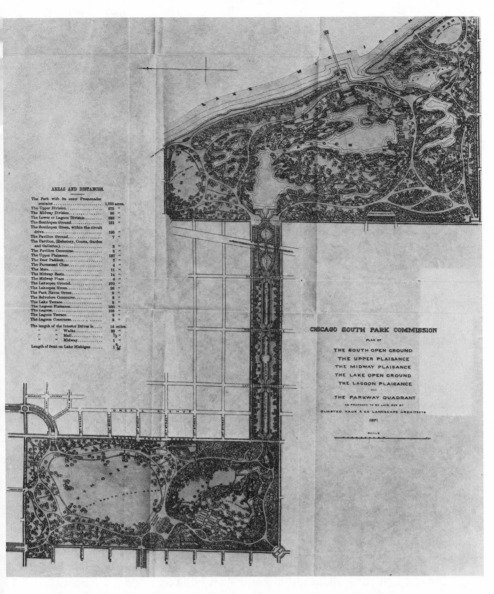

Figure 25. Plan of the South Parks, Chicago, Illinois, by Olmsted, Vaux & Company, 1868. 1871 map. (Courtesy, Center for Landscape Studies, Dumbarton Oaks, Trustees for Harvard University, Washington, D.C.)

vated earth to create a lagoon. Distributing the rich fill thus obtained they created the depth and quality of soil that would support stands of large trees. The designers also perceived that Lake Michigan provided an unusual means of access to the park: in the future, they predicted, "the toiling population of Chicago, relieved from work at an early hour on the last of the week, will be carried [in steamboats] to the South Park by many tens of thousands at the cost of a few cents." There they might walk, swim, play, or hire boats and follow an interior watercourse from the lagoon across the Midway to the smaller lake in the upper park.[19]

The land selected for the south park was flat and barren. As a result, Olmsted and Vaux could not create in Chicago the kind of naturalistic park they had in other cities. They did landscape the shores of the lagoon with lush tropical plants to convey to visitors a sense of the abundance of nature, and they shaped a sweeping expanse of lawn, the 100-acre "Southopen ground," in the upper division. But because they were planning only part of a much larger park system, Olmsted and Vaux could not make a series of parks differentiated by intended use. Thus, in addition to providing spaces for passive recreation, they also had to crowd a number of structures into the park, including a formal mall and an immense refectory in the upper division and a concourse, boathouse, terrace, Belvedere, aviary, and zoo in the lower. The political limitations of two park commissions and the topographical limitations of the south park site thus prevented Olmsted and Vaux from designing as comprehensive and imaginative a park system as they had in Buffalo.[20]

Jenney's designs for the western parks (fig. 26), however, reasserted the function of the park as educational and associational. Douglas Park, for example, contained a refectory with a massive stone railing, a rotunda and cascade, a dairy and farmstead, a second refectory, and a formal concourse with bandstand. Instead of placing these structures in one part of the park, as Olmsted and Vaux had done at Central Park and as Olmsted later would do at Franklin Park, Jenney distributed them throughout the landscape. Moreover, he wanted each architectural element to be seen from the drive, thereby celebrating the structures that Olmsted and Vaux had conceded to be necessary in their first parks but had carefully hidden from view. In his design for Central (now Garfield) Park, Jenney confronted a problem Olmsted and Vaux had faced in their first collaborative effort: a site divided by roadways. Although he attempted to screen out of the park the traffic on these roads, Jenney was unable to maintain the aesthetic unity of the plan. The middle portion of the park was highly ornamental, with a large architectural terrace, a "byzantine" bandstand, a concourse, a refectory, and gardenesque beds of flowering plants. The southernmost part, intended to be educational, included

Figure 26. Plan of Central Park, Chicago, Illinois, by William LeBaron Jenney, 1871. (Courtesy, Library of Congress, Washington, D.C.)

a zoo, a botanical garden, and the site for a museum. Humboldt, the southernmost of the three parks, had a formal promenade and drive, a refectory, a carriage concourse, and an enormous bandstand adjacent to the lake. Most of these elements had appeared in Central Park or Prospect Park, but Olmsted and Vaux had abandoned them when designing the Buffalo system only the previous year.[21]

In his plans for Chicago's west parks Jenney revealed his French training in landscape engineering and architecture. His formal boulevards clearly owed more to Haussmann and Alphand than did Olmsted and Vaux's parkways, and his conception of the park was far closer to the ideas of another student of a French *école*, Richard Morris Hunt, than to those of the "dreamers" who in 1858 had designed New

York's Central Park. Indeed, whereas Olmsted and Vaux attempted to redefine city form by shaping the park as a naturalistic landscape, with sweeping expanses of pastoral scenery, Jenney devoted the largest expanses of his parks to water that served as foreground to architectural elements: he introduced only one important lawn in his three parks, a portion of the twenty-acre northernmost section of the Central Park—a space more limited than even the smallest of the constricted areas in the southern end of New York's Central Park.[22]

The development of the Chicago parks thus represents the recurrence of the debate over park form that began with the 1858 competition for designs of New York's Central Park and that reached a critical point in the battle over Richard Morris Hunt's proposed monumental gateways. The differences separating the Olmsted-Vaux and Jenney plans might have invited comparison, perhaps even clarified park purposes and design, but neither the south nor the west parks took the shape their designers intended. The great fire of 1871 halted most park construction by diverting resources into the rebuilding of the city; then the economic panic of 1873 exacerbated Chicago's financial distress. Twenty years later, when Olmsted returned to the city to help plan the site of the World's Columbian Exposition, he found Jackson Park still, for the most part, a swampy morass. Olmsted modified his earlier design to create an appropriate setting for the exhibition, and under the direction of Daniel H. Burnham a group of talented architects created the monumental white city that rose there in 1892 and 1893.[23]

Like other major eastern cities, Boston began applying the lessons demonstrated in Central Park soon after public acknowledgment of the Olmsted and Vaux design. Upon acquiring the Public Garden from private investors in 1859, and designating that land for park purposes, the City Council advertised a competition for designs. They awarded the prize to George F. Meacham, but his plan, complete with buildings, fountain, and formal axis, was closer in intent to Fort Greene Park and to Downing's Washington Mall than it was to a naturalistic landscape. It was really more an extension of the city than an escape from it. Nevertheless, the Public Garden, together with the Boston Common, was important in any program of park development in Boston. H. W. S. Cleveland pointed out that because of the proximity of these spaces to the center of population, Boston was better provided with parks than any city in the country. But because the city was already so intensively developed, the creation of a single park as large as New York's within the corporate limits would be impossible.[24]

Boston began developing the Public Garden according to Meacham's plan in 1859. After the Civil War, however, civic leaders recognized the need for a much larger park. In 1869 the City Council appointed a special committee to study the park issue, newspapers were inundated with letters outlining design proposals, citizens expressed their desires in public hearings, and H. W. S. Cleveland and others offered suggestions for park development. Cleveland rightly recognized that, because of the limited amount of available space, any large park for Boston would have to be located outside the city. Boston had "neither the necessity or the power to create a park such as New York's," he wrote, "without going so far beyond her limits as to render it comparatively of little value." Instead of a large, centrally located park, he advocated the improvement of roads and avenues outside the city with parklike scenery that might provide residents some of the sights and sounds of the country.[25]

Cleveland's proposal anticipated Boston's metropolitan park system, but he presented it at a time when the city was still largely confined to the peninsula. Its major shortcoming was the city's inability to acquire the necessary land beyond its boundaries. Cleveland dealt with this by proposing that the suburban properties remain in private hands, though he did not explain how, without being under the city's control, this area would remain parklike as the process of urban decentralization accelerated. Robert Morris Copeland appreciated the impact of urban and suburban development on these areas, citing Roxbury, a once-charming rural neighborhood that had been transformed into "rows and blocks of very inferior houses, too many of them tenantless." Copeland also outlined a plan for a ring of suburban parks in 1869, as did attorney Uriel H. Crocker, but again Boston lacked the authority to develop an ambitious series of parks beyond the city line.[26]

As debate over the location of parks continued, supporters invited Olmsted to Boston, and on February 25, 1870, he delivered an address at the Lowell Institute entitled "Public Parks and the Enlargement of Towns." Olmsted pointed out the necessity of a metropolitan solution to the city's recreational needs: "The Boston of today is the mere nucleus of the Boston that is to be. It is practically certain that it is to extend over many miles of country now thoroughly rural in character." Thus it would be foolhardy to limit consideration of park sites to the town, because continued urban and suburban growth would surely increase the distance separating country and city.[27]

Three months after Olmsted's lecture, the state legislature approved an act enabling Boston to establish a metropolitan park system, including a ring of suburban parks. But the law required that two-thirds of the city's voters support the measure in referendum, which failed because too many residents of working-class areas feared that they would be taxed to pay for recreational spaces that would be inaccessible to them. It was only after Boston began annexing surrounding territories in 1870 and 1873 that a comprehensive metropolitan park system became a political possibility.[28]

Despite this initial setback the park issue retained considerable support in Boston. Copeland followed up his initial suggestions with a book, *The Most Beautiful City in America: Essay and Plan for the Improvement of Boston*, which he published in 1872. In it he modified his earlier proposal and recommended that a series of parks be developed within the newly annexed areas of the city—undoubtedly a concession to the sentiment voters had expressed in the park referendum. Unlike his earlier essays, this advocated specific sites for park development, including an area near the "new lands" of Back Bay at Parker Hill and additional locations in Dorchester and in the recently annexed parts of West Roxbury. Numerous other individuals stepped forward to offer suggestions. These various proposals and activities were the beginnings of what became Boston's Emerald Necklace, the nation's first comprehensive metropolitan park system.[29]

The process of translating these proposals into landscape began in 1874, when Mayor Samuel Cobb appointed a special commission to study the park issue. The commission held public hearings and, in its report, recommended the creation of a park along the Charles River. The commission also expressed the hope that "a series of parks of moderate size, connected by proper roads, be laid out between the third and fourth mile circles; and that the land for a second series of larger size, beyond the first, be secured at once" for future development. This 1874 report thus sketched the outline of a series of peripheral parks united by parkways. It also testified to the effects of urban decentralization: land for park development between the three- and four-mile circles was limited because suburbanization was proceeding so rapidly. Thus, the only available land for large naturalistic parks was located on the advancing urban frontier.[30]

Following the publication of this report the City Council passed a second Park Act. This law stipulated acquisition of land only within the limits of Boston. Upon approval of the measure by citizens, Cobb appointed a municipal park commission, chaired by Charles H. Dalton, to oversee development. The new commission studied suggestions for park locations and examined numerous plans but found none that measured up to its expectations of what a park should be. The commissioners then invited Olmsted to offer advice on the land being considered for park use, and on two occasions he visited the sites and proposed modifications in their boundaries. After Olmsted's second visit the park commission published its initial report, a comprehensive scheme that advocated the establishment of a number of smaller parks in the populated areas of the city and larger recreational spaces in the newly annexed wards, all joined by a system of parkways. The land included in this scheme eventually became the three principal elements of the Boston park system – the Fens, Jamaica Pond, and Franklin Park.[31]

Although financial difficulties delayed implementation of this plan, the Boston park commission acquired the land for the Back Bay park (the Fens) in 1878. This first park was necessary as a sanitary measure to provide adequate drainage of Muddy River and Stony Brook, tidal estuaries that flowed into the Charles River. To obtain the best plan for the Fens, the commissioners held a competition, but, finding all the entries unsatisfactory, rejected them and instead invited Olmsted to undertake the improvements. At the same time, Olmsted was collaborating with Charles Sprague Sargent on a plan for the Arnold Arboretum, which was being developed by Harvard on land leased by the city to the university on condition that the facility be open to the public. These projects launched Olmsted's public design career in Boston and made him the logical choice to develop the five-hundred-acre West Roxbury park later named in honor of Benjamin Franklin.[32]

Olmsted described the most important element of the West Roxbury park site as "a gentle valley nearly a mile in length, and of an average breadth between the steeper slopes of the bordering hills of less than a quarter of a mile." He informed Dalton that, when improved, the site would incorporate "a type of scenery which is perhaps the most soothing in its influence on mankind of any presented by nature"– the sweeping lawns and gently rolling hills, visually endless in extent, that he characterized as pastoral scenery.[33]

Olmsted began devising his plan for Franklin Park (fig. 27) in 1884 and submitted it to the park commission near the end of the following year. As he and Vaux had done in the lower half of Central Park, Olmsted divided the Franklin Park site into two unequal areas according to their topography, scenery, and intended use. The larger part, the Country Park, consisted of heavily wooded areas ranging across the surrounding hills (named the Wilderness) and a sweeping greensward in the valleys below (named the Nazingdale). The Country Park incorporated the breadth of naturalistic scenery Olmsted considered essential in an urban park and provided space for group activities as well as individual contemplation of nature. Unlike the plans he and Vaux had devised for the Buffalo park system, this design did not limit the use of Franklin Park to these purposes only. He devoted a third of the space within the park's boundaries to an antepark and there located playgrounds, a formal pedestrian mall called the Greeting, a music concourse, and a deer paddock. But, as he and Vaux had done at Central and Prospect parks, Olmsted carefully shaped the elements of the design so that these provisions for more active or "gregarious" recreation would not be visible from the naturalistic landscape.[34]

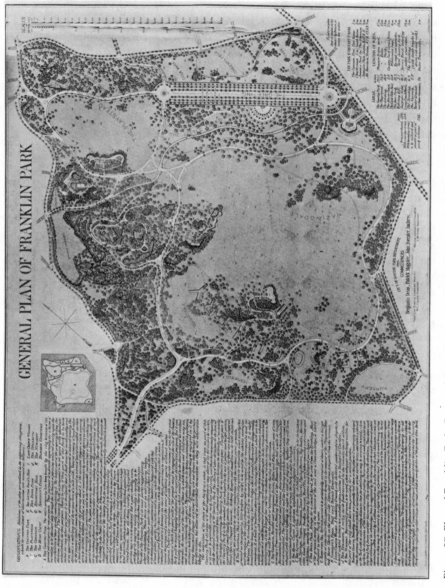

Figure 27. Plan of Franklin Park, Boston, Massachusetts, by Frederick Law Olmsted, 1885. From *Notes on Franklin Park and Related Matters* (Boston, 1886). (Courtesy, National Park Service, Frederick Law Olmsted National Historic Site, Brookline, Massachusetts.)

As the development of Franklin Park continued, Olmsted devoted his attention to completing the Emerald Necklace. During the last eight years of his professional career Olmsted and his growing firm prepared designs for Jamaica Pond, for the Muddy River Parkway, which connected Jamaica Pond with the Fens, for Marine Park and Charlesbank, and for numerous smaller parks in the city. He also undertook a number of designs for suburban areas, including the Brookline Hill subdivision and Planter's Hill and World's End in Hingham. These plans were visionary, but Olmsted continued to be hindered in developing the comprehensive metropolitan park system he had advocated in "Public Parks and the Enlargement of Towns." Despite annexation, Boston's legal limits still incorporated only a fraction of the greater city; and, as Charles Eliot observed near the end of 1890, "the other municipalities within the metropolitan district are allowing their few remaining open estates to be divided and built upon one by one and year by year." Suburban growth was threatening to destroy the natural features that surrounded Boston.[35]

The metropolitan park system envisioned by Cleveland, Copeland, Crocker, and Olmsted was a logical way of providing recreational space for Boston and its neighboring municipalities. But because Olmsted's parks were located within city limits, the more comprehensive program of park development became a reality only in the 1890s. The major promoters of the metropolitan concept were Charles Eliot, son of Harvard president Charles W. Eliot, who had studied landscape architecture with Olmsted, and Sylvester Baxter, a journalist who a year later published *Greater Boston*, a pamphlet that pointed to the necessity of comprehensive solutions to problems long unsolved because of political boundaries that had created artificial divisions and had impeded common action. On March 5, 1890, Eliot published in *Garden and Forest* a letter entitled "The Waverly Oaks: A Plan for their Preservation for the People." This letter advocated the establishment of an organization that would preserve "surviving fragments of the primitive wilderness of New England...as the Public Library holds books and the Art Museum pictures—for the use and enjoyment of the public." The same year, Eliot solicited the support of members of the Appalachian Mountain Club. He called public meetings, publicized the need for open spaces, and orchestrated the campaign to introduce a bill in the General Court creating the Trustees of Public Reservations. That bill became law on May 21, 1891, and Eliot was appointed secretary to the trustees.[36]

Following Eliot's recommendations the trustees surveyed the existing open spaces in Massachusetts, paying particular attention to long-neglected coastal areas, and attempted to promote a more comprehensive treatment of parks in the Boston metropolitan area. The trustees called a meeting of all park authorities from the Boston area in December of 1891, and on that occasion Eliot spoke bluntly about political interference. He described the "ridiculous town boundary difficulty" that "prevents concerted action" in framing metropolitan solutions to metropolitan problems. Numerous speakers echoed Eliot's remarks, and after the meeting the trustees petitioned the General Court to establish a park system that transcended local boundaries. The legislature approved a bill to form a temporary metropolitan park commission, which the governor signed in June of 1892. Then Eliot's work really began, because the temporary commission had to submit a comprehensive report at the next session of the General Court. As secretary to that commission, Eliot suggested that a metropolitan park system embrace five types of areas—oceanfront beaches, the shores and islands of the bay, tidal rivers and estuaries, large expanses of native forest, and smaller parks in the built areas of the city. The commission adopted Eliot's recommendations and forwarded them to the General Court, which enacted a bill that, when approved by the governor, established the Metropolitan Park Commission. Between his appointment as landscape architect to the commission and his untimely death in 1897, Eliot directed the creation of America's first metropolitan park system (fig. 28). In some ways he built upon earlier proposals—especially those that foresaw the need for parks located on the periphery in anticipation of urban growth—and in other ways he grafted on to the evolving ideology of the public park the conservationist principles of the Progressive Era.[37]

During the years in which Olmsted and Eliot labored in Boston, other cities developed park systems of commendable extent and design—H. W. S. Cleveland's proposal for Minneapolis is an example, as is the Olmsted firm's plan for open spaces and residential neighborhoods in Atlanta—but Boston's metropolitan park system marked the culmination of the evolution of the naturalistic urban landscape in nineteenth-century America. Charles Sprague Sargent gave classic expression of this park ideal in an 1888 essay published in *Garden and Forest*.

> An urban park is useful in proportion as it is rural. The real, the only reason why a great park should be made, is to bring the country into the town, and make it possible for the inhabitants of crowded cities to enjoy the calm and restfulness which only a rural landscape and rural surroundings can give. . . all other objects must, in a great park, be subordinated to the one central, controlling idea of rural repose, which space alone can give.[38]

As Sargent's remarks demonstrate, what began as a somewhat vague and generalized belief that parks were necessary measures for protecting public health and providing recreational opportunities gradu-

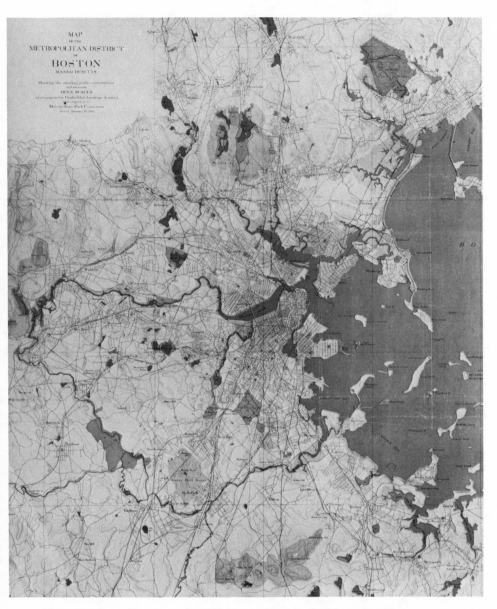

Figure 28. Metropolitan Boston in 1893. Prepared by Charles Eliot for the Metro-
politan Park Commission, showing existing and proposed open spaces. (Courtesy,
National Park Service, Frederick Law Olmsted National Historic Site, Brookline,
Massachusetts.)

ally became a coherent program predicated on what Olmsted and others believed was the psychological impact of viewing natural scenery. Thus, in the hands of Olmsted, Cleveland, Jacob Weidenmann, Eliot, and others—but, of course, not everyone—the conception of the park evolved from an associational and educational space that was essentially an extension of the city into a naturalistic landscape that in its very rusticity was the antithesis of the urban environment.

Promoters and landscape architects alike, however, conceded that large naturalistic parks needed to be complemented by parkways and smaller recreational areas to which people could resort in the course of their daily lives. The plans for Buffalo, Chicago, and Boston represented the effort—with varying degrees of success—to create comprehensive park systems and provided, in Buffalo's case, for the differentiation of recreational spaces according to use. Moreover, the parkways and boulevards were consciously conceived not only as linear extensions of the parks but also as a means of providing openly built neighborhoods for residential development.

Because most urban areas in nineteenth-century America retained the traditional boundaries of the walking city—three to four square miles—not even the most imaginative municipal park systems could provide adequate recreational spaces in anticipation of urban expansion. As early as 1869 the spokesmen advocating park development in Boston had recognized the need for such planning, but the vision of a metropolitan park system was not realized until the 1890s, by which time the effects of unplanned decentralization were unmistakable. Only then did politicians and citizens heed the advice of Olmsted and Eliot and forsake community control, only then did they invest authority for park development in a commission that could plan comprehensively for the needs of a modern metropolis. In the last decade of the century Charles Eliot expanded on Olmsted's park ideal by forming the Trustees of Public Reservations, a private organization dedicated to preserving what remained of New England's wilderness. The ideology of the public park had evolved from tenuous beginnings to embrace the Progressive conservation movement: though physically distant from them, metropolitan park systems had become conceptually related to the Adirondacks and the national parks.

PART THREE

The New Urban Landscape

CHAPTER VIII

URBAN DECENTRALIZATION
AND THE DOMESTIC LANDSCAPE

I enjoy this suburban country beyond expression.
—FREDERICK LAW OLMSTED

Neither the competition for the design of Central Park nor the debate over appropriate gateways resolved the question of what an urban public park should be. Nor did the execution of other major public landscapes in the nineteenth century. To be sure, almost everyone agreed that parks, in some form, were necessary palliatives or correctives to the evils of the city; but there agreement ended. Others, especially Olmsted, regarded the park as complete in itself, a consciously contrived "natural" landscape that would have an "unconscious influence" on the visitor.

In retrospect Olmsted's vision that the park could be an oasis of rural beauty within but free from the intrusions of the urban environment seems, to some critics, a hopelessly naive legacy of the Victorian era. Indeed, over the last century Central Park and its progeny have been altered—perhaps irrevocably—to accommodate changing uses of park space and the evolution of modern recreation. As a result of the expansion of the Metropolitan Museum of Art, the transformation of pastoral meadows into athletic fields, and the placement of statues, skating rinks, carousels, and playgrounds in the formerly naturalistic landscape, New York's park is fundamentally different from that conceived by the designers whom Richard Morris Hunt long ago castigated as "dreamers." Nevertheless, Central Park is, in the assessment of historian Carl Condit, "perhaps the greatest civic achievement of the United States in the nineteenth century." More broadly, the parks, parkways, and park systems it inspired are undoubtedly also that century's greatest contribution to city planning in America.[1]

But Olmsted and Vaux admitted the park's limitations in refining and civilizing the urban environment. Even while directing initial improvements on Central Park they found wanting its relationship to the city; but because of taste, politics, or financial considerations the Central Park commissioners ignored their arguments for, among other things, a better system of transportation to the park. As their 1866 and 1868 reports to the commissioners of Brooklyn's Prospect Park demonstrate, however, when given a more sympathetic audience Olmsted and Vaux presented the park as an integral part of a radically new arrangement of urban space. The system of parks and parkways they proposed for Brooklyn, like the boulevards Baron Haussmann was then constructing in Paris, was an attempt to create a more openly built city, to redefine urban form by incorporating large expanses of rural beauty that might help correct the congestion of the city and serve as institutions of social reform. But while Haussmann labored to provide an imperial setting for Napoleon III and to facilitate the rapid movement of troops, Olmsted and Vaux platted large new areas within the city as appropriate locations for middle-class homes. Parks, parkways, and openly built residential neighborhoods, they believed, would make obsolete the traditional criticism of the city as the locus of congestion, corruption, filth, and disease.[2]

What finally made possible the realization of Olmsted and Vaux's conception of the modern metropolis was the development of new forms of transportation that effectively shattered the limits of the walking city and reversed traditional patterns of land use. In the preindustrial city the wealthy usually lived in the center of town and the poor on the periphery, but an increase in "urban nuisances" during the nineteenth century rendered once fashionable neighborhoods less and less desirable. New transportation systems—at first omnibuses and ferries, later horse-drawn streetcars, steamboats, and locomotives—literally turned the city inside out, making possible the separation of residential and commercial neighborhoods, enabling the rich to move to homes in the suburbs, while the poor huddled in increasingly congested downtown areas. The resulting change in the physical geography of cities was dramatic. Historian Kenneth T. Jackson has identified a clear pattern of urban decentralization in northeastern cities as early as 1830, and throughout the remainder of the nineteenth century New York's suburbs "actually maintained a higher rate of growth than that of neighboring Manhattan."[3]

The process of urban decentralization began inconspicuously enough: at first people just moved farther and farther from their places of work. A Bostonian observed in 1838, "A number of our merchants have found that it is not absolutely necessary that their dwellings should be within five minutes' walk of their counting houses. Nay, they have even discovered that a daily walk from a cottage in an adjacent town is not a very frightful task." Though such a walk hardly would have struck terror into the hearts of most working-class men, few evidently found the rewards of a suburban home within their means. A number of historians and urban geographers have demonstrated convincingly that during the antebellum years most laborers lived within a mile of their places of work, which likewise were clustered near similar establishments inside the city, because of considerations of time and the instability of job tenure. Moreover, most resided in rented quarters because the cost of purchasing or building a home on the periphery usually was prohibitive.[4]

Thus, at first only those people who owned carriages could afford the luxury of living beyond the limits of the walking city. Manhattan's fabled march uptown was led by the wealthy and fashionable, who relocated in less congested and more attractive neighborhoods. In Philadelphia it was also the rich who moved to outlying areas. Sidney George Fisher identified a rapidly increasing "taste for country life" among his genteel peers. "New and tasteful homes are built every year," he observed in 1847, especially in Germantown, which was desirable for being "perfectly healthy & the scenery very handsome."[5]

If at first it was predominantly the wealthy who enjoyed the opportunity to escape crowded urban areas, mass transportation systems made possible the development of middle-class residential neighborhoods some distance from centers of business and from tenement districts. For those who could pay the fares—usually five or six cents, which was too expensive for the poor—the street omnibuses that became widely used in the 1830s and 1840s effectively enlarged the limits of the city. The Baltimore *Sun* praised the omnibus for enabling "persons to reside at a distance from their places of business in more healthy locations without loss of time and fatigue in walking." The impact of even so rudimentary a transportation innovation as the omnibus was galvanic. Sir Charles Lyell discovered in 1846 that during a five-month absence from New York "whole streets had been built, and several squares finished in the northern or fashionable end of town, to which the merchants are now resorting, leaving the business end, near the Battery, where they formerly lived."[6]

More significant as a cause of decentralization were the horse-drawn street railways that came to dominate urban transportation networks in the 1850s. These streetcars were much larger than omnibuses and carried a greater number of people. By riding on rails they afforded a more comfortable trip than was possible on cobbled or unpaved city streets, and their greater speed enabled people to live in homes even farther from the center of town. On a drive through Germantown in August of 1857, Fisher reported that what was once a village had been transformed into an attractive suburb, "adorned with elegance & supplied with all the conveniences of a city—shops, gas, water-works, with none of the annoyances of town, but quiet, country scenery and trees everywhere." Two years later he astutely ascribed the growth of Philadelphia's numerous suburbs to the "horse rail-roads," which enabled "anyone to enjoy the pleasures of country life and at the same time attend business in town." According to Fisher, by making possible the development of residential neighborhoods on the urban periphery, the streetcar brought about a decisive change in the arrangement of cities. The advantages of suburbs, he wrote,

> are so obvious that this villa & cottage life has become quite a passion and is producing a complete revolution in our habits. It is dispersing the people of the city over the surrounding country, introducing thus among them, ventilation, cleanliness, space, healthful pursuits, and the influences of natural beauty, the want of which are the sources of so much evil, moral & physical, in large towns.

Because streetcars had rendered suburban homes so convenient, Fisher wondered "how any can bear to stay in town."[7]

The development of commuter railways extended still further the possibilities of suburban growth. Lewis Mumford has argued persuasively that the railroad served as a centralizing device by causing the concentration of population and industry in urban areas. But as much as it contributed to the dominance of central cities, the railroad also telescoped distances, bringing country and city closer together. Emerson praised this new improvement in transportation for the "increased acquaintance it has given the American people with the boundless resources of their own soil." To him the railroad was less noteworthy for its centralizing tendencies than for its ability to bring Easterners into contact with the "tranquilizing, sanative influences" of nature. H. W. S. Cleveland also noted the duality of the railroad's impact. In 1855 he observed, "Every railroad becomes a salient point of the city, and the busy mart, which heretofore has been so called, is now but the heart of this widely extended metropolis."[8]

Thus, while it caused concentration of activity, the railroad also resulted in urban decentralization and the separation of commercial and residential neighborhoods. Andrew Jackson Downing, who castigated the practice of building cities "as though there was a frightful scarcity of space," recognized the potential of this new form of transportation. He reasoned that, although they were originally built for commerce, railroads "cannot wholly escape doing some duty for the Beautiful, as well as the Useful," by opening land for nonurban development. In his estimation, travel by train "half annihilated" old notions of time and space and enabled thousands of city workers to reside in a "country cottage, several miles distant." This surely was the case in Boston, where the railroad was at first the primary means of transportation to outlying areas: by 1850 there were eighty-three commuter stations within a fifteen-mile radius of the city, some with as many as thirty-two trains per day carrying passengers to and from Boston.[9]

What might be termed the "urban transportation revolution" dramatically altered the spatial arrangement of cities. Following the paths of the streetcar lines, Bostonians moved to Roxbury and Dorchester, Philadelphians to Germantown, and New Yorkers to northern Manhattan. Regularly scheduled ferry service rendered Brooklyn and New Jersey attractive residential options. Fredrika Bremer observed that some of New York's merchants had chosen to "have their house and home" in Brooklyn. Walt Whitman's "Crossing Brooklyn Ferry" paid poetic tribute to the "hundreds and hundreds that cross, returning home." Others moved to Jersey in order to "enjoy those solid comforts which can only be obtained away from the tainted atmosphere of a city life." The English visitor Lady Emmeline Stuart Wortley learned that in New York, "incessant communication is kept up between the city and its picturesque, prosperous, and rapidly increasing suburbs, by means of steam ferry-boats, the Harlem Railroad, and omnibuses." So great were the pace and extent of decentralization, in New York and in virtually every other city, that by 1870 Cincinnati journalist Sidney Denise Maxwell could describe urban growth as a new form of imperialism: "In all directions the city is moving on to conquest, the flower of her population deployed as skirmishers, who steadily advance upon a country that little thinks or knows what powers of expansion and absorption belong to the cities of this country."[10]

Unfortunately, in most cities the "conquest" of surrounding country took the form of extending over it the old urban landscape, the icon of commercial rather than domestic values, the gridiron. The relentless, unplanned expansion of urban rectilinearity led the editor of the *Crayon* to lament the absence of walls surrounding America's cities: "There is something in a wall which divides the city from the country, and while it shuts man into the former, by a kind of stimulant to contrariness drives him out into the latter. Here city grows into country; we never know when we leave one or enter into the other." As the process of decentralization inevitably increased the value of property on the periphery, real estate promoters and railroad and streetcar companies purchased distant tracts, laid out rectangular streets, and sold house lots in what they described as ideal suburban communities. Too often these developments were the work of speculators in search of a fast profit or of companies unwilling or unable to defer return on the cost of buying and improving the land, and the results were regrettable. Although they promised buyers a combination of rural pleasures and ease of access to the city, such suburbs sacrificed the advantages of urban life.[11]

The development of the village of Dearman (now Irvington), New York, demonstrates the least appealing aspects of suburban speculation. A large, hilly tract overlooking the Hudson, Dearman was located in Westchester County, twenty miles north of New York City,

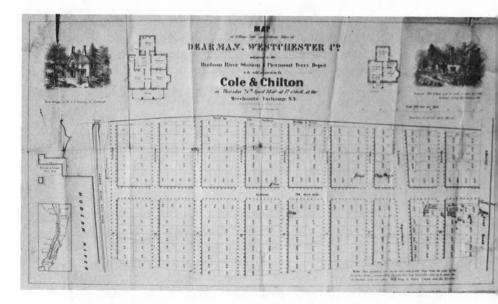

Figure 29. Plan of Dearman (now Irvington), Westchester County, New York, 1851, Cole and Chilton, Promoters. (Courtesy, Collection of the Hudson River Museum, Yonkers, New York.)

and was connected to the metropolis by the Hudson River Railroad, the Albany Post Road, and frequent steamboat excursions. The site possessed all the requisites for advantageous development in what Downing called the "modern" or "natural" style of landscape gardening. Such a plan, with curvilinear streets and irregularly shaped lots following the contour of the land, would not only have enhanced the site's attractiveness but would have reduced the cost of grading and filling the property. Dearman's promoters, Cole and Chilton, instead imposed on the hilly topography the rectangular grid (fig. 29). The speculative intent was obvious: from the time John Randel laid out Manhattan's street system, every fast-growing city had learned of the gridiron's advantages for *"buying, selling,* and *improving* real estate." Following this precedent, Cole and Chilton planned a central avenue, seventy feet wide, running east from the river (directly up a hill), and eight narrower intersecting streets running parallel to the Hudson. Throughout the tract they placed uniform lots of fifty by one hundred feet.[12]

Downing had special cause for concern over the Dearman plan. Although the developmental scheme violated every precept of landscape theory he had promulgated in the preceding decade, Cole and Chilton nevertheless attempted to capitalize on his enormous popularity by placing engravings from Downing's *Cottage Residences* (1842) in the upper left and right corners of their plan. Downing must have been enraged and, with this misrepresentation as incentive, offered a devastating critique of the speculative village. His response, the essay "Our Country Villages," proceeded to outline a theoretical plan that codified the suburban ideal in nineteenth-century America.[13]

Because of the rapid development of cities and territories throughout the United States, Downing reasoned that "the plan and arrangement of new towns ought to be a matter of national importance." He was particularly distressed by the development of recently platted suburbs along the Hudson, which claimed to combine "the advantages of the country with easy railroad access" to the city. In a veiled reference to Dearman, Downing wrote that fifty-foot lots and rows of houses along shaded streets composed "the sum total of the rural beauty, convenience and comfort of the latest plan for a rural village in the Union." In forsaking the city the purchaser acquired only "his little patch of back and front yard, [and] a little peep down the street, looking one way at the river, and the other way at the sky." A resident sacrificed the urban amenities, yet found himself in a place with "houses on all sides, almost as closely placed as in the city, which he has endeavored to fly from."[14]

Other arbiters of taste echoed Downing's criticism of the gridiron suburb. From the "Editor's Easy Chair" at *Harper's*, George William Curtis excoriated the "taste which would carve up such a town site as Dearman or Abbotsford, upon the steep slope of a river bank, into rectangular squares." He asserted that "roads in country villages *ought to wind*," because such streets were cheaper to build and increased the number of scenic views. Similarly did the authors of *Village and Farm Cottages* scorn the speculator who laid out a suburban community with the "checker-board exactness" of a city. Even worse was the builder of "city tenements" in the country, the villain who "covers the ground with narrow cells, and advertises to sell or rent them as charming rural residences." H. W. S. Cleveland lamented the "experiments of speculators, who lay out rectangular villages with the aid of a surveyor, and offer rural felicity for sale in lots of thirty by fifty feet." John Jay Smith was also among the critics of promoters whose desire for profits justified the application of a rectangular grid to the urban periphery.[15]

Significantly, each of these commentators thought of the gridiron as urban form and considered its use in suburban development especially reprehensible. If a suburb were to be a place where families escaped the "turmoil of cities," Downing reasoned, it must take on aspects of the country. Thus, in "Our Country Villages" he asserted that a suburban community must be more than "mere rows of houses upon streets crossing each other at right angles, and bordered with shade trees." Admitting that "people must live in towns and villages," he charged his readers with the task of improving them. The most important desideratum of a community, Downing believed, was a large, centrally located "open space, common, or park." This area, jointly owned by all lot holders, "would be the nucleus or *heart of the village*, and would give it an essentially rural character." Downing recommended that the largest and finest residences front the park and that, by the "imperative arrangement" of other streets and houses, the village proprietors secure "sufficient space, view, circulation of air, and broad, well-planted avenues of shade trees." John Jay Smith also insisted that suburban developers include in their plans space for a "healthful promenade," and instead of a rectangular grid he suggested the treatment of the entire town as a residential park.[16]

To Downing and to other spokesmen who articulated the suburban ideal at mid-century, the suburb was more than a speculative subdivision: it was a community that, by conscious design and allocation of public and private spaces, attempted to reconcile the family's desire for a home amid natural surroundings with the trenchant realities of urban growth and change. A house in such a suburb enabled a family to escape the congestion, disease, and "immoral influences" of the city and to rear children in more beneficial surroundings, while retaining ease of access to urban jobs and to the social and cultural attractions of the metropolis.[17]

One of the most extraordinary of nineteenth-century planned suburban communities was Evergreen Hamlet (fig. 30), established in 1851 on an eighty-five-acre site at Millvale, Pennsylvania, near Pittsburgh. William M. Shinn, promoter and first trustee, joined with five other friends to form the nucleus of what they anticipated would become a sixteen-family village. In a remarkable real estate prospectus, Shinn announced that the purpose of the hamlet was to secure "the advantages and comforts of the country, at moderate cost, without doing violence to the social habits incident to city life." Such a community would unite "some of the benefits of country and city" and "avoid some of the inconveniences and disadvantages of both." To this end Shinn organized Evergreen Hamlet as a joint-stock corporation committed to communitarian principles. Excepting the sixteen house lots, all land was held in common. Families shared the cost of maintaining a schoolhouse (where children were trained "under a system approximating to 'Home Education'"), an icehouse, a farm building, and other facilities. Only six families constructed dwellings at Evergreen Hamlet, however, and after Shinn's death in 1865 the town dissolved its joint-stock status.[18]

One of the first and undoubtedly the most influential early suburb established according to Downing's precepts was Llewellyn Park, New Jersey, located twelve miles west of New York City on the eastern

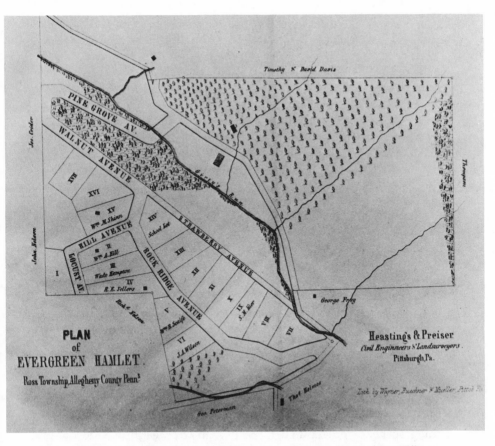

Figure 30. Plan of Evergreen Hamlet, Allegheny County, Pennsylvania, 1851, William Shinn, Trustee. From *Constitution of Evergreen Hamlet* (Pittsburgh, 1851). (Courtesy, Historical Society of Western Pennsylvania, Pittsburgh, Pennsylvania.)

slope of Orange Mountain. According to a real estate prospectus, the site combined "healthfulness of climate," beauty of situation, and "ease of access" to the metropolis. Intended as the location of "country homes for city people," Llewellyn Park was planned "with special reference to the wants of citizens doing business in the city of New York, and yet wishing accessible, retired, and healthful homes in the country." Those families who relocated in Llewellyn Park also retained most of the amenities of the city: although the site was "fairly in the country" the proximity of the town of Orange ensured that residents could "secure the necessaries of life with the greatest possible convenience."[19]

This residential park was the creation of Llewellyn S. Haskell, a New York drug importer, who occasionally was assisted by the architect Alexander Jackson Davis. In 1853 failing health led Haskell

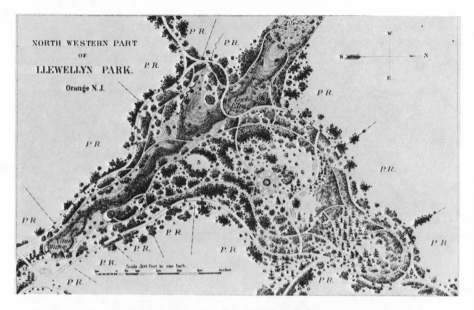

Figure 31. Plan of Llewellyn Park, New Jersey, 1853, showing park with space for private residences arranged around it. From A. J. Downing, *A Treatise on the Theory and Practice of Landscape Gardening, Adapted to North America...* (1841; New York, 1875). (Courtesy, The Henry Francis duPont Winterthur Museum Library, Collection of Printed Books, Winterthur, Delaware.)

to purchase as the site for his home a property known as Eagle Rock, a forty-acre tract on Orange Mountain, which was noted for its stunning scenery and reputed to be particularly healthful. Soon after building his own residence Haskell, perhaps at Davis's suggestion, conceived the idea of organizing a suburban community and began acquiring adjacent farms. By 1857 he had amassed 350 acres of "well-wooded and beautifully broken and diversified" land; thirteen years later Llewellyn Park embraced almost 750 acres. Together with Davis and landscape gardeners Eugene A. Baumann and Howard Daniels, Haskell began to shape what he considered the ideal residential village.[20]

Like Downing, Haskell considered a park essential to the success of a suburban community, and in 1857 he donated to the newly organized village trustees a centrally located park of fifty acres (fig. 31). This area, known as the "Ramble," was jointly owned by all lot proprietors, who paid an annual assessment (not to exceed ten dollars per acre) for maintenance of the park and of the roads and walks of the village. Extending almost a mile in length, the park included a "finely wooded ravine" and a brook, which was dammed to form artificial ponds. A circuit drive girded the Ramble, and such ornamental structures as kiosks, summerhouses, rustic seats, and bridges embellished the in-

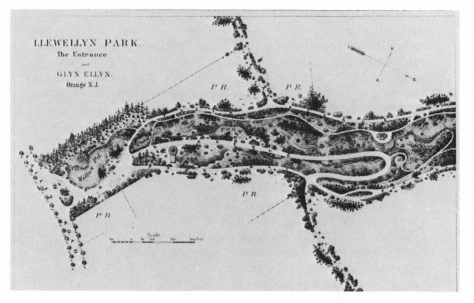

Figure 32. Llewellyn Park, the Glen. From A. J. Downing, *Treatise on the Theory and Practice of Landscape Gardening, Adapted to North America...* (1841; New York, 1875). (Courtesy, The Henry Francis duPont Winterthur Museum Library, Collection of Printed Books, Winterthur, Delaware.)

terior (fig. 32). One contemporary visitor noted that the park's "irregularity of form" afforded great "variety of surface and feeling of size" and furnished "secluded and quiet nooks and most pleasant surprises."[21]

Surrounding the Ramble, Haskell and his associates placed sites for suburban homes. Llewellyn Park was designed to accommodate one hundred families on lots varying in size from one to twenty acres, with a six-acre plot being the average holding. No fences separated individual properties, which contributed to "the appearance of a single very large landscaped estate." Throughout the village Haskell placed ten miles of gently curving roads and walks. The result, he asserted, was more than a community affording urban amenities amid rural surroundings, or handsome sites for suburban homes combined with ready access to the city. Because of the Ramble and the absence of fences demarcating property lines, Llewellyn Park enabled a "family occupying a small place in the country, costing only a few thousands of dollars, to enjoy all the advantages of an extensive country-seat, without the expense or trouble attending the latter."[22]

At about the same time Haskell was acquiring the land for Llewellyn Park, Nathaniel Parker Willis suggested a plan (never implemented) for a suburban community, Highland Terrace, to be located on the west bank of the Hudson River between Cornwall and

Newburgh. For Willis, the completion of the Erie Railroad and frequent steamboat excursions on the Hudson made the river an extension of Broadway, enabling individuals and their families to live in rural surroundings fifty miles from New York while maintaining access to urban amusements, conveniences, and society. Echoing Downing and others, Willis envisioned Highland Terrace as a retreat for those "who have rural tastes and metropolitan refinements rationally blended—who have families which they wish to surround with the healthful and elegant belongings of a home, while, at the same time, they wish to keep pace with the world." Residence at Highland Terrace, he assured his readers, would be a "mixture of city and country, *with the home in the country.*"[23]

Similar in arrangement to Llewellyn Park and in conception to Downing's and Willis's suburban ideal was the village of Irving Park, established in 1859 as a one-hundred-acre residential community overlooking the Hudson at Tarrytown, New York. Repeating Haskell's earlier claims, Irving Park's promoter, Charles H. Lyon, praised the site as "entirely healthy and free from fever and ague." He pointed out that the location was especially desirable because of its "extensive views" of river scenery. Tarrytown was advantageous as a residential area, he announced, because "the distance from the city is entirely in its favor, being near enough for the requirements of business men, and yet far enough away to escape some well-known annoyances, and to realize all the retirement that constitutes the great charm of rural life." At his own expense Lyon constructed gateways, lodges, ornamental structures, and roads and offered for sale lots of from one to eight acres in extent (fig. 33). He reserved almost fifty acres of the property for a park "to be used in common by all the occupants." Thus at Irving Park a purchaser acquired a site for a home in the country, accessible to the city, as well as joint ownership of an extensive pleasure ground. A writer in *Harper's Weekly* praised the site as admirably "adapted to the purpose of a *Neighborhood Park,*" one especially appropriate for the man who conducted his business in the city but who saw "no reason why he should establish his household in the same tumultuous arena." The editor of the *Horticulturist* predicted that this "system of united effort will become the custom when its advantages are more disseminated."[24]

Dozens, perhaps hundreds of subdivisions or planned communities were begun in the 1850s, but outbreak of the Civil War retarded the realization of the suburban ideal. For antebellum generations, the ownership of land in cities and on their periphery was a safe and remunerative investment. As cities grew, even vacant land increased in value, bringing owners what Henry George later called "unearned increments" on their capital. Developing a suburban community, however, was a different kind of venture, requiring substantial initial

NORTH VIEW FROM THE SUMMIT NEAR THE PAVILION

Figure 33. View of Irving Park, Tarrytown, New York, 1859. From *Description of Irving Park, Tarrytown; The Property of Charles H. Lyon* (New York, 1859). (Courtesy, Frances Loeb Library, Graduate School of Design, Harvard University, Cambridge, Massachusetts.)

expenditures for the purchase and preparation of land and the construction of roads, a park, and ancillary structures. Haskell, for example, is said to have spent as much as one hundred thousand dollars landscaping Llewellyn Park, and Charles Lyon's preliminary improvements at Irving Park demanded a "very considerable pecuniary outlay." These promoters expected to recoup expenses and eventually earn a profit through the sale of building lots which had been made more desirable by their efforts.[25]

Wartime economy, however, disrupted such investment. Historian Allan Nevins reports the failure, in 1861, of almost six thousand Northern businesses holding liabilities of some 178.5 million dollars. Although by 1863 this financial instability was replaced by what Nevins calls the "great boom in the North," the war obviously had a decided impact on the national economy. State and local governments paid bounties to meet recruitment quotas, the federal government borrowed 830 million dollars through the sale of bonds, new levies on goods and income drained cash away from consumers, and inflation sent prices soaring. Moreover, wartime spending redirected the flow of capital formerly invested in land to industries providing materials needed for the prosecution of the war—munitions factories and military suppliers, of course, but also oil producers and distributors, mechanization of agriculture, and countless new industries promising fabulous dividends. But although economic concentration in such enterprises intensified after the war, interest in the domestic environment and the creation of suburban communities revived with the return of peace.[26]

Because of its comprehensive design and national influence the most important suburb developed in the immediate postbellum years was the community at Riverside, Illinois. Three years after Appomattox, Emery E. Childs invited the firm of Olmsted, Vaux & Company to submit a design for a suburb to be located on a sixteen-hundred-acre farm, formerly owned by David A. Gage, nine miles west of Chicago on the banks of the Des Plaines River. Included on the property would be the first suburban station of the Chicago, Burlington, and Quincy Railroad, which would provide convenient access to the city. After studying the environs for beauty of scenery and characteristics conducive to health, Olmsted and Vaux pronounced Riverside "the only available ground near Chicago which does not present disadvantages of an almost helpless character."[27]

In their preliminary report to the Riverside Improvement Company, Olmsted and Vaux rejected the Llewellyn Park model of development, and in this they differed in significant ways from Downing and other early proponents of the suburban ideal. This change of approach took place over a short period of time: in 1865 Olmsted had informed Vaux that he was designing Berkeley Neighborhood "upon the Llewellyn plan," but within four years he had found the design of Haskell's residential park lacking, particularly in its proscribing of fences dividing properties. "I think that the want of fences, of distinct family separation," he informed Edward Everett Hale, "is the real cause of the ill-success or want of great success of Mr. Haskell's undertaking." Properly designed suburban homes required "*private outside apartments*," Olmsted asserted, and as a result he came to consider the fence "a sort of outer wall of the house."[28]

Olmsted believed, then, that a suburban community should be more than a park divided into building lots. Although both the park and the suburb offered alternatives to the "constantly repeated right angles, sharp lines, and flat surfaces" of the city, he and Vaux asserted that the purposes of recreational grounds and residential neighborhoods were distinct. In their design for the Long Meadow at Prospect Park, for example, Olmsted and Vaux had created a sweeping greensward surrounded by trees and pools of water. The function of such a park space was to convey to the visitor a sensation of spaciousness, of rural tranquility not otherwise obtainable within the city. By contrast, they explained, the "essential qualification of a suburb is domesticity," the privacy of the family home in congenial surroundings. Handsome houses in well-designed suburbs, Olmsted and Vaux noted, exemplified the "most attractive, the most refined and the most soundly wholesome forms of domestic life, and the best application of the arts of civilization to which mankind has yet attained."[29]

The improvements Olmsted and Vaux deemed necessary to make the Riverside tract conform to the suburban ideal would be expensive, and to argue their case more persuasively they placed community development within the context of urban growth. The "most prominent characteristic of the present period of civilization," they informed the Riverside promoters, "has been the strong tendency of people to flock together in great towns." According to Olmsted and Vaux the response to urban growth in the nineteenth century was twofold: first was the development of new concepts of city planning that promoted the separation of compact business districts and residential areas with "rural spaciousness"; second was a countermigration from city to suburb. The landscape architects astutely reminded Riverside's promoters that the growth of suburbs was part of the process of urbanization, a movement that sought "not a sacrifice of urban conveniences, but their combination with the special charms and substantial advantages of rural conditions of life." The qualities of a refined suburban environment thus marked "not a regression from, but an advance upon, those which are characteristic of town life."[30]

Following this explication of the purposes of a suburb, Olmsted and Vaux addressed the question of Riverside's means of access to the city. To supplement the railroad they suggested construction of a broad pleasure drive, varying in width from two hundred to six hundred feet, planted with clumps of trees and made convenient by occasional shelters and watering places along the road. As they had proposed for the parkways in Brooklyn and other cities, Olmsted and Vaux again suggested separation of pedestrian, equestrian, carriage, and commercial traffic on Riverside's grand promenade. On pleasant days this drive would afford the businessman opportunity for "taking air and exercise" amid delightful surroundings on the journey to and from work. For the community the promenade would be a kind of umbilical cord, providing conveyance to the city and the "essential, intellectual, artistic, and social privileges which specially pertain to a metropolitan condition of society."[31]

Olmsted and Vaux then turned to the design of the suburb (fig. 34). The initial requirement of such a village, they noted, was the construction of "good roads and walks, pleasant to the eye within themselves, and having at intervals pleasant openings and outlooks, with suggestions of refined domestic life, secluded, but not far removed from the life of the community." Because in a suburb comfort was far more important than speed of travel, they recommended that

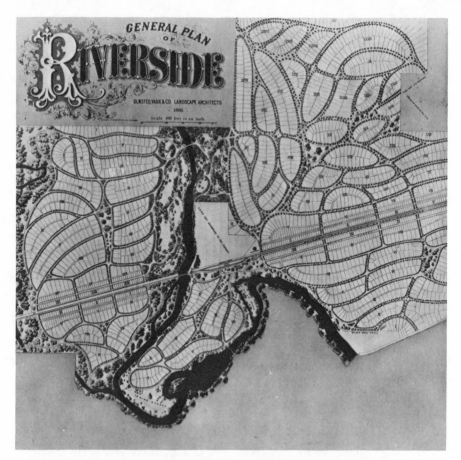

Figure 34. Plan of Riverside, Illinois, by Olmsted, Vaux & Company, 1868. (Courtesy, National Park Service, Frederick Law Olmsted National Historic Site, Brookline, Massachusetts.)

thoroughly drained roads and walks follow gently curving lines. To enhance their attractiveness the designers suggested that the roadways be spacious and that thick plantings of trees and an abundance of turf embellish their borders. Olmsted and Vaux further advised that each house be placed at least thirty feet from the street, and that each owner plant one or two handsome trees between his house and the road. Such a plan, they predicted, would lend to the village "an aspect of secluded peacefulness and tranquility."[32]

Along the primary drive through the village Olmsted and Vaux reserved a large tract of land, the long common, for public purposes, and at the center of town they designated a square for community facilities. On this latter site, adjacent to the railroad station, the Riverside Improvement Company erected a storage tower to distribute fresh water to every home. Near the train depot the promoters also constructed a commercial block, which enabled residents to purchase needed goods without traveling to Chicago, and across the common from the business center they built William LeBaron Jenney's Riverside Hotel.[33]

Olmsted and Vaux lent a sense of community to Riverside by placing throughout the suburb a series of small parks, areas possessing the "character of informal village-greens, commons and playgrounds." The main provision for public recreation, however, was a 160-acre park located along a three-mile stretch of the Des Plaines River as it meandered through the village. Near the river they arranged a drive and walk, and to enhance the park's attractiveness they recommended the construction of "pretty boat-landings, terraces, balconies overhanging the water, and pavilions at points desirable for observing regattas, mainly of rustic character, and to be half overgrown with vines."[34]

The Riverside Improvement Company adopted the plans prepared by Olmsted, Vaux & Company, though not without lengthy debate. Unfortunately, the designers almost immediately encountered difficulties with the promoters. Childs defaulted on payments to the firm and, even worse, threatened to violate the unity of the plan by building his own house in the center of the most important public space, the long common. By October of 1869 a disgusted Olmsted termed the development a "regular fly away speculation," and Frederick C. Withers, Vaux's architectural partner, informed the designers that progress was so abysmal that the firm was losing potential business as a result. On April 30, 1870, Olmsted, Vaux & Company negotiated a release from their agreement with the Riverside promoters.[35]

Riverside's woes were not over. The great Chicago fire of 1871 destroyed the company's records, and the economic panic of 1873 struck with such severity that the promoters defaulted on their obligations. Recovery was long delayed because capital previously available for suburban development instead was needed to finance the rebuilding of Chicago. But despite these difficulties, the village proprietors built upon the foundation Olmsted and Vaux established and Riverside eventually became the successful suburban community the designers had envisioned. Today, long since engulfed by the expanding city, Riverside's tree-lined curvilinear streets stand amidst a sprawling gridiron, but the community remains a bastion of domesticity and a monument to the nineteenth-century attempt to reconcile country and city.[36]

The invention of the suburb in the nineteenth century, both in Europe and America, was part of the process of decentralization that fundamentally reshaped the urban environment. What once had been closely built areas—usually only three or four miles square—followed the extension of transportation lines and spread indiscriminately over the surrounding countryside. Decentralization reversed the traditional relationship of center and periphery, and those who could afford the cost often chose to move to suburban homes. Decentralization also demonstrated the importance of domesticity during the nineteenth century: "There is a fixed tendency among civilized men," Olmsted pointed out, "to place more and more value upon the cleanliness and purity of the condition of their domestic life." These conditions may have suffered in a gridiron city, but decentralization made possible an alternative to compact urban building and the creation of discrete residential neighborhoods more appropriate to domesticity.[37]

Unfortunately, most suburban development in the nineteenth century was as unplanned as the linear expansion of the city. Too often it was undertaken with the expectation of reaping handsome profits, and, in the absence of a clearly defined public policy, those individuals who selected such locations for their homes and the contractors who built them collectively determined irrevocably the landscape of the modern city. Sam Bass Warner's investigation of urban growth in Boston, for example, demonstrates that the twentieth-century metropolis is the "product of hundreds of thousands of separate decisions."[38]

Even so successfully designed a community as Riverside, which codified the suburban ideal and which served as a model for similar development in other cities, had drawbacks. The affluent who moved to the more congenial environment of the suburbs turned their backs on those whom Charles Loring Brace called the "dangerous classes," and, partly as a result, the city fragmented into a series of discrete residential neighborhoods divided by race, ethnic origins, and economic activities. This flight to the suburbs, at first a trickle but later an exodus, included individuals who were turning away from the city as physical form and from the complexity of new work and interpersonal relationships. In their quest for personal security and domestic bliss amid suburban surroundings, these people made personal decisions that had public implications, ignoring the effect they might have on broader social problems and the quality of urban life. To the supremacy of privatistic values Warner ascribes the breakdown of the city as community. Tragically, the nineteenth-century search for an urban compromise failed to bring about a new balance of country and city. To do so the suburb would have to be planned comprehensively, as an integral part of the modern metropolis rather than an escape from it.[39]

CHAPTER IX

THE NEW CITY:
A HOUSE WITH MANY ROOMS

The principle of a division of labor may, with advantage, be meas-
urably applied to the plan of a city; one part of it being laid out
with a view to the development of one class of utilities, another to
a different class, according as natural circumstances favor.
— *FREDERICK LAW OLMSTED and JOHN JAMES ROBERTSON CROES*

Neither decentralization nor suburbanization was adequate to the task of refining and civilizing America's cities. To be sure, the move to a home on the urban periphery enabled those families that could afford it to escape urban congestion, but in relocating a distance from cities those individuals too often turned their backs on the persisting problems of urban life—tenements, filth, corruption, and disease. Nor, in the absence of comprehensive planning, did decentralization and suburbanization even have much of a positive impact on the spatial arrangement of cities. Most development on what Kenneth T. Jackson has called the "crabgrass frontier" was, like Dearman and Chicago's Hyde Park, really nothing more than linear extension of the urban gridiron. Instead of creating more openly built cities these communities increased the distance separating town and country. And, as Olmsted and Vaux learned at Riverside, not even the most imaginative plans and the best intentions were commensurate to the needs of the modern metropolis. The properly designed suburb was too costly, too likely to be victimized by changing economic conditions, and too ready a target for the designs of speculators and their "Gold Exchange and Erie [Railroad] principles" to be a panacea for the challenges confronting the nineteenth-century city.[1]

Although at first decentralization was so unplanned that it compounded rather than solved the problem of urban congestion, Olmsted shrewdly recognized that modern transportation systems made possible the implementation of a new pattern of city form. In his estimation, streetcar and railway lines, together with parks and parkways, could bring about the "suburbanizing" of the residential sections of large towns and provide "elbow room about a house without going into the country, without sacrifice of butchers, bakers & theatres." But if these new residential neighborhoods were to be integral parts of the modern metropolis, Olmsted realized, they would have to be platted in anticipation of urban growth.[2]

Olmsted first clearly defined the components of the new city in "Public Parks and the Enlargement of Towns," an address delivered in 1870 at a meeting of the American Social Science Association held in Boston. In this paper Olmsted asserted that a "strong drift townward" was the most prominent characteristic of the age, and he attributed the growth of cities in part to the depopulation of agricultural districts. Several once prosperous New England neighborhoods, he pointed out, resembled nothing so much as the pathetic landscapes of Goldsmith's "Deserted Village." Society had all but disappeared from these places, and towns fell into disrepair as people moved to cities. Technological improvements also affected the quality of life in rural areas. The introduction of labor-saving machinery, after all, acted to "reduce the man-power required on the farms." Such devices not only displaced many agricultural workers; they also made large scale operations economically advantageous, which tended to increase the size of farms and the distance separating households in the country. As the number of farms declined and rural homesteads became increasingly isolated, the attractions of such a way of life diminished. Olmsted quoted a woman who remarked, "If I were offered a deed of the best farm that I ever saw, on condition of going back to the country to live, I would not take it. I would rather face starvation in town."[3]

Olmsted was certain that the rapid growth of cities and the "withdrawal of people from rural conditions of living" were caused by circumstances of a "permanent character." These increments in the urban population were only to be expected, he reasoned, because cities provided distinct advantages in terms of access to such educational and cultural institutions as libraries, schools, museums, and halls of the performing arts. "People of the greatest wealth can hardly command as much of these in the country," Olmsted reminded his audience, "as the poorest work-girl is offered here in Boston." Specialization of labor, availability of services, improvements in transportation and sanitary conditions—all contributed to the superiority of city to country. And this disparity would only become more pronounced, he predicted, because innumerable advances in "enterprise and the progress of invention" were sure to "add rapidly to the economy and convenience of town life, and thus increase its comparative attractions."[4]

Despite such improvements, the prospect of sustained urban growth remained threatening. The numerous evils which continued to plague cities would not be cured without enormous effort. In crowded neighborhoods, vitiated air carried "highly corrupt and irritating matters," and the incessant energy of street contact had a harmful impact on the "nerves and minds" of the people. Fortunately, Olmsted reported, sanitary improvements and modern "Science" had "beyond all question determined many of the causes of the special evils by which men are afflicted in towns, and placed means in our hands for guarding against them." Foremost among such remedies was the development of public parks, which purified the disease-ridden atmosphere of the congested city. "Air is disinfected by sunlight and foliage," he declared, and trees eliminated those elements most dangerous to health. Thus the primary purpose of a park was "to give the lungs a bath of pure sunny air, to give the mind a suggestion of rest from the devouring eagerness and intellectual strife of town life."[5]

Provisions for parks, though essential, were but preliminary steps in the creation of a more healthful, more openly built urban landscape. If urban areas were to continue to spread, however, leaders in every city must seize the opportunity to avoid the mistakes of the past and to plan a modern metropolis free of congestion and the tyranny of the gridiron.[6]

In this address and in subsequent reports Olmsted cited the example of New York's street arrangement to demonstrate how the gridiron promoted congestion and thus was inappropriate to residential neighborhoods. Indeed, he attributed the use of the gridiron to an earlier period when considerations of defense necessitated enclosing a town within walls. As population increments matched the increasing economic dominance of cities, the finite amount of space made crowding unavoidable. Nevertheless, it was only a short walk from the center of population to the fields beyond the town. Though sharply defined, country and city were proximate. Not so confined, Manhattan marched uptown, and as it did so the gridiron proved disastrous. The Commissioners Plan of 1811, Olmsted asserted, was devised at a time when New York was a "small, poor, remote provincial village." It was a utilitarian design, determined by "chance occurrence": a mason's sieve was placed over a map of Manhattan Island, and its rectangular grid determined the arrangement of streets. The result, Olmsted concluded, was perhaps the worst city plan ever invented.[7]

Olmsted castigated the gridiron, the old urban landscape, for its regrettable social and economic impact on Manhattan. Because of the high cost of grading and filling the island's irregular topography, and because of the resulting exorbitant ground rents, lots in uniform, two-hundred-foot blocks were divided and subdivided, creating endless rows of contiguous houses, extensive in depth but often occupying only twelve or fourteen feet of street frontage. Poorly lighted and ventilated, and with no service alley to permit access to the rear yard, these inconvenient and unhealthy buildings all too often deteriorated into slum-like quarters. Even worse was the product of the gridiron and the cupidity of builders, the tenement house, which Olmsted called calamitous and demoralizing to the working classes.[8]

These same factors affected the housing of the middle and upper classes. Their homes were "only a more decent sort of tenement house, nearly half of their rooms being without direct light and ventilation." In such buildings the interior spaces were usually occupied by stairwells and water closets, functions for which they were least suited. "Decent, wholesome, tidy dwellings" for the laboring classes, Olmsted concluded, were "sadly wanting" in New York. Not even the most elegant of the city's houses could escape the tyranny of the imperious gridiron. He repeated Henry W. Bellows's characterization of the typical substantial private dwelling as a "slice of house fifteen feet wide, slid into a block with seven long flights of stairs between the place where the cook works and sleeps." Because of the spatial limitations of building lots, even the finest brownstones, with their fashionable bay windows and high stoops, were "really a confession that it is impossible to build a convenient and tasteful residence in New York, adapted to the civilized requirements of a single family, except at a cost which even rich men find generally prohibitory."[9]

Aesthetically Olmsted criticized the gridiron's failure to provide adequate sites for noble and imposing buildings. "There is no place under the system in New York," he observed, "where a stately building can be looked up to from base to turret, none where it can even be seen full in the face and all at once taken in by the eye; none where it can be viewed in advantageous perspective." The 1811 plan, Olmsted concluded, "defies the architect to produce habitable rooms of pleasing or dignified proportions" and necessitates "methods of building which are at issue with all the lessons of civilized experience."[10]

Moreover, the Commissioners Plan of 1811 impeded New York's commercial development (by strangling traffic), endowed the city with a drearily monotonous street plan, and directed the region's population growth into the surrounding suburbs. The builders who employed this rectangular street arrangement inflicted these tribulations on the generations that followed. "If one sagacious despot had wished to make life in towns as much as possible repulsive to common sense," Olmsted concluded, "he would have forced just such a method of building" as New York's street plan imposed on that city.[11]

Despite the obvious limitations of the grid, Olmsted admitted that it was a permanent fixture of New York's cityscape. Experience taught that once a plan had been determined little could be done to alter or improve it. After London's disastrous fire of 1666, for example,

Sir Christopher Wren had proposed to rebuild the city according to a Baroque plan. His scheme received the approval of the king, but because its streets would have violated existing property lines short-sighted merchants and residents blocked its implementation. Yet less than one hundred years after reconstruction of the medieval city, London's merchants, at great expense, began to provide some of the conveniences the Wren plan had offered. After a similarly disastrous fire in 1835, New York's merchants might have profited from London's mistake. Here, Olmsted noted, was "a rare opportunity for laying out a district expressly with a view to facilitate commerce," but again the city was rebuilt in its former shape. The reluctance to alter street and property lines he attributed to "the difficulties of equalizing benefits and damages among the various owners of the land." Remedy for a bad plan, Olmsted concluded, was impractical, and New York's grid-iron remained inviolate (with the singular exception of Broadway) despite the "enormous changes in the modes of commerce, of means of communication, and of styles of domestic life which this century has seen." Olmsted lamented that the gridiron inflicted on American cities the tyrannous burden of the past, that much of what had been done in the name of urban design "has to be undone, and much of what cannot be undone is permanent injury."[12]

The gridiron might be a permanent fixture of the commercial city, but urban growth and decentralization made possible potentially less dense building and the adoption of different patterns of street arrangement. The initial stages of decentralization merely extended the gridiron into the surrounding countryside. Olmsted knew that the modern metropolis would need to adopt some other form of residential planning. The street railways and commuter trains that shattered the boundaries of the walking city could also eliminate the stranglehold of urban congestion. Accomplishing this was vitally important, he reasoned, because the "future progress of civilization" would depend on "the influences by which men's minds and characters" would be affected in the large towns and cities where they lived and worked. By the 1870s the future welfare of the United States would be determined not by its agrarian heritage or by some romantic attachment to "the country"; it would be dependent on the "convenience, safety, order and economy of life in its great cities."[13]

Olmsted's essential precondition for the creation of this new urban landscape was the complete separation of commercial and residential neighborhoods. The exigencies of business might require compact development in certain areas, but he saw no reason why all parts of the urban environment must suffer the same fate. Some areas must be designed to accommodate "humanity, religion, art, science and scholarship," others the requisites of domesticity. Unsurprisingly, it was the efficient home that Olmsted chose as metaphor for the modern city: "If a house to be used for many different purposes must have many rooms and passages of various dimensions and variously lighted and furnished," he explained, "not less must such a metropolis be specifically adapted at different points to different ends." Such a city would be composed of discrete commercial and industrial districts, a series of large public parks tied together by a system of parkways, handsomely designed residential subdivisions laid out to anticipate urban expansion, and suburban communities—all conceived as integral, interdependent parts of the same metropolis.[14]

Olmsted and Calvert Vaux had a fleeting opportunity to design a major residential subdivision of New York during the summer of 1860. They were selected as landscape architects by the commissioners appointed to lay out streets and avenues in Manhattan north of 155th Street. This area, the only part of the city north of 14th Street that was not included in the 1811 gridiron, was still largely undeveloped. Bounded by the Hudson and Harlem rivers and by Spuyten Duyvil Creek, it was, as Olmsted described it, "1800 acres of very rugged & beautiful ground—impracticable to be brought into the square street & avenue system of the rest of the island."[15]

Olmsted and Vaux realized that, because of its topography and distance from the centers of population and business, northern Manhattan could be developed most advantageously as a suburb within the corporate limits of the city. By planning this area as a residential enclave for villas and cottages, the designers attempted to attract those middle-class families who might otherwise move to suburbs in Brooklyn or New Jersey. The Washington Heights area possessed all the "essential rural requirements" for such homes, but scenery was not enough: Olmsted and Vaux explained that the natural beauty of the neighborhood must be combined with the "advantages of society, of compact society," yet without sacrificing "tranquility and seclusion." To do so was difficult because, in the absence of modern zoning ordinances, access to the city also made possible intrusion by the city.[16]

In a letter to one of the commissioners, Henry Hill Elliott, which is the sole surviving document revealing his and Vaux's prescriptions for the development of the area, Olmsted pointed out that the only way to protect the residential character of Washington Heights was by controlling the placement of streets in the area. Any road that led too directly to the city, he warned, would become a "noisy, dusty, smoking, shouting, rattling and stinking" thoroughfare. Instead of attracting the better sort of family, the street would be lined with "cheap tenement & boarding houses" for the cartsmen, mechanics, and laborers who provided service to the neighborhood.[17]

Nevertheless, some provision for service access was essential, and to meet the exigencies of commerce Olmsted suggested that

Tenth and (as far as possible) Eleventh avenues be extended on a straight line northward through the island. Because of their directness these roads would attract the carts of tradesmen, who, upon nearing their destinations, would take smaller, less direct "tributary roads" to the residential areas of the Heights. The principal means of communication within the neighborhood was a carriage drive that would wind "circuitously or indirectly," following the contours of the hilly topography. As this road would be unsuitable for through traffic Olmsted believed that it would be "resorted to for pleasure driving." Such a street arrangement, he predicted, would minimize the intrusions of business and ensure that northern Manhattan would long remain a desirable location for handsome residences.[18]

No documents explain precisely what happened to Olmsted and Vaux's plan for the development of Washington Heights, but if the sentiments expressed in this letter to Elliott were formalized in an unpublished report their recommendations were ignored. The state-appointed commission was disbanded, and its responsibilities transferred to the Board of Commissioners of the Central Park. On behalf of the commissioners, Andrew H. Green later wrote an extensive report on laying out streets in the area, but this document failed to comprehend what Olmsted understood intuitively: that without protection against unwanted development, without assurance of a permanent rural character, Washington Heights would never fulfill its potential as a residential neighborhood.[19]

A decade later Olmsted had another opportunity to plan a major residential subdivision in the New York metropolitan area. Together with physician Elisha Harris, civil engineer J. M. Trowbridge, and architect Henry Hobson Richardson, he was engaged by the Staten Island Improvement Commission to prepare a preliminary plan of development. Despite its proximity to Manhattan, Staten Island was not benefiting from the rapid decentralization of the urban population. In part this was the result of inadequate transportation facilities, but far more important was the island's reputation as a disease-ridden place. Olmsted and his colleagues undertook a complete sanitary survey of the island and investigated what changes might promote residential development. Their report, undoubtedly written primarily by Olmsted, argued that Staten Island possessed "a special character for domestic purposes." Despite its distinct advantages for suburban growth, Olmsted predicted, the island would become a desirable place of residence only if it were reserved almost exclusively for that use. The suggestions for improvement that Olmsted and his colleagues presented would have been expensive, especially for a speculative land company, and even though the report predicted that proper development would pay handsome dividends in the future, nothing came of the comprehensive program it outlined.[20]

Although Olmsted was denied the chance to transform the picturesque heights of northern Manhattan into his conception of the suburban subdivision within the city and to develop the rolling hills of
Staten Island as a proper residential community, he would have another opportunity to redirect the pattern of urban decentralization in
the metropolitan area. On January 1, 1874, New York took the first
tentative step in its evolution as a consolidated city by annexing the
southern portion of Westchester County, known today as the Bronx.
At that time southern Westchester was predominantly rural in character, a scattering of small towns interspersed amid numerous farms.
But despite its size—the Bronx was nearly as large in area as
Manhattan—its population and the assessed value of its real estate
were dwarfed by those of New York City. Here was a rural backwater,
without the leadership or the resources to determine its own future,
threatened by the unplanned expansion of the metropolis to the
south and by that of Yonkers to the north.[21]

The state legislature, ever wary of strengthening the power of city
Democrats, entrusted development of the Bronx (designated the
Twenty-third and Twenty-fourth wards) to the Department of Public
Parks, successor to the Board of Commissioners of the Central Park.
On November 5, 1875, the department's board adopted a resolution
proposed by its president, William R. Martin, and requested that
Olmsted prepare a comprehensive plan for developing the annexed
district. Thus Olmsted received, for the first time in his career, the opportunity to develop a major urban subdivision of a metropolitan
area. The board conferred upon Olmsted the power to employ "as his
assistant, an engineer to act directly under his orders." He selected
John James Robertson Croes, a civil and topographical engineer already in the employ of the department, who had conducted the
preliminary survey of the northern end of the Bronx.[22]

In his reports on the development of the new wards Olmsted
demanded that New Yorkers look beyond the 1811 plan and envision
the rich potential of their city if organized according to a different spatial arrangement. The familiar but lamented gridiron was inadequate
to the social and aesthetic requirements of the new urban landscape:
an arbitrary rectangular street arrangement, which promised to
"make all parts of a great city equally convenient for all uses," instead
made all parts of the urban environment equally inconvenient. Moreover, in the Twenty-third and Twenty-fourth wards, use of the gridiron would have necessitated destroying the natural features of the
landscape, at enormous expense. Olmsted and Croes thus determined that the topography of the Bronx was an asset to be exploited
rather than an inconvenience to be eliminated, that "variety of surface
offers variety of opportunity." To be effective, their plan would have to
anticipate the inevitable expansion of the city while at the same time

The New Urban Landscape

reconciling urbanization with a ruggedly picturesque terrain. The task would obviously be a difficult one: "A judicious laying out of the annexed territory," Olmsted admonished, "requires a certain effort of forecast as to what the city is to be in the future. In this respect, there is a great danger in attempting too much as in attempting too little."[23]

In a series of reports to the Department of Public Parks, Olmsted and Croes divided the Twenty-third and Twenty-fourth wards into three discrete sections, the village of Morrisania, the heights overlooking the Hudson at Riverdale, and the central district. Unfortunately, the plan of Morrisania was irremediable. Like those parts of New York laid out in 1811, it was already covered with a closely built gridiron. Nevertheless, Olmsted envisioned this area as a flourishing commercial community, a marketplace that would provide necessary services to the adjacent suburban quarters.[24]

The remainder of the Twenty-third and Twenty-fourth wards was still largely undeveloped, and Olmsted applied a device he had first implemented while developing the Buffalo park system—the organization of recreational spaces according to intended use—by proposing the complete differentiation of neighborhoods and urban space in the Bronx. For example, because the topography of the Riverdale area made it unsuitable for a rectangular street arrangement, Olmsted and Croes chose to develop it as a permanent suburban retreat within the expanded city. This they characterized as a neighborhood divided into large lots, with curvilinear streets following the slopes of the hills. Riverdale, they suggested, would become a rural oasis for "that class of citizens to whom the confinement, noise, and purely artificial conditions of the compact city are oppressive, and who are able to indulge in the luxury of a villa or suburban cottage residence." The designers justified this type of development in economic as well as aesthetic terms. Not only would it cost less to subdivide the area for suburban homes than to grade it for rectangular streets, but because it could be developed quickly and soon attract those residents who might otherwise move to Brooklyn or New Jersey, the district eventually would make a substantial contribution to the city treasury.[25]

Olmsted and Croes proposed a different treatment for the central area of the Twenty-third and Twenty-fourth wards, which lay directly north of the village of Morrisania. Because its topography varied they divided this area into four sections. The southernmost they designated a business district and arranged its streets in rectilinear blocks—but with the blocks oriented to the north and south rather than to the east and west as in Morrisania and Manhattan. For the area west of Webster Avenue they proposed a modified grid, with some of the streets following the contour of the land. The rough and irregular section to the north, a plateau overlooking the Harlem River, they set aside as a residential district, and the northernmost reaches of the central area, still devoted primarily to agriculture, they designed wholly in accord with its topography. Olmsted and Croes concluded by pointing out that their plan for this area provided for "business sections in the valleys of the Mill Brook and Cromwell Creek, for a section for residences on the elevated ground along the center of the district, [and] for a section for suburban homes at the northern limit." Olmsted hoped also to plan a system of parks and parkways that would extend throughout the annexed territory, but political differences within the Department of Public Parks resulted in the termination of his services before such a report could be prepared. Nevertheless, Olmsted and Croes devised for the Bronx a comprehensive plan that utilized fully the differentiation of urban space made possible by innovations in transportation.[26]

But Olmsted realized that, however ingenious the design for the annexed territory, without efficient communication with Manhattan the Bronx's development as a residential subdivision of New York would be delayed, perhaps forever. Thus, he and Croes advocated the construction of a steam-powered rapid transit network that would unite all parts of the Twenty-third and Twenty-fourth wards and provide convenient access to the metropolis. Croes, who assumed primary responsibility for designing the transportation system, proposed that a loop of tracks encircle the annexed territory and that additional lines cut through the middle of the district. These tracks would in turn connect with existing railroad and elevated streetcar lines running south toward Manhattan and would become an integral part of a metropolitan transportation network. Following the precedent of the transverse roads at Central Park, Croes and Olmsted suggested that the railroad tracks be placed in trenches cut beneath the surface of the land (fig. 35). This separation of grades would provide for greater safety in operation, allow the trains to travel at optimal speed, which was impossible in the congested streets of Manhattan, and ensure that the railroad intruded on everyday life as little as possible.[27]

All of these elements of the plan—adaptation of streets to the natural topography, a multipurpose land use pattern that provided for differentiation of commercial, residential, and recreational functions, the separation of commercial traffic from recreational drives and pedestrian paths, and a comprehensive transportation system connecting the Twenty-third and Twenty-fourth wards to the city— attempted to provide for the future growth of the Bronx in a way that would be compatible with the developmental needs of the metropolis. The plans prepared by Olmsted and Croes were comprehensive and imaginative proposals to bring order to the process of urban decentralization, to create an alternative to the New York Edith Wharton later characterized as "this cramped horizontal gridiron of a town

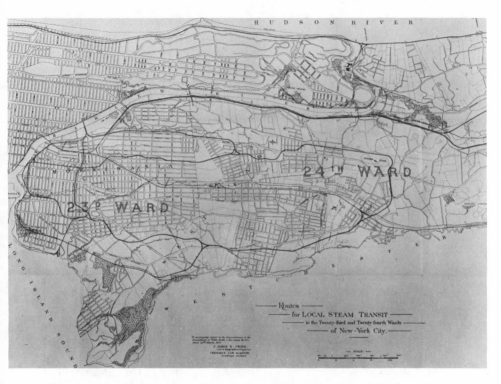

Figure 35. Proposed plan for steam-powered rapid transit lines throughout the Twenty-third and Twenty-fourth wards, Bronx, New York, by J. J. R. Croes and F. L. Olmsted, 1876–77. (Courtesy, Center for Landscape Studies, Dumbarton Oaks, Trustees for Harvard University, Washington, D.C.)

without towers, porticoes, fountains or perspectives, hide-bound in its deadly uniformity to mean ugliness."[28]

Unfortunately, but for part of the plans for the central district of the Twenty-fourth Ward, the Olmsted-Croes proposals were never implemented. The comprehensive development of the Bronx was too expensive for a city reeling from the profligate spending of the Tweed administration and suffering the effects of the panic of 1873. Indeed, major opposition to uptown development was led by Andrew H. Green, who had labored heroically to put the city's finances in order after Tweed's demise, and by Henry G. Stebbins, his longtime ally on the Board of Commissioners of the Central Park and its successor, the Department of Public Parks. Green argued that spending the city's limited resources on development in the Bronx before it was immediately necessary was fiscally irresponsible. "Can we afford to lavish more millions up town," he asked, "and continue to neglect the ways of traffic and travel down town, where the majority of the population live, and where the commerce that sustains the city is chiefly executed?" Stebbins criticized the Olmsted-Croes plans for their extravagance and for being potentially detrimental to existing property owners. Aesthetically he denounced the "irregularly warped and curved" roads and "tortuous" lines of the streets. These "innovations," he charged, ignored the "principle of obtaining direct and rectangular streets to as great an extent as the geography will permit," and would result in the division of the land into "fanciful" but utterly useless shapes.[29]

Green and Stebbins were undoubtedly correct in arguing that a substantial portion of the city's expenditures for public works must be allocated to southern Manhattan, where congestion was becoming intolerable. But they failed to grasp what Olmsted had learned, that once the gridiron was adopted any major alteration in street arrangement was impossible. Moreover, in failing to provide for the comprehensive planning of the Bronx in advance of the city's expansion, Green and Stebbins effectively doomed that area to piecemeal development. In the street plan eventually adopted, the blocks are small and compact, similar to those laid out by the Commissioners Plan of 1811, and, excepting the village of Riverdale, the curvilinearity so important to Olmsted is eliminated. The compact development surely contributed to the eventual deterioration of the South Bronx into one of the city's worst slums. Absent too is the suburban character Olmsted and Croes saw in the irregular topography of the land north of Morrisania, an area long since engulfed by the sprawling metropolis. The outcome of this short-sighted planning, according to John C. Olmsted, who, under his stepfather's supervision, drafted the proposed street arrangement, was New York's sentence "to endure for all time a bad system of main streets." The resulting development of the Bronx, he concluded, was "a fine example of the shocking waste of our poor human civilization."[30]

A few years after the termination, in 1878, of Olmsted's service with the Department of Public Parks, the city's Rapid Transit Commission rejected the transportation network he had designed in collaboration with Croes. Notwithstanding Croes's service as engineer to the commission, that body ignored the plan to locate a system of railroad tracks below grade and instead built elevated railroads, at enormously increased cost, which contributed to the aesthetic demise of the urban landscape. Years later John C. Olmsted attributed the subsurface transportation plan to Croes and asserted that, as a result of the decision to build the elevated railroad, "the community now has to pay for subways in rock at 5 times what his rapid transit system would have cost." The failure to implement Croes's plans he blamed on politics, the lobbying of elevated railroad franchises, and the opposition of property owners.[31]

Only in the matter of park development did the Twenty-third and

Twenty-fourth wards take shape according to the lines Olmsted and Croes projected. The 1884 commission appointed by the state legislature to locate parks in the annexed territory followed the precepts Olmsted had articulated during his years of work in New York. The commission's report, in fact, echoed Olmsted's justification for the development of parks in terms of increased public health, higher property values, and contributions to the social environment of the city. Based on this report the city eventually did locate major parks at the old Van Cortlandt estate, along the Bronx River, and in the northern part of the central district, as well as several smaller parks in the more populous quarters of the Twenty-third Ward.[32]

The success of the 1884 park commission notwithstanding, there can be little doubt that Olmsted would have prepared a more comprehensive plan. Rather than locating parks primarily in the northern reaches of the Bronx (the area farthest from the center of population), Olmsted probably would have distributed open spaces throughout the new wards. If his designs for the development of Brooklyn and Buffalo can be considered examples, by a more ambitious system of parks and parkways Olmsted would have extended the benefits of open space throughout the entire borough.

The plans that Olmsted and Croes prepared for the development of the Twenty-third and Twenty-fourth wards are the most complete articulation of the vision of a new urban landscape. They are not anti-urban, but instead attempt to reshape the city to accommodate a variety of uses. These plans make provision for a commercial district, for separate residential neighborhoods that would provide house lots suitable for domesticity, for parks and parkways, and for an efficient transportation system both within the annexed territory and connecting it to the metropolis. Had it been developed according to the Olmsted-Croes proposals, the Bronx would have demonstrated a rational alternative to the gridiron and been the culmination of the nineteenth-century effort to reconcile country and city. Alas, these plans were swamped in the maelstrom of New York City politics. Never again would Olmsted—or any other designer in nineteenth-century America—have a comparable opportunity to create so important a part of a metropolis in anticipation of urban decentralization. Tragically, the comprehensively designed new urban landscape, the civilized city Olmsted and many of his contemporaries envisioned, would never be realized.

CHAPTER X

TRANSFORMATION:
THE NEOCLASSICAL CITYSCAPE

*The Commissioners of 1807, as we call them, though in fact their
map, authorized in that year, was not filed until 1811, were public malefactors of high degree.*
—MONTGOMERY SCHUYLER

As the winter of 1861 faded, as civil war loomed on the horizon,
Henry W. Bellows took time from ministerial duties and philanthropic
efforts to write about Central Park. Bellows considered this first great
urban park a testament to democracy, a system of government soon to
be contested not in the halls of Congress or on recreational grounds
but on battlefields. Whether or not he knew of the responsibilities he
would assume as wartime head of the United States Sanitary
Commission, Bellows welcomed the opportunity to describe the
manifestly civilizing and humanizing influence that he found in the
park. In analyzing its importance to the evolution of democracy in
America, Bellows noted exactly what made Central Park so exceptional, its singular role in documenting a transformation in American
life. Settlers on the frontier ravaged the environment. They cut trees
with the enthusiasm of Cooper's fictional Billy Kirby—whose heroic
efforts cleared forests in the name of "progress" with such efficiency
that Natty Bumppo fled west to escape the settlers' axe—and then
these pioneers imposed on the landscape the rectangular street
arrangement they considered symbolic of urban form. But while the
conquest of the continent may have been the saga of the West, Bellows
considered the reformation of the land in the center of Manhattan
Island a manifestation of the evolving civilization of the East. Instead
of chopping down trees, instead even of preserving them, as George
P. Morris's famous poem had advocated, citizens of New York were
planting trees by the thousands, in a naturalistic manner, in order to
provide an alternative environment to the straight lines and sharp
angles that otherwise defined the city.[1]

What Bellows applauded about Central Park was its embodiment
of a particular vision of what a city should be, and in this he agreed

wholeheartedly with its principal designer. Like Olmsted, Bellows considered the park not only a naturalistic landscape but an experiment in republican institutions. In his estimation the park was a large and handsome yet accessible expanse of nature scientifically designed to meet the daily needs of the urban population. Olmsted had attempted to shape the landscape to affect park visitors unconsciously, through the contemplation of seemingly limitless natural scenery. In this respect the park was a reform, an attempt to redress the fundamental environmental failures that he found in the modern commercial city. It was predicated on a particular vision of civilization, in which the designed urban landscape approximated "the country," tempered the excesses of human nature, and raised humanity to a higher level of social interaction. This formulation of the psychological impact of scenery, which contemporaries often described as the restorative power of nature, determined that the park should be the physical antithesis of conditions in the city. But the park was not an expression of anti-urbanism; it was designed to be another element in the complex physical fabric and "the general municipal economy of a great City."[2]

Bellows continued the attempt to resolve the persistent ambivalence toward country and city in American culture through a series of essays published between 1867 and 1872. He began by assaulting the longstanding tradition of hostility toward urban life that was one legacy of the revolutionary generation. "It is common enough for moralists of the Jeffersonian type to deplore the existence of great cities," he wrote, "and to denounce them as sores on the body politic, while they enlarge on the superior innocency and happiness of life in the country." Such criticism invariably ignored both the problems of a rural existence and the promise of the city. A more realistic appraisal of the country, Bellows asserted, would be "very gloomy," because civilization there "lags far behind that of the city." According to Bellows, few of the conveniences and improvements in the "art of comfortable living" had made their way outside the metropolis.[3]

Although the census of 1870 documented the increasing concentration of people in urban areas, Bellows was not alarmed. Instead he predicted that the "causes which are giving city life its present dominance" would continue indefinitely. Whereas critics of the Jeffersonian persuasion might have offered prophesies of imminent urban doom, Bellows, like Olmsted, advised his readers to "accept the tendency and invest it with the best conditions." As cities were growing they were improving. During the previous twenty-five years, sanitary reform, urban transportation systems, and new fire prevention techniques had brought about an immense "advance in healthfulness and comfort of city residence." Foremost among these improvements, of course, was the development of the new urban landscape.[4]

Bellows could praise the growth of cities because he equated civilization with urban life. He was certain that the culture of cities was decidedly superior to that of the country, as it provided "more intellectual and moral facilities; more opportunities for employment, amusement, and locomotion; more resources against drudgery and monotony; better division of labor, better household appliances, more order, neatness, and control of one's time." Among the institutions that enhanced the appeal of cities, Bellows enumerated public libraries, art museums, and music conservatories. Most important were public parks and parkways, which provided large spaces for healthful recreation and contributed to the achievement of a more openly built urban landscape. For Bellows these public recreational grounds comprised the "true essence of the attractiveness of city life, inasmuch as they wed the best charms of the country to the practical advantages of the town."[5]

Neither city nor country was without serious limitations. Bellows noted the railroad's impact, causing at once "consolidation in towns and cities" and a scattering of population to outlying areas. Improved transportation brought country and city closer together, thereby enabling people to live in a suburban environment without sacrificing urban conveniences. Like Olmsted, Bellows believed that a metropolitan area must provide for all three ways of life—the compactness essential to the economy of cities, the open spaces and pastoralism of the country, and the middle ground of the suburb, a landscape consciously contrived to provide the optimal surroundings for domesticity.[6]

The conception of the new urban landscape evolved and became more comprehensive as it was implemented during the second half of the nineteenth century. What began as an attempt to provide city residents with large open spaces that would promote public health and afford opportunities for recreation gradually embraced the planning of the metropolis as a totality. Parks, parkways, park systems, suburbs, and residential neighborhoods in urban subdivisions—all laid out in anticipation of the linear extension of the gridiron—promised to recast city form and naturalize the urban environment.

But while many of the nation's cultural leaders found this vision of the new urban landscape appropriate in the years preceding and immediately following the Civil War, during the 1880s and 1890s a different conception of the city emerged. In the early 1880s the nation's principal metropolitan areas began a dramatic recovery from the economic panic of 1873. During the next two decades New York's merchants and civic leaders commissioned construction of many buildings that shaped the metropolis of the early twentieth century. As Clarence Cook had done thirty years earlier, architectural critic

Mariana Griswold van Rensselaer surveyed the impact of this new construction on the fabric of the city. The business area of downtown New York, she noted, "is being so rapidly remodeled that small trace will be left in the year 1900 of the work that stood but ten years ago." Recently erected commercial buildings, in her estimation, were much more successful aesthetically than the existing public or domestic ones, because utilitarian considerations had resulted in the functional massing of form rather than the application of showy decoration. Mrs. van Rensselaer's architectural theory resonates with such mid-nineteenth-century ideas as truth to materials and expression of purpose, but she was also aware of more recent developments in city planning, especially those undertaken by Baron Haussmann. She recognized that, even as new construction reshaped New York, as Central Park was being surrounded by tall apartment buildings and massive private residences, it was the gridiron that dictated architectural design. Mrs. van Rensselaer described the typical city street in terms of "barren ugliness or hideous deformity," and lamented the inflexibility of the gridiron. The new Metropolitan Opera House, for example, was located on so restricted a site that, despite the architect's efforts, it could not achieve monumentality, a limitation the author contrasted with the success of Garnier's L'Opera, completed only a few years earlier in Paris.[7]

The gridiron left few spaces for noble buildings or groups of structures, creating aesthetic problems, and in the hands of speculators without a comprehensive vision of the city it also promoted congestion. The nation's cities had become more complex as physical and social spaces than they were when Cook wrote about New York thirty years earlier, and the rectangular street arrangement compounded urban problems. Thus, in the closing decades of the century a younger generation of civic leaders confronted what contemporaries considered a new urban barbarism: municipal governments dominated, to a greater degree than ever before, by corrupt political machines; levels of poverty that would have made the revolutionary generation despair for the fate of the republic; shortages of adequate housing for city residents, which consigned millions to squalid tenements; the environmental effects of coal-powered industrial capitalism, which polluted the atmosphere and so discolored buildings that the layers of soot inspired Lewis Mumford's metaphorical title, *The Brown Decades*; and the increasing congestion of carts, carriages, pedestrians, and trolleys on city streets and avenues. The demographic complexion of the nation's principal urban areas also changed as the rate of immigration accelerated. Many of those who crowded into New York's Lower East Side and similar neighborhoods came not from countries that traditionally had contributed to the American populace but from southern and eastern Europe.[8]

The United States was becoming, in English commentator James F. Muirhead's apt phrase, a "land of contrasts," and nowhere were the disparities in income and quality of life greater than in the nation's cities. Urban and industrial growth created fabulous new wealth, to be sure, but it created as well the squalid living conditions William Dean Howells recorded in *A Hazard of New Fortunes* and Jacob Riis captured in a series of haunting photographs. One response to the changing demographic profile of the city was the rise of forms of popular entertainment that socialized residents to life in America's urban areas. Active recreation replaced the passive contemplation of natural scenery, and a new athleticism answered Theodore Roosevelt's call for the "strenuous life." As the diversity of the city and its people increased, the world of genteel reformers and that of P. T. Barnum gave way to the exoticism and titillation of Coney Island. Broadways everywhere became, as Mumford noted in the 1920s, the linear extension of the amusement park—places that, he felt, deadened the senses and offered a glittering but temporary relief from the wretchedness of the urban existence. To the nation's principal cultural leaders at the turn of the century, popular amusements aggravated rather than alleviated the problems the poor confronted in America's cities. For them the task was to create institutions that would instruct and improve residents of cities.[9]

Another measure of the contrasts appearing in the nation's cities at the end of the nineteenth century was the differentiation of urban space. Since the 1850s lower Manhattan had been the province of commercial buildings, warehouses and tenements, but by the 1880s the island had fragmented into a series of discrete neighborhoods increasingly divided by economic use, race, class, and ethnic origin. Wealthy and white-collar workers followed streetcar lines or elevated railroads uptown or to the urban periphery, seeking the "broader, lower and more open building" Olmsted thought appropriate for residential neighborhoods. At the same time the city's commercial district began invading midtown—a development epitomized by the construction of Daniel H. Burnham's Flatiron Building (1901) on the southern side of Madison Square, which once had been a handsome residential area. The skyscraper, surely the most dramatic symbol of urban optimism and of the commercial forces that dominated New York, achieved the "more compact and higher" building Olmsted predicted for business areas, but at the expense of fundamentally altering the scale of the city.[10]

These developments were part of a broad transformation in American culture that occurred at the end of the nineteenth century. One manifestation of accommodation to change was the growing acceptance, among the nation's principal cultural leaders, of a different conception of what the city should be. Olmsted's vision of the naturalistic city may have been appropriate at an earlier time, but to Progressive reformers it must have seemed as naive as Richard Morris Hunt had predicted when he castigated the designers of Central Park as hopeless dreamers. Conditions in the expanding commercial city, the chaotic city with its increasingly foreign-born population, demanded not a nostalgic pastoralism or the silent influence of natural scenery but a new civic order and a different urban form that would refine and civilize residents of the tumultuous cities. Indeed, as historian Paul Boyer has pointed out, civicism became the ultimate urban moral reform crusade of the Progressive Era, and its supporters embraced "positive environmentalism" as a means of making the city a "moral habitat." In the hands of this younger generation New York was becoming, Thomas Bender and William R. Taylor recently observed, "the city of progressive urban reform, which involved as one of its principal aims the definition, in the political and architectural realms, of modern public life and culture."[11]

As had been the case at the turn of the nineteenth century and during the years when Olmsted and his collaborators were creating a more openly built urban environment, near the beginning of the twentieth century the question of city design became an important statement of not only the goals and methods but also the cultural vision of reformers. New York's leaders, among the most energetic in the nation, sought to redefine urban form, to control the expansion of their city, and to impose order on its residents. Like Olmsted and his contemporaries these Progressive reformers criticized the gridiron. Montgomery Schuyler described New York's 1811 plan as an exhibition of "dense ignorance of the art of city-making." But instead of a naturalistic city these new reformers applied the lessons of the Ecole des Beaux Arts to American urban space in order to create a city scale characterized by ensembles of neoclassical monuments. As the architect John Wellborn Root noted, such structures could "convey in some large elemental sense an idea of the great stable, conserving forces of modern civilization."[12]

The most immediate manifestation of this new conception of civic culture and city design was the transformation of the great urban parks created before and after the Civil War. As the evolution of Prospect Park demonstrates, this change began several years before the date with which historians traditionally mark the commencement of the Progressive Era and before the great White City rose in Chicago. In 1882 "reform" mayor Seth Low refused to reappoint James S. T. Stranahan, who since 1861 had served as president of the Brooklyn Park Commission. Thereafter the park became a political battleground, its labor force a vast new resource for dispensing patronage. By 1886 the Brooklyn Park Commissioners were "a set of politicians— all Democrats save one & he a Mugwump! They were a poor lot," John

Y. Culyer informed Olmsted, "with one or two exceptions."[13]

Under the aegis of the new commission the Prospect Park Olmsted and Vaux had created in the 1860s became instead a monument to a different conception of what the city should be. C. C. Martin, a park engineer, sent Olmsted a copy of the commission's 1888 *Annual Report*. "It is a literary curiosity," he informed his former employer, "and there are some novel ideas of landscape-Architecture which I think you will enjoy." Martin then described a number of changes the new commission was introducing, noting especially the cutting of trees on the park's perimeter, a demonstration of how little Stranahan's successors understood the purposes of the park: "You will of course remember with what care the borders of the Park were mounded up & thickly planted with the purpose of isolating the park from the surrounding city—These trees have all been trimmed up so that Park Visitors can readily see the buildings and everything outside." Martin concluded, even more ominously, "This is but one instance where the original design has been ridden over rough shod." By the end of October 1888, Olmsted informed his son John that the "present course of the Brooklyn Park Commissioners is sadder than anything else I know of."[14]

The transformation of Prospect Park involved more than the visual invasion of the naturalistic landscape by the city. In response to a changing constituency, park administrators made provision for various forms of modern recreation. The creation of baseball diamonds, hockey fields, and areas for lawn tennis, among other sports, afforded much needed facilities for urban residents, but they did not necessarily have to be placed in the naturalistic parks. As Olmsted pointed out to architect Henry Van Brunt, cities needed such recreational grounds as well as a large expanse devoted to the "pleasant contemplation of natural *scenery*." Thus the rise of active recreation marked a major shift away from the mid-century park ideal.[15]

More important, at the end of the nineteenth century Hunt's vision of the park as monumental civic space gained widespread acceptance, as was evident in the development of Grand Army Plaza. Olmsted and Vaux had conceived of the oval entrance as a large space for the assembling of groups of people and also as a means of directing traffic from surrounding streets into and around the park. But their goal of creating an immediate transition from city to park was replaced by a different use of the space. Mayor Low portended this change in 1885, when he proposed the erection of a memorial arch on the plaza. The 1888 *Annual Report* offered yet another use. The commissioners described this space as a "great failure, suggestive of Siberia in winter and Sahara in summer," and planned to remedy those conditions by remaking the plaza into a public garden similar to the one in Boston. Charles Sprague Sargent rushed to defend the

Figure 36. Memorial Arch, Grand Army Plaza, Brooklyn, New York, by John Duncan, 1889–92. (Courtesy, The Brooklyn Historical Society, Brooklyn, New York.)

integrity of the Olmsted-Vaux plan, and especially the "noble plaza," which, he asserted, was "one of the great features of the park." Nevertheless, the Beaux Arts conception of the park won out, and the cornerstone of John Duncan's Soldiers and Sailors Monument (fig. 36) was laid on October 30, 1889. It was dedicated three years later, with the elaborate ceremony appropriate to a monumental civic space. That same year Duncan designed two massive Doric columns for the entrance to the park at the plaza, for which Frederick MacMonnies added the bronze eagles that rest atop the shafts. The oval entrance thus became, in Richard Guy Wilson's recent judgment, a kind of "national *Valhalla*" honoring the Civil War dead.[16]

The opening of Chicago's World's Columbian Exposition in 1893 accelerated the transformation of the new urban landscape. Visitors to the great fair confronted an architectural space that, as John Kasson has noted, confirmed "the sense of possibility of what a city might be" (fig. 37). The neoclassical order that Henry Adams considered "the

Figure 37.
Court of Honor, World's Columbian Exhibition, Chicago, Illinois, 1893. Photograph by Frances Benjamin Johnston. (Courtesy, Prints and Photographs Division, Library of Congress, Washington, D.C.)

first expression of American thought as a unity" embodied a different urban vision than that of Olmsted and many other Americans who came of age in the antebellum years. Nevertheless, Adams left the great fair with a nagging doubt, a sense that the nation was "driving or drifting unconsciously to some point in thought," as did Montgomery Schuyler. This greatest of American architectural critics attempted to dissuade his contemporaries from misunderstanding, and misapplying, the lessons of the exposition. What accounted for the success of the White City were the qualities of "unity, magnitude and illusion," Schuyler wrote, "and the greatest of these is illusion." The buildings erected in Chicago were "a triumph of occasional architecture," not models to be copied in other cities.[17]

To be sure, less acute minds celebrated rather than questioned the implications of the White City that rose on the prairie adjacent to Lake Michigan, and the result often was a series of indifferently or poorly

The New Urban Landscape

designed buildings that justified Schuyler's fears. Nevertheless, a group of architects familiar with the tenets of the Ecole des Beaux Arts learned at the fair the lessons of unity and magnitude. Indeed, to these architects and to many other civic leaders the very purity of the White City seemed to promise redemption for urban society. Here was a city free of the corruption characteristic of machine rule, a city powered by electricity and thus remarkably untouched by the soot and filth that were the legacy of heavy industry and urban congestion, a city whose transient population virtually excluded Emma Lazarus's "huddled masses." In short, the Columbian Exposition taught a different lesson than did Central Park. The White City promised to supplant the seeming confusion of the Victorian era with a new and grand urban environment. Employing the design principles so successfully implemented at the exposition, architects and reformers returned east where, under the guise of what Charles M.

Robinson called the "science of modern city-making," they initiated the City Beautiful movement. But proponents of the City Beautiful were not seeking a naturalistic urban form; they celebrated the city and attempted to modify its traditional shape by creating a series of public spaces characterized by horizontal monumentality (strikingly similar to the five-story height Clarence Cook thought appropriate in the 1850s) rather than by the verticality of the skyscraper or the congestion that had resulted from the development of the 1811 gridiron. Unfortunately, few places were more vulnerable to such blandishments, such promises of a more enlightened civic order, than the open spaces of the naturalistic parks. Ironically, the architects who transformed the parks ignored the lesson Olmsted taught in his treatment of the wooded island at the great fair—that a city beautiful without appropriate landscaping scaled to human needs was hardly beautiful. [18]

In the aftermath of the White City, the architectural firm of Charles Follen McKim, William Rutherford Mead, and Stanford White continued the process of transforming Prospect Park. They designed each of the principal entrances, but instead of providing for an immediate transition from city to park they erected massive gateways. By every standard of taste, the acanthus columns of Bartel-Pritchard Circle (fig. 38) and the colonnade at Park Circle are handsome structures, yet in many ways they are antithetical to the purposes of a naturalistic landscape, at least as Olmsted and his collaborators envisioned the park. Worse for the mid-century conception of the park as visual and psychological antithesis of cityscape was McKim, Mead and White's design of the classical Peristyle within the park proper, and their reshaping of the Children's Playground and Water into the formal Rose Garden and Vale of Cashmere (figs. 39, 40). Alarmed by these changes, Olmsted warned Frank Squier, president of the Brooklyn Park Commission, against the "unfortunate tendency to crowd Prospect Park too much with statues, monuments, and other architectural structures."[19]

Even more destructive were the numerous neoclassical structures designed by less talented architects. Olmsted and Vaux had always conceded that some buildings were necessary in their parks, but they consciously determined that each would serve a specific function while reinforcing the rural character of the scenery. Nevertheless, the destruction of several of Vaux's rustic buildings and the construction of so many others according to the principles of Beaux Arts classicism transformed Prospect Park into the associational and educational landscape Olmsted and Vaux had guarded against. The City Beautiful invaded the naturalistic landscape and so littered it with mock temples and statuary that instead of being an alternative to the urban environment the park became an extension of it. In the hands of

Figure 38. "Improvement of Plaza, 15th Street and 9th Avenue, Brooklyn." 1915 photograph of Bartel-Pritchard Circle, Prospect Park, Brooklyn, New York, by McKim, Mead, and White. (Courtesy, New York City Department of Parks and Recreation, Prospect Park Administrator's Office, Brooklyn, New York.)

Progressive reformers, the vision of the park that had prevailed in the Central Park competition for designs and in the debate over Hunt's monumental gateways, the vision that had shaped so many urban public spaces in the second half of the nineteenth century, was swept aside. Country, even the conscious evocation of the country within the park, gave way to a celebration of the city.[20]

The same changes affected other major urban public parks constructed during the second half of the nineteenth century. San Francisco's Golden Gate Park became the site of an international exposition, for which several of the buildings were designed to be permanent structures. Central Park was surrounded by neoclassical monuments honoring great deeds and great men (but only one honored its "creator," and, in what was perhaps an unwitting admission of the Progressivist infatuation with efficiency, that was dedicated to Andrew Haswell Green rather than to Olmsted or Vaux). Burnham proposed the location of Chicago's cultural institutions in Grant Park, and Arnold W. Brunner planned a neoclassical structure with formal surroundings for Riverside Park's Inspiration Point. Numerous other structures in cities across the nation testify to the extent to which the City Beautiful movement recast the park in its own terms.[21]

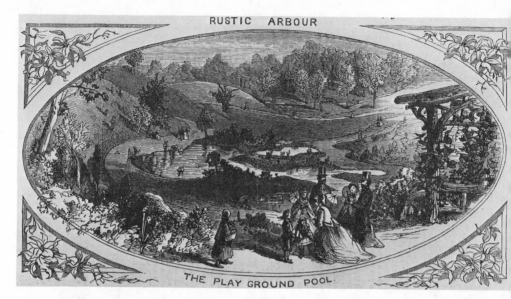

RUSTIC ARBOUR

THE PLAY GROUND POOL.

Figure 39. "The Play Ground Pool," Prospect Park, Brooklyn, New York, 1868. Detail from woodcut by H. Fenn, "Prospect Park, Brooklyn, New York," *Harper's Weekly,* September 12, 1868. (Courtesy, The Brooklyn Historical Society, Brooklyn, New York.)

Even as they were transforming the naturalistic parks, proponents of the City Beautiful movement ambitiously strove to create a dramatic new form for America's cities. The plan Daniel H. Burnham and his collaborators prepared in 1909 for the Windy City on Lake Michigan tried to turn "grubby commercial Chicago into Parisian boulevards and Venetian lagoons." His designs for the redevelopment of Cleveland and San Francisco similarly outlined monumental, neoclassical civic centers that attempted to bring order to the tumultuous cities. Nevertheless, these plans embodied a vision of urban life that was far removed from the realm of business or the harsh reality of tenements and sweatshops.[22]

New York could not escape the tyranny of the gridiron, even at the turn of the twentieth century. To be sure, several architects proposed radical alterations in the rectangular street arrangement, and in its 1907 report the New York City Improvement Commission sought to control urban growth and modify civic form. But as Olmsted had discovered a generation earlier, the value of urban real estate made large-scale departures from an existing city plan prohibitively expensive. The gridiron, the icon of commercial values, frustrated the attempts of Progressive reformers to reshape the city, just as it had the efforts of earlier reformers.[23]

Because they were unable to change the street plan established almost a century earlier, proponents of the City Beautiful movement in

The New Urban Landscape

Figure 40. The Vale of Cashmere, Prospect Park, Brooklyn, New York, by McKim, Mead, and White, c. 1895. (Courtesy, The Brooklyn Historical Society, Brooklyn, New York.)

New York attempted to redefine civic space through the use of monumental architecture. Various improvement associations campaigned for appropriate embellishment of public buildings, the municipal government established commissions to review and evaluate the design of structures and spaces, and the city became a veritable museum of didactic art—triumphal arches, monuments, and statuary intended to instruct residents in civic virtue.[24]

Perhaps the most obvious manifestations of this transformation of urban space were the changes in location and design of a number of New York's principal cultural institutions. Columbia University, for example, moved from its second (midtown) campus to a new educational acropolis, designed by McKim, Mead, and White, on Morningside Heights. Like Columbia, New York University and City College relocated uptown, far from the commerce which sustained their endowments, and were redesigned as ensembles of neoclassical architecture. Similarly, in 1880 the Metropolitan Museum of Art moved from its downtown location to a new structure in Central Park. Construction of the museum was part of a broader crusade to create urban cultural institutions, but its placement within the naturalistic landscape marked the reassertion of the idea of the park as an omnibus educational and cultural institution. That initial building, designed by Calvert Vaux, employed the structural polychromy popular during the Victorian era. By the 1890s, however, Vaux's rather modest building was sacrificed to changing tastes and a new conception of what the city should be: it was almost totally enclosed within a massive neoclassical facade designed by Richard Morris Hunt for the Fifth Avenue entrance. No longer was the museum a place that would elevate the working classes, as its original charter had promised. Instead, as if paralleling the Metropolitan's shift from collecting copies and casts to enshrining old masters, the building became a monument to the wealthy benefactors who were erecting mansions on nearby streets. The same fate awaited Vaux's original design for the American Museum of Natural History, which had its beginnings in the 1870s and which was supplanted by a more ambitious architectural project during these years. Around the turn of the century other cultural institutions located on the borders of Central Park, as the handsome Beaux Arts facades of the New-York Historical Society and the National Academy of Design attest. Like the city's principal universities, institutions of culture were moving uptown, away from the congestion of lower Manhattan and from the commercial activities that were extending northward on the island.[25]

The transformation of Prospect Park and the relocation of many of New York's cultural institutions stand as metaphors for the new conception of urban form that dominated civic culture at the end of the nineteenth century. Through its various constituencies the City Beautiful movement created the imposing sites for noble structures and the monumental public spaces that were so lacking in the Commissioners Plan of 1811. Numerous building projects in midtown at the beginning of the twentieth century created a civic scale vastly different from the commercial scale represented by the spectacular skyline of lower Manhattan. With the construction of the massive railroad terminals with their underground track systems and with the opening of the first subway in 1904, the streets and their buildings at last defined urban space in New York—at the very time when the skyscraper was aggravating congestion.[26]

But if "the days of the Italian Renaissance were revived on Manhattan Island," as the painter Theodore Robinson observed, those achievements came at the expense of creating separate realms of culture and commerce, which is ironic, because many leaders of the City Beautiful movement were businessmen as well as patrons of the arts. As a result, the great achievements of the City Beautiful movement were, in New York, limited to the construction of discrete ensembles of Beaux Arts monuments and to the creation of imposing plazas and other civic spaces. The rectangular street arrangement, with its manifest structural and aesthetic flaws, remained to haunt future generations of reformers.[27]

That would not be the case in Washington, D.C. There the configuration of energy, idealism, and urban optimism that characterized the City Beautiful movement finally gave an aspect of dignity to the nation's capital, long a source of embarrassment to cosmopolitan Americans. Three factors account for that success: with only a few notable exceptions the radial streets and public spaces of L'Enfant's plan remained intact; commerce was less important in the capital than in other cities; and the federal government, which owned much of the land, possessed powers greater than those of New York City. Thus, in the early years of the twentieth century the McMillan Commission employed a team of architects, landscape designers, and sculptors, headed by Daniel H. Burnham, Charles Follen McKim, Frederick Law Olmsted, Jr., and Augustus St. Gaudens, which attempted to create a capital worthy of the new American empire. These city planners swept aside much of the development that had taken place in Washington during the nineteenth century (including the remnants of Downing's design for the public grounds) and over the course of decades realized, for the first time, the magnificent intentions L'Enfant had projected. Ironically, the Washington L'Enfant had platted in the 1790s is, in physical form, a monument to the Progressive Era's search for a new urban order. Ironically, the city plans that were so inappropriate at the turn of the nineteenth century became, at the beginning of the twentieth, symbols of the neoclassical civic form that supplanted the mid-nineteenth-century vision of a naturalistic urban landscape.[28]

NOTES

Unless otherwise noted, all citations to Olmsted correspondence, reports, and manuscripts will refer to materials in the Frederick Law Olmsted Papers, Manuscript Division, Library of Congress, Washington, D.C.

Introduction

1. Gunther Barth, *City People: The Rise of Modern City Culture in Nineteenth-Century America* (New York, 1980), p. 15. See also Oscar Handlin, "The American City as a Field of Historical Study," in Oscar Handlin and John Burchard, eds., *The Historian and the City* (Cambridge, Mass., 1963), pp. 1–26, which frames a number of questions this book addresses.

2. See Leo Marx, *The Machine in the Garden: Technology and the Pastoral Ideal in America* (New York, 1964), passim.

3. See, for example, George B. Tatum, *Philadelphia Georgian: The City House of Samuel Powel and Some of Its Eighteenth-Century Neighbors* (Middletown, Conn., 1976), passim, as well as the vast literature on Italian and English country houses and villas.

4. Paul Boyer, *Urban Masses and Moral Order in America, 1820–1920* (Cambridge, Mass., 1978), passim.

5. [Clarence C. Cook], "New-York Daguerrotyped. Private Residences," *Putnam's Monthly* 3 (Mar. 1854): 246; Olmsted, Vaux & Co., draft report to the Commissioners of Fairmount Park, c. 1871.

6. See, for example, Sam Bass Warner, Jr., "If All the World Were Philadelphia: A Scaffolding for Urban History," *American Historical Review* 74 (Oct. 1968): 26–43; idem, *The Private City: Philadelphia in Three Periods of Its Growth* (Philadelphia, 1968), passim.

7. Olmsted, "Observations on the Future of New-York," manuscript draft, 1879; idem, "The Future of New-York," *New-York Daily Tribune*, Dec. 28, 1879; idem, "Passages in the Life of an Unpractical Man," manuscript draft, c. 1878; idem, *Public Parks: Being Two Papers Read Before the American Social Science Association in 1870 and 1880, Entitled, Respectively, Public Parks and the Enlargements of Towns and A Consideration of the Justifying Value of a Public Park* (Brookline, Mass., 1902), p. 29.

8. Olmsted explained his opposition to active recreation on many occasions, but especially in his "Address to the Prospect Park Scientific Association," unpublished manuscript, May 1868, Frederick Law Olmsted National Historic Site, Brookline, Mass.; Olmsted and Vaux to Henry G. Stebbins, Apr. 16, 1872, in *Frederick Law Olmsted: Landscape Architect, 1822–1903*, ed. Frederick Law Olmsted, Jr., and Theodora Kimball, 2 vols. (New York, 1922–28), 2: 381; Olmsted to Stebbins, n.d. [c. 1873]; Olmsted to Stebbins, May 14, 1874, in *Frederick Law Olmsted: Landscape Architect*, 2: 421–23; Olmsted to Henry Van Brunt, Jan. 22, 1891. Geoffrey Blodgett, "Frederick Law Olmsted: Landscape Architecture as Conservative Reform," *Journal of American History* 62 (Mar. 1976): 869–89 and Boyer, *Urban Masses and Moral Order*, offer a perceptive discussion of social control (pp. 54–64), as, from a much different perspective, does Roy Rosenzweig, *Eight Hours for What We Will:*

Workers and Leisure in an Industrial City, 1870–1920 (Cambridge, Mass., 1983), pp. 127–28. See also Christopher Stone, "Vandalism: Property, Gentility, and the Rhetoric of Crime in New York City, 1890–1920," Radical History Review 26 (1982):13–34.

9. Andrew Jackson Downing, "The New-York Park," reprinted in Rural Essays. By A. J. Downing. Edited, With a Memoir of the Author, by George William Curtis; and a Letter to His Friends, by Fredrika Bremer (New York, 1853), pp. 147–53.

10. Olmsted to Charles Loring Brace, Aug. 1, 1853, in The Papers of Frederick Law Olmsted, vol. 2, Slavery and the South, 1852–1857, ed. Charles E. Beveridge, Charles Capen McLaughlin, and David Schuyler (Baltimore, 1981), pp. 232–36; Calvert Vaux to Edwin Lawrence Godkin, Mar. 14, 1878, Olmsted Papers.

11. Calvert Vaux, Villas and Cottages (New York, 1857), pp. 22, 38; Vaux to Olmsted, July 6, 1865, June 3, 1865; The Papers of Frederick Law Olmsted, vol. 3, Creating Central Park, 1857–1861, ed. Charles E. Beveridge and David Schuyler (Baltimore, 1983), pp. 63–68.

I. Flawed Visions: The Lessons of Washington and New York

The epigraphs are from Captain Frederick Marryat, Diary in America, ed. Jules Zanger (1839; Bloomington, Ind., 1960), p. 188, and from Edith Wharton, A Backward Glance (New York, 1934), p. 55

1. Henry Adams, History of the United States of America during the First Administration of Thomas Jefferson, 1801–1805, 2 vols. (1889; New York, 1921), 1: 49, 59; Eric McKitrick, "The City in History," in Columbia University, The University Committee on General Education, Proceedings of the General Education Seminar: The City and the University 7 (Fall 1978): 5–10.

2. For accounts of the early history of the federal city see Elizabeth S. Kite, L'Enfant and Washington, 1791–1792 (Baltimore, 1929); Constance McLaughlin Green, Washington: Village and Capital, 1800–1878 (Princeton, 1962); and John W. Reps, Monumental Washington: The Planning and Development of the Capital Center (Princeton, 1967), pp. 1–25. Frederick Gutheim's review of Reps's book suggests that L'Enfant and his collaborators did not envision so "monumental" a city (Landscape 17 [Spring 1967]: 26–28). See also J. P. Dougherty, "Baroque and Picturesque Motifs in L'Enfant's Design for the Federal Capital," American Quarterly 26 (Mar. 1974): 23–26, and J. L. ,Sibley Jennings, Jr., "Artistry as Design: L'Enfant's Extraordinary City," Quarterly Journal of the Library of Congress 36 (Summer 1979): 225–78.

3. McKitrick, "The City in History," p. 8.

4. Thomas Jefferson, Notes on the State of Virginia (1784–85; New York, 1964), p. 103.

5. Edmund S. Morgan, American Slavery, American Freedom: The Ordeal of Colonial Virginia (New York, 1975), esp. pp. 215–337.

6. Jefferson, Notes on the State of Virginia, p. 157. The Adams quotation, from a letter to Mercy Otis Warren of April 16, 1776, is printed in John R. Howe, Jr., The Changing Political Thought of John Adams (Princeton, 1966), p. 31.

7. Jefferson, Notes on the State of Virginia, p. 158. On Washington see Thomas Bender, Toward an Urban Vision: Ideas and Institutions in Nineteenth-Century America (Lexington, Ky., 1975), p. 3. For Adams's statements on cities see Frank Freidel, "Boosters, Intellectuals, and the American City," in Oscar Handlin and John Burchard, eds., The Historian and the City (Cambridge, Mass., 1963), pp. 115–20.

8. C. McL. Green, Washington: Village and Capital, pp. 10–11.

9. Ibid., pp. 11–19.

10. Adams, *History of the United States*, 1: 30–31; Moore is quoted in C. McL. Green, *Washington: Village and Capital*, p. 39; James Sterling Young, *The Washington Community, 1800–1828* (New York, 1966), p. 13.

11. Young, *The Washington Community*, passim; C. McL. Green, *Washington: Village and Capital*, pp. 64–65; Charles Dickens, *American Notes for General Circulation* (1842; London, 1850), p. 81; E. T. Cook, *A Subaltern's Furlough: Descriptive of Scenes in Various Parts of the United States, Upper and Lower Canada, New-Brunswick, and Nova Scotia, During the Summer and Autumn of 1832*, 2 vols. (New York, 1833), 1: 96; Theodore Dwight, *Summer Tours; Or, Notes of a Traveler Through Some of the Middle and Northern States* (1834; New York, 1847), p. 17. Upon arriving in Washington in 1844, Edward Everett Hale found the capital "an agreeable country town." Hale, *A New England Boyhood and Other Bits of Autobiography*, in *The Works of Edward Everett Hale*, 10 vols. (Boston, 1900), 6: 218.

12. Alexis de Tocqueville, *Democracy in America*, ed. Phillips Bradley, 2 vols. (1835–40; New York, 1945), 1: 299–300; McKitrick, "The City in History," pp. 5–10.

13. Tocqueville, *Democracy in America*, 1: 299–300; McKitrick, "The City in History," pp. 5–10; George Wilson Pierson, *Tocqueville and Beaumont in America* (New York, 1938), p. 667.

14. See, for example, McKitrick, "The City in History," pp. 5–10, and John J. McDermott, "Nature Nostalgia and the City: An American Dilemma," *Soundings* 55 (Spring 1972): 1–20.

15. I. N. Phelps Stokes, *The Iconography of Manhattan Island, 1498–1909*, 6 vols. (New York, 1915–28), 1: 470–73, 3: 869; John W. Reps, *The Making of Urban America: A History of City Planning in the United States* (Princeton, 1965), p. 297.

16. Stokes, *Iconography of Manhattan Island*, 5: 1442–54; New York (State), Legislature, *Laws of the State of New York, 1801–1812*, 6 vols. (Albany, 1804–12), 5: 125–27.

17. Gouverneur Morris et al., "Remarks of the Commissioners for Laying Out Streets and Roads in the City of New York, Under the Act of April 3, 1807," Mar. 26, 1811, reprinted in New York (City), Common Council, *Manual of the Corporation of the City of New York, 1866*, comp. D. T. Valentine (New York, 1866), pp. 756–57.

18. Ibid., pp. 757, 762.

19. Ibid., pp. 759–62.

20. Ibid., p. 759.

21. John Randel is quoted in *Manual of the Corporation of the City of New York, 1864*, comp. D. T. Valentine (New York, 1864), p. 878.

22. C. McL. Green, *Washington: Village and Capital*, passim.

23. Tocqueville, *Democracy in America*, 1: 299–300; Pierson, *Tocqueville and Beaumont in America*, p. 667; Allan Pred, *Urban Growth and City Systems in the United States, 1840–1860* (Cambridge, Mass, 1980), p. 4.

24. De Witt Clinton, quoted in Charles N. Glaab, ed., *The American City: A Documentary History* (Homewood, Ill., 1963), p. 71. See also John W. Reps, *Town Planning in Frontier America* (Princeton, 1969), pp. 198–203, and Edward K. Spann, *The New Metropolis: New York City, 1840–1857* (New York, 1981), passim.

25. Spann, *New Metropolis*, pp. 117–19; *The Papers of Frederick Law Olmsted*, vol. 3, *Creating Central Park, 1857–1861*, ed. Charles E. Beveridge and David Schuyler (Baltimore, 1983), passim; Olmsted, "The Future of New-York," *New-York Daily Tribune*, Dec. 28, 1879.

26. John R. Stilgoe, *Common Landscape of America, 1580 to 1845* (New

Haven, 1982), pp. 99–107; Richard C. Wade, *The Urban Frontier: Pioneer Life in Early Pittsburgh, Cincinnati, Lexington, Louisville, and St. Louis* (Cambridge, Mass., 1959), passim.

II. Toward a Redefinition of Urban Form and Culture

The epigraph is from Edward Everett Hale, "The Congestion of Cities," *Forum* 4 (Jan. 1888): 529.

1. Sociologist Robert K. Merton's analysis of manifest and latent functions provides one mechanism for understanding the structural flaws of American urban and political culture that resulted in part from the location of the capital in Washington, D.C. According to Merton, the political machine evolved in nineteenth-century cities to provide the services and opportunities that could not be delivered within the existing governmental structure. George Washington Plunkitt's memoirs are, in many respects, a veiled critique of the absence of metropolitanism in American life. This sachem of Tammany Hall justified the urban political machine as a countervailing force to the power of rural legislators in state government. See Robert K. Merton, *Social Theory and Social Structure* (1949; rev. ed., Glencoe, Ill., 1957), pp. 71–82; William Riordan, *Plunkitt of Tammany Hall* (1905; Bridgeport, Conn., 1976), passim.

2. Anselm L. Strauss, *Images of the American City* (New Brunswick, 1976), p. 107; Morton and Lucia White, *The Intellectual versus the City: From Thomas Jefferson to Frank Lloyd Wright* (Cambridge, Mass., 1962), pp. 13–17.

3. For criticisms of the Whites' thesis see Charles N. Glaab, "The Historian and the American Urban Tradition," *Wisconsin Magazine of History* 67 (Autumn 1963): 12–25, and Lewis Mumford's assessment in *The Letters of Lewis Mumford and Frederick J. Osborn: A Transatlantic Dialogue, 1938–1970* ed. Michael Hughes (New York, 1972), pp. 446–47. See also Henry Nash Smith, *Virgin Land: The American West as Symbol and Myth* (Cambridge, Mass., 1950), passim.

4. Gunther Barth, *City People: The Rise of Modern City Culture in Nineteenth-Century America* (New York, 1980), passim.

5. [Andrew Jackson Downing], "Cultivators, The Great Industrial Class of America," *The Horticulturist, and Journal of Rural Art and Rural Taste* 2 (June 1848): 537–39.

6. George Jacques, "The Morale of Rural Life," ibid. 3 (Feb. 1849): 377; Frederick Law Olmsted to John Hull Olmsted, June 23, 1845, in *The Papers of Frederick Law Olmsted*, vol. 1, *The Formative Years, 1822–1852*, ed. Charles Capen McLaughlin and Charles E. Beveridge (Baltimore, 1977), pp. 217–20; "Rural Taste in North America," *Christian Examiner* 69 (Nov. 1860): 350.

7. James Fenimore Cooper, *Home as Found*, in *The Complete Works of J. Fenimore Cooper*, Leatherstocking Edition, 32 vols. (New York, 1893?), 14: 326, 424; Alexis de Tocqueville, *Democracy in America*, ed. Phillips Bradley, 2 vols. (1835–40; New York, 1945), 2: 144–45; Andrew Jackson Downing, *Treatise on the Theory and Practice of Landscape Gardening, Adapted to North America...*, 6th ed. (1841; New York, 1859), p. vii; and idem, "The Influence of Horticulture," *Horticulturist* 2 (July 1847): 10. See also Marvin Meyers, *The Jacksonian Persuasion: Politics and Belief* (1957; New York, 1960), pp. 57–100.

8. Percy W. Bidwell, "The Agricultural Revolution in New England," *American Historical Review* 26 (July 1921): 683–702; George Rogers Taylor, *The Transportation Revolution, 1815–1860* (New York, 1951), passim; Robert A. Gross, " 'The Most Estimable Place in the World': A Debate on Progress in Nineteenth-Century Concord," *Studies in the American Renaissance* 1 (1978): 1–15.

9. Sidney George Fisher, *A Philadelphia Perspective: The Diary of Sidney George Fisher Covering the Years 1834–1871*, ed. Nicholas B. Wainwright (Philadelphia, 1967), p. 202.

10. Raymond J. O'Brien, *American Sublime: Landscape and Scenery of the Lower Hudson Valley* (New York, 1981), pp. 102–26ff; *Papers of Frederick Law Olmsted*, 1: 100.

11. David J. Rothman, *The Discovery of the Asylum: Social Order and Disorder in the New Republic* (New York, 1971), pp. 69–78, 112–14, passim; James M. Newman, "Report on the Sanitary Police of Cities," American Medical Association, *Transactions* 9 (1856): 432–33; Alexis de Tocqueville, *Democracy in America*, ed. J. P. Mayer and Max Lerner, trans. George Lawrence (New York, 1966), p. 510; Fredrika Bremer, *Homes of the New World: Impressions of America*, trans. Mary Howitt, 2 vols. (New York, 1853), 1: 15; "First Annual Report of the Committee on Public Hygiene," American Medical Association, *Transactions* 2 (1849): 431: Olmsted, Vaux & Co., draft report to the Commissioners of Fairmount Park, c. 1871.

12. Henry W. Cleaveland, William Backus, and Samuel D. Backus, *Village and Farm Cottages*, reprint edition, with a new introduction by David Schuyler (1856; Watkins Glen, N.Y., 1982), pp. 12–14; C.L.D., "Random Thoughts on Rural Life," *Horticulturist* 5 (Sept. 1850): 109; Thomas Thomas, Jr., *The Working-Man's Cottage Architecture, Containing Plans, Elevations, and Details for the Erection of Cheap, Comfortable, and Neat Cottages* (New York, 1848), p. 4.

13. Henry Ward Beecher, *A Discourse Delivered at Plymouth Church, Brooklyn, New York* (New York, 1847), reviewed and quoted in *Horticulturist* 2 (Feb. 1848): 377; Lewis F. Allen, *Rural Architecture. Being a Complete Description of Farm Houses, Cottages, and Out Buildings* (New York, 1852), pp. 16–17; "Farming Life in New England," *Atlantic Monthly* 2 (Aug. 1858): 334.
In his essay "Farming" Emerson wrote: "The city is always recruited from the country. The men in cities who are the centers of energy, the driving wheels of trade, politics, or practical arts, and the women of beauty and genius, are the children or grandchildren of farmers, and are spending the energies which their father's hardy, silent life accumulated in frosty furrows, in poverty, necessity, and darkness." "Farming," in *The Viking Portable Emerson*, selected and arranged with an introduction and notes by Mark Van Doren (New York, 1946), p. 239.

14. Stuart Blumin, *The Urban Threshold: Growth and Change in a Nineteenth-Century Urban Community* (Chicago, 1976), p. 1; Allan Pred, *Urban Growth and City Systems in the United States, 1840–1860* (Cambridge, Mass., 1980), p. 4.

15. On Lowell see Thomas Bender, *Toward an Urban Vision: Ideas and Institutions in Nineteenth-Century America* (Lexington, Ky., 1975), pp. 55–128, and John F. Kasson, *Civilizing the Machine: Technology and Republican Values in America, 1776–1900* (New York, 1976), pp. 55–106.

16. Kenneth T. Jackson, "The Crabgrass Frontier: 150 Years of Suburban Growth in America," in Raymond A. Mohl and James F. Richardson, eds., *The Urban Experience: Themes in American History* (Belmont, Calif., 1973), pp. 199–200, and Edward K. Spann, *The New Metropolis: New York City, 1840–1857* (New York, 1981), passim.

17. Neil Harris, *The Artist in American Society: The Formative Years, 1790–1860* (New York, 1966), pp. 261–66; idem, *Humbug: The Art of P. T. Barnum* (Boston, 1973), passim; [Andrew Jackson Downing], "The New-York Park," *Horticulturist* 6 (Aug. 1851): 346–48, reprinted in Downing, *Rural Essays...* (New York, 1853); Paul Boyer, *Urban Masses and Moral Order in America, 1820–1920* (Cambridge, Mass., 1978), pp. 3–21.

18. Edwin Hubbell Chapin, *Moral Aspects of City Life: A Series of Lectures* (1853; 5th printing, New York, 1856), pp. 13–19; Boyer, *Urban Masses and Moral Order*, pp. 72–74; Eugene Arden, "The Evil City in American Fiction," *New York History* 52 (July 1954): 259–79. See also Perry Miller, *The Life of the Mind in America: From the Revolution to the Civil War* (New York, 1965), p. 87.

19. John Jay Smith, "Reciprocity: The Country Visiting the City," *Horticulturist*, n.s. 8 (Aug. 1858): 345; Frederick W. Sawyer, *A Plea for Amusements* (New York, 1847), pp. 97–98; "Great Cities," *Putnam's Monthly* 5 (March 1855): 256.

20. R. Richard Wohl, "The 'Country Boy' Myth and Its Place in American Urban Culture: The Nineteenth-Century Contribution," ed. Moses Rischin, *Perspectives in American History* 3 (1969): 82–95; Boyer, *Urban Masses and Moral Order*, pp. 70–75; Arden, "Evil City," pp. 259–79.

21. Ralph Waldo Emerson, "The Young American," in *Emerson's Complete Works*, Riverside Edition, 12 vols. (Boston, 1888–93), 1: 345, 348–49. See also Kasson, *Civilizing the Machine*, pp. 55–106, which points out how Emerson's early optimism for technology changed after visiting England.

22. Michael Cowan, *City of the West: Emerson, America, and Urban Metaphor* (New Haven, 1967) pp. 2, 182–83, 215.

23. Hale is quoted at length in "Editor's Drawer, City Life Compared to that in the Country," *Horticulturist*, n.s. 10 (May 1860): 247–48.

24. Thomas Cole, "Essay on American Scenery," manuscript copy, box 5, folder 1; Cole manuscript journals, entries dated Oct. 7 [1835] and Nov. 8 [1834], box 4, folder 4; Cole to A. B. Durand, Sept. 12, 1836, box 1, folder 2, Thomas Cole Papers, New York State Library, Albany, New York.

25. See Perry Miller, "Nature and the National Ego," in *Errand into the Wilderness* (Cambridge, Mass., 1956), pp. 204–16, for a suggestive discussion of these paintings and their context. For Cole's intent in painting *The Course of Empire* see Lewis L. Noble, *The Course of Empire, Voyage of Life, and Other Pictures of Thomas Cole, N.A. With Selections from his Letters and Miscellaneous Writings: Illustrative of his Life, Character, and Genius* (New York, 1853), pp. 176–79ff.

26. Noble, *Course of Empire*, p. 71; Cole to Durand, Sept. 12, 1836, Cole Papers. Among the more plaintive of Cole's letters to Durand are those of June 12, Aug. 30, and Nov. 18, 1836, all to be found in the Thomas Cole Papers.

27. Nathaniel Parker Willis, *Letters from Under a Bridge* (New York, 1844), pp. 1–17, 38; Willis to John Bigelow, May 12, 1858, John Bigelow Papers, Manuscripts and Archives Division, Rare Book & Manuscripts Division, The New York Public Library, Astor, Lenox and Tilden Foundations, New York City.

28. [George William Curtis], "Editor's Easy Chair," *Harper's New Monthly Magazine* 11 (July 1855): 271–72.

29. Nathaniel Hawthorne, *The Blithedale Romance* (1852; New York, 1960), pp. 180–81.

30. Miller, "Nature and the National Ego," pp. 204–16; "Exhibition of the National Academy," *Literary World* 1 (May 15, 1847): 348.

31. Henry Whitney Bellows, "Cities and Parks: With Special Reference to the New York Central Park," *Atlantic Monthly* 7 (Apr. 1861): 417.

32. Henry P. Tappan, *A Step from the New World to the Old, and Back Again; With Thoughts on the Good and Evil in Both*, 2 vols. (New York, 1852), 1: 78–79; "City Public Parks," *Scientific American*, n.s. 1 (Nov. 19, 1859): 377; [Olmsted], "Description of the Central Park," in New York (City), Board of Commissioners of the Central Park, *Second Annual Report. January, 1859* (New York,

1859), p. 60, reprinted in *The Papers of Frederick Law Olmsted*, vol. 3, *Creating Central Park, 1857–1861*, ed. Charles E. Beveridge and David Schuyler (Baltimore, 1983), pp. 204–19.

33. Pierrepont is quoted in Jackson, "Crabgrass Frontier," p. 199; [Andrew Jackson Downing], "Hints to Rural Improvers," *Horticulturist* 3 (July 1848): 10; [Curtis], "Editor's Easy Chair," p. 272.

III. The Didactic Landscape: Rural Cemeteries

The epigraph is from Andrew Jackson Downing, "Additional Notes on the Progress of Gardening in the United States," *Gardener's Magazine* 17 (Mar. 1841): 146–47.

1. Philippe Ariès, *Western Attitudes toward Death: From the Middle Ages to the Present*, trans. Patricia M. Ranum (Baltimore, 1974), pp. 15–25, and Philippe Ariès, *The Hour of Our Death*, trans. Helen Weaver (New York, 1981), passim. That Americans were familiar with the classical origins of rural burial is indicated in Joseph Story's *Address Delivered on the Dedication of the Cemetery at Mount Auburn, September, 24, 1831* (Boston, 1831), p. 9, and "Mount Auburn Cemetery. Report of the Massachusetts Horticultural Society upon the Establishment of an Experimental Garden and Rural Cemetery. Boston. 1831," *North American Review* 33 (Oct. 1831): 403.

2. Ariès, *Western Attitudes toward Death*, pp. 69–74; Scipione Piatolli, *An Essay on the Danger of Interments in Cities* (New York, 1824), pp. 79–82. An alternative to creating new cemeteries was, of course, cremation, but this was deemed unacceptable in Catholic France in the eighteenth century. For the advocacy of cremation in the 1790s, however, see Jacques de Cambry, *Rapport sur les sépultures présenté à l'administration centrale du Département de la Seine* (Paris, 1799).

3. George Collison, *Cemetery Interment*. . .(London, 1840), p. 93; Ariès, *Western Attitudes toward Death*, p. 73; N. B. Penny, "The Commercial Garden Necropolis of the Early Nineteenth Century and Its Critics," *Garden History* 2 (Summer 1974): 62; Theodore Ledyard Cuyler, "The Cemeteries of Paris and London," *Godey's Magazine and Lady's Book* 30 (Jan. 1845): 10; "Père la Chaise," *New-England Magazine* 7 (Nov. 1834): 395; "Loose Leaves by a Literary Lounger: No. 4. Gatherings from the Grave-Yard," *Democratic Review* 14 (April 1844): 417. See also David Schuyler, "The Evolution of the Anglo-American Rural Cemetery: Landscape Architecture as Social and Cultural History," *Journal of Garden History* 4 (July–Sept. 1984): 291–304.

4. Timothy Dwight, *Travels in New England and New York*, ed. Barbara Miller Solomon, 4 vols. (1822; Cambridge, Mass, 1969), 2: 360; John Jay Smith, "Memorandum Respecting the Foundation of Laurel Hill Cemetery," unpublished manuscript journal, entry dated Nov. 1835, The John Jay Smith Historical Collection, Paoli, Pennsylvania; Story, *Address at Mount Auburn*, p. 10; Irving's remarks, from "Rural Funerals" in his *Sketch-Book*, are quoted in [John Jay Smith], *Guide to Laurel Hill Cemetery, Near Philadelphia* (Philadelphia, 1844), p. 19.

5. J. J. Smith, "Memorandum," entries dated Nov. 1835, June 30, 1836, Oct. 24, 1836; Frederick Law Olmsted and Calvert Vaux, "Description of a Plan for the Improvement of the Central Park, 'Greensward,' " in *The Papers of Frederick Law Olmsted*, vol. 3, *Creating Central Park, 1857–1861*, ed. Charles E. Beveridge and David Schuyler (Baltimore, 1983), p. 120; Herman Melville, *Pierre; Or, The Ambiguities* (1852; New York, 1964), p. 302; "A Cemetery Broken Up," *New-York Daily Tribune*, Sept. 18, 1850, p. 3.

6. Timothy Dwight, *Travels*, 2: 360; Francis D. Allen, *Documents and Facts, Showing the Fatal Effects of Interments in Populous Cities* (New York, 1822),

pp. iii, 9; Edward H. Barton, "Sanitary Report of New Orleans, La.," American Medical Association, *Transactions* 2 (1849): 594. For other statements describing cemeteries within cities as injurious to public health see John H. Griscom, M.D., *The Sanitary Condition of the Laboring Population of New York. With Suggestions for its Improvement. A Discourse (With Additions) Delivered on the 30th of December, 1844, at the Repository of the American Institute* (New York, 1845), pp. 53ff.

7. Zimmermann is quoted in Charles E. Beveridge, "Frederick Law Olmsted's Theory of Landscape Design," *Nineteenth Century* 3 (Summer 1977): 39–40.

8. Ibid.; Henry David Thoreau, *Walden; Or, Life in the Woods* (1854; Garden City, N.Y., 1960), pp. 113–14; Wilson Flagg, *Mount Auburn: Its Scenes, Its Beauties, and Its Lessons* (Boston, 1861), p. 295.

9. Stanley French, "The Cemetery as Cultural Institution: The Establishment of Mount Auburn and the 'Rural' Cemetery Movement," *American Quarterly* 26 (March 1974): 37–59.

10. Jacob Bigelow, *A History of the Cemetery of Mount Auburn* (Boston, 1860), pp. 4–5; J. J. Smith, "Memorandum," entry dated Nov. 1835.

11. Allan Johnson and Dumas Malone, eds., *Dictionary of American Biography*, 20 vols. (New York, 1937), s.v. "Bigelow, Jacob."

12. Jacob Bigelow, autobiographical paper, quoted in George E. Ellis, "Memoir of Jacob Bigelow, M.D., Ll.D.," *Proceedings of the Massachusetts Historical Society* 17 (1879–1880): 424; Jacob Bigelow, *History of the Cemetery of Mount Auburn*, pp. 2–5; Zebedee Cook, Jr., *An Address Pronounced Before the Massachusetts Horticultural Society. In Commemoration of its Second Annual Festival, the 10th of September, 1830* (Boston, 1830), p. 27.

13. Massachusetts Horticultural Society, *History of the Massachusetts Horticultural Society, 1829–1878* (Boston, 1880), p. 76; Jacob Bigelow, *History of the Cemetery of Mount Auburn*, pp. 5–15; Edward Everett, "The Proposed Rural Cemetery," reprinted in ibid., p. 135; see also Henry A. S. Dearborn's "Report on the Garden and Cemetery," reprinted in ibid., p. 168; Flagg, *Mount Auburn*, p. 276. Barbara Rotundo points out that the name "Sweet Auburn" was derived from Oliver Goldsmith's "The Deserted Village." Rotundo, "Mount Auburn: A Proper Boston Institution," *Harvard Library Bulletin* 22 (July 1974): 270.

14. Jacob Bigelow, *History of the Cemetery of Mount Auburn*, pp. 15, 21, 17; Flagg, *Mount Auburn*, p. 276; *History of the Massachusetts Horticultural Society*, p. 92; Olmsted, *Report to the Trustees of the Mountain View Cemetery*, in *Organization of Mountain View Cemetery Association, Oakland, California* (San Francisco, 1865), p. 45.

15. Dearborn, "Report on the Garden and Cemetery," p. 173; *History of the Massachusetts Horticultural Society*, pp. 96–102.

16. [Andrew Jackson Downing], "Public Cemeteries and Public Gardens," *Horticulturist* 4 (July 1849): 9, 11; Jacob Bigelow, *History of the Cemetery at Mount Auburn*, pp. 29–30.

17. [Downing], "Public Cemeteries and Public Gardens," p. 9; Keith N. Morgan, "The Landscape Gardening of John Notman, 1810–1865," (M.A. thesis, University of Delaware, Winterthur Program in Early American Culture, 1973), pp. 13–31; Constance M. Greiff, *John Notman, Architect 1810–1865* (Philadelphia, 1979), pp. 53–60; J. J. Smith, *Guide to Laurel Hill Cemetery*, pp. 12–14.

18. J. J. Smith, *Guide to Laurel Hill Cemetery*, pp. 8, 48; Sidney George Fisher, *A Philadelphia Perspective: The Diary of Sidney George Fisher Covering the Years 1834–1871*, ed. Nicholas B. Wainwright (Philadelphia, 1967), p. 46;

Nathaniel Parker Willis, *Letters from Under a Bridge* (New York, 1844), p. 30; R. A. Smith, *Smith's Illustrated Guide To and Through Laurel Hill Cemetery. . .* (Philadelphia, 1852), pp. 29–31; [Downing], "Public Cemeteries and Public Gardens," pp. 9–10.

19. [Downing], "Public Cemeteries and Public Gardens," pp. 9–10; Fredrika Bremer, *Homes of the New World: Impressions of America*, trans. Mary Howitt, 2 vols. (New York, 1853), 1: 15. See also Nehemiah Cleaveland, *Green-Wood Illustrated* (New York, 1847), and Donald Simon, "Green-Wood Cemetery and the American Park Movement," in Irving Yellowitz, ed., *Essays in the History of New York City: A Memorial to Sidney Pomerantz* (Port Washington, N.Y., 1978), pp. 61–77.

20. [Downing], "Public Cemeteries and Public Gardens," p. 9.

21. Sir Joshua Reynolds, *Discourses*, ed. Stephen O. Mitchell (Indianapolis, 1965), p. 204; Archibald Alison, *An Essay on the Nature and Principles of Taste* (Edinburgh, 1790), p. 411. The most important secondary readings include B. Sprague Allen, *Tides in English Taste, 1619–1800*, 2 vols. (Cambridge, Mass., 1937); Walter Jackson Bate, *From Classic to Romantic: Premises of Taste in Eighteenth-Century England* (Cambridge, Mass., 1946); Christopher Hussey, *The Picturesque: Studies in a Point of View* (London, 1927); Samuel H. Monk, *The Sublime: A Study of Critical Theory in Eighteenth-Century England* (1935; Ann Arbor, 1960); and Walter J. Hipple, *The Beautiful, the Sublime, and the Picturesque in Eighteenth-Century British Aesthetic Theory* (Carbondale, Ill., 1957).

22. Richard G. Carrott, "The Egyptian Revival: Its Sources, Its Monuments, and Its Meaning," (Ph.D. dissertation, Yale University, 1961), passim.

23. Ibid.

24. Erwin Panofsky, "Et in Arcadia Ego: Poussin and the Elegiac Tradition," in *Meaning in the Visual Arts* (Garden City, N.Y., 1955), pp. 295–320.

25. Edmund Burke, *A Philosophical Enquiry into the Origin of Our Ideas of the Sublime and Beautiful*, ed., with an introduction and notes, by J. T. Boulton 1757; London, 1958), p. 37.

26. Wilson Flagg, "Rural Cemeteries," *Magazine of Horticulture* 19 (Nov. 1853): 486; Cook, *Address Pronounced Before the Massachusetts Horticultural Society*, p. 27; "Mount Auburn," *New-England Magazine* 4 (May 1833): 384; G.T.C., "Mount Auburn," ibid. 7 (Oct. 1834): 316–17; Flagg, *Mount Auburn*, pp. 35–36. Adolph Strauch pointed out that a rural cemetery "should form the most interesting of all places for contemplative recreation." Strauch, letter to the President and Directors of Spring Grove Cemetery, Oct. 1, 1856, quoted in Spring Grove Cemetery, *The Cincinnati Cemetery of Spring Grove. Reports, Forms, etc. Enlarged Edition* (Cincinnati, 1862), p. 31.

27. Henry Wadsworth Longfellow, *Hyperion, A Romance*, 15th ed. (1839; Boston, 1855), pp. 332–35, 276.

28. G.T.C., "Mount Auburn," p. 319; Albany Rural Cemetery, *Albany Rural Cemetery Association: Its Rules, Regulations, &c., with an Appendix* (Albany, 1846), p. 31; Laurel Hill Cemetery, *Rules and Regulations of Laurel Hill Cemetery, Near Philadelphia; Together with a List of Lot-holders, to November, 1864* (Philadelphia, 1865), p. 14; "Ornamental Cemeteries," *Yale Literary Magazine* 21 (Nov. 1855): 50; [Downing], "Public Cemeteries and Public Gardens," p. 10.

29. Thomas Bender, *Toward an Urban Vision: Ideas and Institutions in Nineteenth-Century America* (Lexington, Ky., 1975), pp. 81–88; Green-Wood Cemetery, *Exposition of the Plan and Objects of the Green-Wood Cemetery, An Incorporated Trust Chartered by the Legislature of the State of New York* (New York, 1839), pp. 11–12; Willis's essay was printed in *Cemetery of Cypress Hills, 1851* (New York, 1850), pp. 39–40; Flagg, *Mount Auburn*, pp. 35–36.

30. Downing, "Additional Notes," pp. 146–47.

31. [Downing], "Public Cemeteries and Public Gardens," p. 9; Stephen Duncan Walker, *Rural Cemetery and Public Walk* (Baltimore, 1835), pp. 6–7. Walker had earlier published these papers in the *Baltimore American* in 1833. See also Downing, "Additional Notes," pp. 146–47; "Central Park," *Scribner's Monthly* 6 (Sept. 1873): 529.

32. [Andrew Jackson Downing], "A Talk About Public Parks and Gardens," *Horticulturist* 3 (Oct. 1848): 157; idem, "Public Cemeteries and Public Gardens, p. 10; Olmsted, "Park," in *Papers of Frederick Law Olmsted*, 3: 357. See also Olmsted to William Robinson, Spring 1875; Olmsted to Jonathan D. Crimmins, Aug. 2, 1888; Olmsted, Deposition in the Case of Jacob Weidenmann vs. Mount Hope Cemetery, Feb. 1888.

33. [Downing], "Public Cemeteries and Public Gardens," pp. 11–12.

34. Brooklyn *Eagle*, quoted in Donald Simon, "The Public Park Movement in Brooklyn, 1824–1873," (Ph.D. dissertation, New York University, 1972), pp. 187–90.

35. Calvert Vaux to Olmsted, June 3, 1865.

IV. The Ideology of the Public Park

The epigraph is from James Fenimore Cooper, *The Pioneers; Or, The Sources of the Susquehanna* (1823; New York, 1964), p. 202.

1. Great Britain Parliament, *Report from the Select Committee*, quoted in George F. Chadwick, *The Park and the Town: Public Landscapes in the Nineteenth and Twentieth Centuries* (New York, 1966), pp. 50–51.

2. John Claudius Loudon, "Hints respecting the manner of laying out the grounds of the Public Squares in London, to the utmost picturesque advantage," *Literary Journal* 2 (Dec. 31, 1804): cols. 739–42, reprinted in Peter Willis, ed., *Furor Hortensis: Essays on the History of the English Landscape Garden in Memory of H. F. Clark* (Edinburgh, 1974), p. 85; T. Rutger, "Some Remarks on the Suburban Gardens of the Metropolis and on the Mode of Laying out and Planting the Public Squares," *Gardener's Magazine* 11 (Oct. 1835): 515; "The Lungs of London," *Edinburgh Magazine* 46 (1839): 214, typescript copy in the Olmsted Papers; "Parks and Pleasure-Grounds," *Westminster Review*, Apr. 1841, quoted in *Gardener's Magazine* 17 (May 1841): 282; Charles H. J. Smith, *Parks and Pleasure Grounds; Or, Practical Notes on Country Residences, Villas, Public Parks, and Gardens* (London, 1852), pp. 156–57.

3. *The Boston Common, Or Rural Walks in Cities. By a Friend of Improvement* (Boston, 1838), pp. 21–22; Howard Daniels, "European Parks," *Horticulturist*, n.s. 10 (Nov. 1860): 530; Thomas B. Fox, "The Education of the Public Taste," *Christian Examiner* 53 (Nov. 1852): 367; John H. Rauch, *Public Parks: Their Effect Upon the Moral, Physical and Sanitary Condition of the Inhabitants of Large Cities; With Special Reference to the City of Chicago* (Chicago, 1869), p. 6. See also [William J. Stillman], "Sketchings. Park Hints for 'the Manhattan,' " *Crayon* 3 (Aug. 1856): 253, and "City Public Parks," *Scientific America*, n.s. 1 (Nov. 19, 1859): 377.

4. See especially *Lemon Hill and Fairmount Park. The Papers of Charles S. Keyser and Thomas Cochran, Relative to a Public Park for Philadelphia*, ed. Horace J. Smith (Philadelphia, 1886), p. 4; J. W. Harshberger, "Correspondence. The Wissahickon Woods," *Garden and Forest* 4 (Mar. 18, 1891): 129; Nelson Blake, *Water for Cities: A History of the Urban Water Supply Problem in the United States* (Syracuse, 1956), pp. 131–33; and John W. Reps, *The Making of Urban America: A History of City Planning in the United States* (Princeton, 1965), passim.

5. "First Annual Report of the Committee on Public Hygiene," American Medical Association, *Transactions* 2 (1849): 431, 438; Edward H. Barton,

"Sanitary Report of New Orleans, La.," ibid., p. 594; John H. Griscom, "Committee on Public Hygiene. Hygiene of New York City," ibid., p. 458. See also Isaac Parrish, "Report on the Sanitary Condition of Philadelphia," ibid., p. 477; "City Public Parks," p. 377; and Charles Rosenberg, *The Cholera Years: The United States in 1832, 1849, and 1866* (Chicago, 1962), passim.

6. [Andrew Jackson Downing], "The State and Progress of Horticulture," *Horticulturist* 6 (Dec. 1851): 540; H. J. Smith, *Lemon Hill and Fairmount Park*, p. 22; Swann's address was printed in *Inaugural Ceremonies and Address of Hon. Thomas Swann. On the Opening of Druid Hill Park, October 19, 1860, Compiled from the Baltimore American* (Baltimore, 1860), pp. 20–21.

7. [Andrew Jackson Downing], "The New-York Park," *Horticulturist* 6 (Aug. 1851): 345, reprinted in Downing, *Rural Essays...* (New York, 1853); "Mr. Downing's Letter from England," ibid. 5 (Oct. 1850): 153; H. J. Smith, *Lemon Hill and Fairmount Park*, p. 25.

8. For a description of Five Points in the 1840s, see Ned Buntline (pseudonym for E.Z.C. Judson), *The Mysteries and Miseries of New York: A Story of Real Life* (New York, 1848), part 1, pp. 75–92. See also Robert Bremner, *From the Depths: The Discovery of Poverty in the United States* (New York, 1956), passim. The Channing quotation is from William Ellery Channing, *Lectures on the Elevation of the Labouring Portion of the Community* (Boston, 1840), p. 64; the final quotation is from H. J. Smith, *Lemon Hill and Fairmount Park*, p. 23.

9. *American Sketches; By a Native of the United States* (London, 1827), p. 18; Ralph Waldo Emerson, "The Young American," in *Emerson's Complete Works*, 12 vols. (Boston, 1888–93), 1: 347; [Olmsted], *Walks and Talks of an American Farmer in England*, 2 vols. (New York, 1852), 1: 133; Stephen Duncan Walker, *Rural Cemetery and Public Walk* (Baltimore, 1835), p. 5; J. O. Choules, *Young Americans Abroad; Or, Vacations in Europe...* (Boston, 1852), p. 160. See also N. H. Carter, *Letters from Europe, Comprising the Journal of a Tour through Ireland, England, Scotland, France, Italy, and Switzerland, in the Years 1825, '26, and '27*, 2 vols. (New York, 1829), 1: 130.

10. [Catharine Maria Sedgwick], *Letters from Abroad to Kindred at Home*, 2 vols. (New York, 1841), 1: 53–54; Emerson, "The Young American," p. 347; Caroline Kirkland, *Holidays Abroad; Or, Europe From the West*, 2 vols. (New York, 1849), 1: 93–94.

11. William Cullen Bryant, *Letters of a Traveller; Or, Notes of Things Seen in Europe and America* (New York, 1851), pp. 169–70. Bryant expressed the same sentiments in an editorial in the New York *Evening Post* of July 3, 1844.

12. Horace Greeley, *Glances at Europe: In a Series of Letters from Great Britain, France, Italy, Switzerland, &c. During the Summer of 1851. Including Notices of the Great Exhibition, or World's Fair* (New York, 1851), pp. 67–68.

13. Henry P. Tappan, *A Step from the New World to the Old, and Back Again; with Thoughts on the Good and Evil in Both*, 2 vols. (New York, 1852), 1: 78–79.

14. [Andrew Jackson Downing], "A Talk About Public Parks and Gardens," *Horticulturist* 3 (Oct. 1848): 154–55; Francis J. Grund, *The Americans in their Moral, Social, and Political Relations* (Boston, 1837), p. 39; C. H. J. Smith, *Parks and Pleasure Grounds*, American Edition, with notes by Lewis F. Allen (New York, 1860), p. 255; [Downing], "The New-York Park," p. 348; [Andrew Jackson Downing], "Our Country Villages," *Horticulturist* 4 (June 1850): 541. A writer in the *Scientific American* claimed that, before the creation of Central Park, public parks had been "so small as to excite the derision of foreigners." "City Public Parks," p. 377.

15. [Downing], "A Talk About Public Parks and Gardens," pp. 154–56; Walker, *Rural Cemetery and Public Walk*, pp. 5–6.

16. [Downing], "The New-York Park," p. 348; Walker, *Rural Cemetery and*

Public Walk, p. 6; [Downing], "A Talk About Public Parks and Gardens," pp. 154–55; [Downing], "Our Country Villages," p. 541; [Downing], "The New-York Park," pp. 348–49.

17. Olmsted to Charles Loring Brace, Dec. 1, 1853.

18. H.W.S. Cleveland, "Landscape Gardening," *Christian Examiner*, 4th ser., 23 (May 1855): 398; James C. Sidney and Andrew Adams in Philadelphia, City Councils, Committee on City Property, *Description of a Plan for the Improvement of Fairmount Park, by Sidney and Adams* ... (Philadelphia, 1859), p. 3; "City Public Parks," p. 377; "New York Central Park," *Magazine of Horticulture* 26 (Dec. 1860): 529; Henry David Thoreau, *Journals*, entry dated Oct. 15, 1859, in *The Writings of Henry David Thoreau*, ed. Bradford Torrey, 20 vols. (Boston, 1906), 12: 387; [Downing], "The New-York Park," p. 347.

19. Donald Simon, "The Public Park Movement in Brooklyn, 1824–1873," (Ph.D. dissertation, New York University, 1972), p. 234; Cynthia Zaitzevsky, *Frederick Law Olmsted and the Boston Park System* (Cambridge, Mass., 1982), pp. 15, 33.

20. Christian Hines, quoted in John Clagett Proctor, "The Tragic Death of Andrew Jackson Downing and the Monument to his Memory," *Records of the Columbia Historical Society* 27 (1925): 250. One contemporary testified that the "great object to be accomplished [by drainage] was to render the neighborhood of the Executive Mansion healthy enough to enable the President and his family to reside there without endangering their lives." *Congressional Globe*, 32nd Congress, 1st sess., (March 24, 1852), p. 854.

21. Smithsonian Institution, "Annual Report of the Board of Regents of the Smithsonian Institution, 1846," in *Senate Executive Documents*, 29th Congress, 2nd sess., doc. 211, esp. p. 29.

22. Transcription from Joseph Henry's "Locked Book" diary, entry dated Nov. 25, 1850, Archives of the Smithsonian Institution, Washington, D.C. See also Wilcomb E. Washburn, "Vision of Life for the Mall," *AIA Journal* 47 (March 1967): 52–59, and John W. Reps, "Romantic Planning in a Baroque City: Downing and the Washington Mall," *Landscape* 16 (Spring 1967): 6–11, which present contrasting assessments of Downing's plan. Details of Taylor's death are drawn from Allan Nevins, *The Ordeal of the Union*, 2 vols. (New York, 1948), 1: 332–33.

23. Henry, "Locked Book" diary, Nov. 25, 1850. At the bottom of Downing's plan Fillmore wrote: "I hereby adopt so much of the annexed plan for the improvement of the public grounds of the City of Washington south of the President's House to the west of Seventh Street subject to such modifications as may be deemed advisable in the progress of the work; and the remainder of the plan for the portion lying east of Seventh Street is reserved for future consideration." Downing's plan is preserved in the Maps Division, Library of Congress. See also Smithsonian Institution, "Fifth Annual Report of the Board of Regents of the Smithsonian Institution" [March 1, 1851], in *Senate Executive Documents*, 32nd Congress, special sess., March 1–7, 1851, misc. rpt. no. 1, p. 63, and "Report of the Secretary of the Interior" [A. H. Stuart], in *Senate Executive Documents*, 32nd Congress, 1st sess., exec. doc. no. 1, pp. 509–10.

24. Quotations in this and the following paragraph are drawn from A. J. Downing, "Explanatory Notes to Accompany the Plan for Improving the Public Grounds at Washington," National Archives, Records of the Commissioners of Public Buildings, Letters Received, vol. 37, letter 3158 1/2. The report is conveniently reprinted in Washburn, "Vision of Life for the Mall."

25. A. J. Downing to Millard Fillmore, June 12, 1851, National Archives, Records of the Commissioners of Public Buildings, Letters Received, vol. 32,

letter 3196; Downing to Joseph Henry, June 14, 1851, Archives of the Smithsonian Institution; Henry, "Locked Book" diary, July, 1, 1851; Washburn, "Vision of Life for the Mall," p. 56. See also Downing to W. W. Corcoran, June 11, 1851, W. W. Corcoran Papers, Manuscript Division, Library of Congress, Washington, D.C.

26. *Congressional Globe*, 32nd Congress, 1st sess., (Aug. 26, 1852), p. 2375; Olmsted , "Report to the Architect of the Capitol on laying out the Capitol Grounds," in *Annual Report of the Architect of the Capitol, House Executive Documents*, 47th Congress, 2nd sess., doc. 1, part 5, (1882) pp. 914–15.

27. Downing, "Explanatory Notes"; [Downing], "The New-York Park," pp. 345–46; Downing to Henry, June 14, 1851.

28. [Stillman], "Sketchings. Park Hints for 'the Manhattan,' " p. 254; idem, "Sketchings. City Parks," *Crayon* 2 (July 18, 1855): 40; H. J. Smith, *Lemon Hill and Fairmount Park*, pp. 19–20; [George William Curtis], "Editor's Easy Chair," *Harper's New Monthly Magazine* 11 (June 1855): 125.

29. [Downing], "The New-York Park," p. 347.

30. Olmsted and Calvert Vaux, "Circular Proposing the Erection in Central Park of a Memorial to Andrew Jackson Downing, Apr. 5, 1860," in *The Papers of Frederick Law Olmsted*, vol. 3, *Creating Central Park, 1857–1861*, ed. Charles E. Beveridge and David Schuyler (Baltimore, 1983), p. 251.

31. Olmsted, manuscript draft introduction to Downing's *Treatise on Landscape Gardening*; Olmsted, appendix to the *Annual Report of the Architect of the United States Capitol for the Fiscal Year Ending June 30, 1882...*, reproduced in House of Representatives, *Documentary History of the Construction and Development of the United States Capitol Building and Grounds*, 58th Cong., 2nd sess., rpt. 646 (Washington, D.C., 1904), p. 1187.

V. The Naturalistic Landscape: Central Park

The epigraph is from Calvert Vaux, letter to Frederick Law Olmsted, July 31, 1865.

1. Andrew Jackson Downing, "Explanatory Notes to Accompany the Plan for Improving the Public Grounds at Washington," National Archives, Records of the Commissioners of Public Buildings, Letters Received, vol. 37, letter 3158 1/2.

2. Olmsted, *Public Parks: Being Two Papers Read Before the American Social Science Association in 1870 and 1880, Entitled, Respectively, Public Parks and the Enlargement of Towns and A Consideration of the Justifying Value of a Public Park* (Brookline, Mass., 1902), p. 50; Greeley is quoted in Clarence C. Cook, *A Description of the New York Central Park* (1869; New York, 1972), p. 110.

3. "Report of Egbert L. Viele, Engineer-in-Chief," in "Communication from the Commissioners of the Central Park," in New York (City), Board of Aldermen, *Documents* 24 (1857), doc. 5, Jan. 19, 1857, p. 12; Olmsted, "Description of the Central Park" [Jan. 1859], in *The Papers of Frederick Law Olmsted*, vol. 3, *Creating Central Park, 1857–1861*, ed. Charles E. Beveridge and David Schuyler (Baltimore, 1983), pp. 205–12; "Central Park," *Scribner's Monthly* 6 (Oct. 1873): 677; Olmsted, "Park," in *Papers of Frederick Law Olmsted*, 3:354–55.

4. See Edward K. Spann, *The New Metropolis: New York City, 1840–1857* (New York, 1981), passim.

5. [Clarence C. Cook], "New-York Daguerrotyped. Group First: Business Streets, Mercantile Blocks, Stores and Banks," *Putnam's Monthly* 1 (Feb. 1853): 121–22; ibid. 1 (Apr. 1853): 358.

6. [C. Cook], "New-York Daguerrotyped. Group First," p. 124;

[Clarence C. Cook], "New-York Daguerrotyped. Private Residences," *Putnam's Monthly* 3 (Mar. 1854): 242..

7. [C. Cook], "New-York Daguerrotyped. Private Residences," *Putnam's Monthly* 3 (Mar. 1854): 247–48, 243.

8. See William Cullen Bryant, "A New Public Park," *The Evening Post for the Country*, July 6, 1844, p. 1; "Communication from the Commissioners of the Central Park," in New York (City), Board of Aldermen, *Documents* 24 (1857): 79–87; Edward Hagaman Hall, "History of Central Park in the City of New York," in American Scenic and Historic Preservation Society, *Sixteenth Annual Report* (Albany, 1911), pp. 450–60; Ian R. Stewart, "Politics and the Park: The Fight for Central Park," *New-York Historical Society Quarterly* 61 (July–Oct. 1977): pp. 135–49.

9. I. N. Phelps Stokes, *The Iconography of Manhattan Island, 1498–1909*, 6 vols. (New York, 1915–28), 5: 1864; "Report of Egbert L. Viele," pp. 35–46; Alexander Pope, "Epistle IV, To Richard Boyle, Earl of Burlington," in *The Poetical Works of Alexander Pope*, ed. A. W. Ward (New York, n.d.), p. 264; C. Cook, *Description of Central Park*, pp. 24–25.

10. Olmsted, "Passages in the Life of an Unpractical Man" [c. 1878], in *Papers of Frederick Law Olmsted*, 3:84–90; Leo Hershkowitz, *Tweed's New York: Another Look* (Garden City, N.Y., 1978), pp. 57–63.

11. New York (City), Board of Commissioners of the Central Park, *Minutes* (New York, 1858), Aug. 27, 1857, pp. 38–39; Olmsted to John Hull Olmsted, Sept. 11, 1857, in *Papers of Frederick Law Olmsted*, 3:79–81; Olmsted, "Passages in the Life of an Unpractical Man," pp. 85–87. Frederick Law Olmsted, Jr., identified the commissioner his father had met at the Morris Cove Inn as Charles Wyllys Elliott. See the introduction prepared by the younger Olmsted for a new edition of his father's work entitled *A Journey in the Seaboard Slave States*, 2 vols. (New York, 1904), 1: xv–xvi.

12. Olmsted, "Passages," pp. 88–90.

13. "Hard Times in the City," *New-York Times*, Oct. 8, 1857, p. 1; Olmsted to Charles Loring Brace, Dec. 8, 1860, in *Papers of Frederick Law Olmsted*, 3:286–87; Olmsted, "Passages," pp. 85–88; Olmsted, "Influence," unpublished manuscript.

14. Olmsted to John Olmsted, Jan. 14, 1858, and Feb. 2, 1858, in *Papers of Frederick Law Olmsted*, 3:113–16; Calvert Vaux, Memorandum, Nov. 1894, Vaux Papers (1967 additions given by Marion Vaux Hendrickson), Manuscripts and Archives Division, Rare Book & Manuscripts Division, The New York Public Library, Astor, Lenox and Tilden Foundations, New York City; Olmsted, "The Central Park," *The American Architect and Building News* 2 (June 2, 1877): 175.

15. C. Vaux to Marshall P. Wilder, Aug. 8, 1852, John Jay Smith Papers, Library Company of Philadelphia, placed on deposit at the Historical Society of Pennsylvania, Philadelphia; George Bishop Tatum, "Andrew Jackson Downing: Arbiter of American Taste, 1815–1852," (Ph.D. dissertation, Princeton University, 1950); Olmsted, *The Spoils of the Park*, in *Frederick Law Olmsted: Landscape Architect, 1822–1903*, ed. Frederick Law Olmsted, Jr., and Theodora Kimball, 2 vols. (New York, 1922–28), 2: 141. See also John David Sigle, "Calvert Vaux: An American Architect," (M.A. thesis, University of Virginia, 1967).

16. Andrew Jackson Downing, "The New-York Park," reprinted in *Rural Essays. By A. J. Downing. Edited, With a Memoir of the Author, by George William Curtis; and a Letter to His Friends, by Fredrika Bremer* (New York, 1853), pp. 150–51; *Frederick Law Olmsted: Landscape Architect*, 2: 41–42.

17. New York (City), Board of Commissioners of the Central Park,

Catalogue of Plans for the Improvement of the Central Park (New York, 1858), especially plans 7, 9, 11, 15, 16, 18, 19, 22, 23, 24, 25, 26, 29, 30, 31 (Crystal Palace); plans 11, 13, 16, 19, 20 (reservoirs); 5 (proposals for columns and a villa near the lake which would "add beauty to the scenery"); 7 (parade ground south of the reservoir, as well as a labyrinth and buildings that would dominate the landscape); 8 (fountains and statuary); 9 (ten temples, ten lodges, three towers, three grand archways, thirteen fountains); 13 (terraces with ornamental fountain, triumphal arches); 17 (suspension bridge, fountains, and flower terraces); 18 (buildings and the design of the lower park as the continents of the earth); 19 (profusion of buildings, fountains, and statuary); 20 (arcaded hall above reservoir and the use of symmetrical forms in the landscape); 21 (archways, fountains, and statuary); 22 (suspension bridge, monumental entrances, fountains); 23 (triumphal arch, prominent theatre); 24 (architectural flower garden, a grand column commemorating the park itself, pavilion, buildings, and fountains); 25 (labyrinth and an Ionic colonnaded entrance gate); 26 (colonnaded terraces, temple for statuary, architectural elements); 28 (grotto); 29 (monuments and a bridge over McGowan's Pass); 30 (grand entranceway with arched gateway, monuments, and buildings); 31 (buildings, monuments, and fountains); and 32 (temples, buildings, and archways). The quotations in this paragraph of text are drawn from plans 18 (p. 1) and 31 (p. 9).

18. Olmsted and Vaux, "Description of a Plan for the Improvement of the Central Park, 'Greensward,' " in *Papers of Frederick Law Olmsted*, 3:120–22; Olmsted to William Robinson, May 17, 1872; Olmsted, "Description of the Central Park," in *Papers of Frederick Law Olmsted*, 3:212–13; Olmsted to the Board of Commissioners of the Central Park, May 31, 1858, in *Papers of Frederick Law Olmsted*, 3:196. See also T. Addison Richards, "The Central Park," *Harper's New Monthly Magazine* 23 (Aug. 1861): 306, and "The Central Park of New York," ibid. 33 (Nov. 1866): 795.

19. Olmsted and Vaux to Henry G. Stebbins, Jan. 1872; Olmsted, "Description of the Central Park," pp. 212–13; Olmsted to the Board of Commissioners of the Central Park, May 31, 1858, in *Papers of Frederick Law Olmsted*, 3:196; [William J. Stillman], "Sketchings. Central Park," *Crayon* 5 (July 1858): 210. "It is clear enough," wrote another journalist, "that the Central Park is to be 'the country,' and the only 'country' which many of our citizens will see during the summer." "General View of the Central Park," *Harper's Weekly*, June 16, 1860, p. 378.

20. Olmsted and Vaux, "Greensward," in *Papers of Frederick Law Olmsted*, 3:121–22, 124, 129–30. See also Charles E. Beveridge, "Frederick Law Olmsted's Theory of Landscape Design," *Nineteenth Century* 3 (Summer 1977): 38–43.

21. Olmsted and Vaux, "Greensward," pp. 121–22.

22. Olmsted and Vaux, "Greensward," pp. 127–29; Olmsted, "Description of the Central Park," p. 214.

23. Olmsted and Vaux, "Greensward," pp. 125–26.

24. Ibid.

25. Ibid., pp. 129–30; Olmsted, "Description of the Central Park," p. 215; Olmsted and Vaux to Henry G. Stebbins, Feb. 1872. Olmsted's description of the view from the terrace follows the eighteenth-century rule of painterly composition, in which landscapes usually incorporated architectural elements or human figures in the foreground, a middle distance, often in the form of a bridge or a sheet of water to carry the eye visually to the background, where subdued colors created the impression of distance. When Olmsted visited Eaton Park in 1850 he described the landscape gardener's art

in terms of painterly composition: "What artist, so noble, has often been my thought, as he, who with far-reaching conception of beauty and designing power, sketches the outline, writes the colors, and directs the shadow of a picture so great that Nature shall be employed upon it for generations, before the work he has arranged for her shall realize his intentions." [Olmsted], *Walks and Talks of an American Farmer in England*, 2 vols. (New York, 1852), 1: 133.

26. Olmsted, *Public Parks*, p. 49; Olmsted and Vaux, "Greensward," pp. 129–30; Olmsted, "Park" [1861], in *Papers of Frederick Law Olmsted*, 3:354–55; "Central Park," *Scribner's Monthly* 6 (Oct. 1873): 683.

27. Olmsted, "Description of the Central Park," pp. 213–14.

28. Olmsted, Vaux & Co., "Report of the Landscape Architects," *Sixth Annual Report of the Commissioners of Prospect Park* [1866], in Brooklyn, Park Commission, *Annual Reports, 1861–1873*...(Brooklyn, 1873), pp. 101–2.

29. Olmsted and Vaux, "Greensward," p. 131; Olmsted, "Park," p. 355.

30. Ibid., p. 119.

31. Beveridge, "Frederick Law Olmsted's Theory of Landscape Design," p. 41.

32. Ibid.; Olmsted, "Park," pp. 354–55; Olmsted to the Board of Commissioners of the Central Park, May 31, 1858, in *Papers of Frederick Law Olmsted*, 3:193–96; Olmsted, "Description of the Central Park," pp. 212–13; Olmsted, Vaux & Co., "Report of the Landscape Architects, 1866," pp. 93–95.

33. Olmsted, "Description of the Central Park," p. 213; Olmsted to Henry Van Brunt, Jan. 22, 1891; Olmsted, *Public Parks*, pp. 37–43.

34. Olmsted, undated manuscript fragment; Olmsted to Parke Godwin, Aug. 1, 1858, Bryant-Godwin Collection, Manuscripts and Archives Division Rare Book & Manuscripts Division, The New York Public Library, Astor, Lenox and Tilden Foundations, New York City.

35. Olmsted to Henry W. Bellows, Oct. 30, 1860, Henry W. Bellows Papers, Massachusetts Historical Society, Boston; Olmsted, "Report to the Board of Commissioners of the Department of Public Parks, Relative to the Police Force of the Department," in New York (City), Board of Commissioners of the Department of Public Parks, *Documents*, doc. 41, Oct. 24, 1872 (New York, 1872), pp. 2–3; on the role of keepers in educating the public see Olmsted, "Notice Posted in Keepers' Room" [Nov. 10, 1860], in *Papers of Frederick Law Olmsted*, 3:279–80. See also Henry W. Bellows, "Cities and Parks: With Special Reference to the New York Central Park," *Atlantic Monthly* 7 (Apr. 1861): 428–29, and Olmsted, *Public Parks*, p. 71.

36. [Downing], "The New-York Park," pp. 346–47; idem, "A Talk About Public Parks and Gardens," *Horticulturist* 3 (Oct. 1848): 154–55; Bellows, "Cities and Parks," pp. 421–22.

37. New York (City), Board of Commissioners of the Central Park, *Minutes*, (New York, 1859) May 24, 1858; Robert J. Dillon and August Belmont, "The Central Park. Objections of Two of the Commissioners to the Plan Adopted. A Card to the Public," *New-York Times*, June 7, 1858, p. 5, and "The Central Park Board," ibid., May 27, 1858, p. 8.

38. Olmsted to the Board of Commissioners of the Central Park, May 31, 1858, in *Papers of Frederick Law Olmsted*, 3:193–96; on Green see *Papers of Frederick Law Olmsted*, 3:55–59. As late as 1872 Olmsted and Vaux were still resisting efforts to place a grand formal avenue in the park and to make the reservoirs the centerpiece of its design. See Olmsted and Vaux to Henry G. Stebbins, April 16, 1872.

39. [Richard Morris Hunt], *Designs for the Gateways of the Southern Entrances to the Central Park. By Richard M. Hunt, Member of the American*

Institute of Architects. With a Description of the Designs, and a Letter in Relation to Them, Addressed to the Commissioners of the Central Park (New York, 1866), pp. 11–13.

40. Ibid., pp. 9, 13, 6, 15–16.

41. Ibid., pp. 7–8.

42. Vaux to Clarence C. Cook, June 6, 1865, Olmsted Papers; Olmsted and Vaux to Henry G. Stebbins, Jan. 1872; [Clarence C. Cook], "Mr. Hunt's Designs for the Gates of the Central Park," New-York Daily Tribune, Aug. 2, 1865.

43. Vaux to Cook, June 6, 1865.

VI. Cities and Parks: The Lessons of Central Park

The epigraph is from Olmsted, Vaux & Co. to the Chairman of the Committee on Plans of the Park Commission of Philadelphia, Dec. 4, 1867.

1. [William J. Stillman], "Sketchings. Editorial Correspondence," Crayon 1 (Mar. 7, 1855): 155; John Jay Smith, "Editor's Table," Horticulturist, n.s. 8 (July 1858): 329; ibid. n.s., 9 (Dec. 1859): 568; Andrew Jackson Downing, letter to John Jay Smith, n.d. (probably 1847) and Mar. 17, 1850, printed in Horticulturist, n.s., 6 (Apr. 1856): 160; "City Public Parks," Scientific American, n.s., 1 (Nov. 19, 1859): 377; Frederick Law Olmsted, "Park" [1861], in The Papers of Frederick Law Olmsted, vol. 3, Creating Central Park, 1857–1861, ed. Charles E. Beveridge and David Schuyler (Baltimore, 1983), pp. 354–57.

2. Swann's address was printed in Inaugural Ceremonies and Address of Hon. Thomas Swann. On the Opening of Druid Hill Park, October 19, 1860, Compiled from the Baltimore American (Baltimore, 1860), pp. 19–20. Keyser's paper was printed in Lemon Hill and Fairmount Park. The Papers of Charles S. Keyser and Thomas Cochran, Relative to a Public Park for Philadelphia, ed. Horace J. Smith (Philadelphia, 1886), pp. 25, 37.

3. John F. Watson, Annals of Philadelphia, and Pennsylvania, in the Olden Times...Enlarged, with Many Revisions and Additions, by Willis P. Hazard, 3 vols. (Philadelphia, 1884), 3: 397–98; George B. Tatum, "The Origins of Fairmount Park," Antiques 82 (Nov. 1962): 502–9; Isaac Parrish, "Report on the Sanitary Condition of Philadelphia," American Medical Association, Transactions 2 (1849): 477.

4. H. J. Smith, Lemon Hill and Fairmount Park, pp. 4, 6; J. W. Harshberger, "Correspondence. The Wissahickon Woods," Garden and Forest 4 (Mar. 18, 1891): 129.

5. H. J. Smith, Lemon Hill and Fairmount Park, pp. 33, 10, 27–28; Philadelphia, Commissioners of Fairmount Park, Acts of Assembly and Ordinances of Councils Relating to Fairmount Park (Philadelphia, 1912), p. 1.

6. H. J. Smith, Lemon Hill and Fairmount Park, pp. 27–28; Philadelphia, City Councils, Committee on City Property, Special Report of the Committee on City Property, Relative to Sedgley Park (Philadelphia, [1857]), pp. 1–3; Olmsted, "Park," p. 355.

7. For information on the competition for designs see John Jay Smith, "Editor's Table," Horticulturist, n.s., 9 (Feb. 1859): 92, and ibid., n.s., 9 (Apr. 1859): 185; Olmsted, "Park," p. 356. See also James C. Sidney and Andrew Adams in Philadelphia, City Councils, Committee on City Property, Description of a Plan for the Improvement of Fairmount Park, By Sidney and Adams (Philadelphia, 1859), p. 3. The Sidney and Adams plan is reproduced as the frontispiece of Description.

8. Sidney and Adams, Description of Plan, pp. 3, 6, 17.

9. Ibid., pp. 9–12.

10. Olmsted and Calvert Vaux to Henry G. Stebbins, Jan. 1872.

11. Sidney George Fisher, *A Philadelphia Perspective: The Diary of Sidney George Fisher Covering the Years 1834–1871*, ed. Nicholas B. Wainwright (Philadelphia, 1967), p. 409.

12. Philadelphia, Commissioners of Fairmount Park, *A Digest of the Acts of Assembly and Ordinances of Councils Relating to Fairmount Park*, comp. C. H. Jones (Philadelphia, 1872), pp. 19–20, 32; Philadelphia, Commissioners of Fairmount Park, *First Annual Report* (Philadelphia, 1869), pp. 26–27; Philadelphia, Commissioners of Fairmount Park, *Report of the Committee on Plans and Improvements of the Commissioners of Fairmount Park* (Philadelphia, 1868) pp. 6–7.

13. Commissioners of Fairmount Park, *Report of the Committee on Plans and Improvements*, pp. 4–7. The Commissioners of Fairmount Park eventually acquired the dwellings and factories already standing in the park.

14. Ibid., pp. 5–6.

15. Robert Morris Copeland to Olmsted, Oct. 24, 1867; Olmsted to Frederick Knapp, Nov. 21, 1867.

16. H. Dechert to Olmsted, Apr. 29, 1868; Philadelphia, Commissioners of Fairmount Park, *Second Annual Report* (Philadelphia, 1870), p. 12, and John C. Cresson report in ibid., appendix 1, p. 46.

17. Foley to Olmsted and Vaux, July 8 and 13, 1871; Olmsted, draft report on the Philadelphia Park, c. 1871. See also Charles E. Beveridge, "Frederick Law Olmsted's Theory of Landscape Design," *Nineteenth Century* 3 (Summer 1977): 38–43.

18. Theodore Cuyler to Olmsted, Vaux & Co., Oct. 23, 1872; Olmsted, Vaux & Co. to Theodore Cuyler, Oct. 28, 1872.

19. John Maass, *The Glorious Enterprise: The Centennial Exhibition of 1876 and H. J. Schwarzmann, Architect-in-Chief* (Watkins Glen, N.Y., 1973), pp. 20–23; Philadelphia, Commissioners of Fairmount Park, *Third Annual Report* (Philadelphia, 1871), p. 5.

20. James Wynne, "Sanitary Report on Baltimore," American Medical Association, *Transactions* 2 (1849): 567–68.

21. "A City Park," *Baltimore American and Commercial Advertiser*, Mar. 3, 1859, p. 2; "The Park Project," ibid., Mar. 9, 1859, p. 2. The petitions are preserved as item 318 for the year 1860, in the City Records Center, Baltimore.

22. Swann, in *Inaugural Ceremonies*, p. 24; "A City Park," p. 2.

23. Ibid.; Public Good, "City Railways," *Baltimore American*, Mar. 9, 1859, p. 2; "An Ordinance to provide for a public Park or Parks," July 19, 1860, document 1510 for the year 1860, City Records Center, Baltimore.

24. For the city's income from the "park tax" see documents 212 (Apr. 9, 1863), 213 (July 12, 1863), and 214 (Oct. 2, 1863) for the year 1863, City Records Center, Baltimore; for subsequent issues of stock to provide for the purchase and improvement of city parks see documents 1135 for the year 1863 and 973 for the year 1865, City Records Center, Baltimore. See also Swann's address in *Inaugural Ceremonies*, pp. 25–27.

25. Baltimore, Park Commission, *First Annual Report* (Baltimore, 1861), p. 436; Howard Daniels, "A Public Park for Baltimore," *Horticulturist*, n.s., 10 (Sept. 1860): 435–38; Cummins's prayer and Swann's address, both printed in *Inaugural Ceremonies*, pp. 15, 25, 27.

26. Daniels placed an advertisement in at least one issue of the 1855 *Horticulturist* which stated in part: "Having laid out fifteen rural cemeteries and a corresponding number of private grounds, he feels confident that he will be able to please his employers. Plans for Parks, Cemeteries, Country Seats, Villas, Farms, Orchards, Cottages, Conservatories, Green-houses, Rustic Structures, &c." *Horticulturist*, n.s., 5 (1855), unpaginated advertise-

ment bound at the back of the volume. See also "Editor's Chair," ibid., n.s., 6 (Feb. 1856): 98. For Daniels's work at Llewellyn Park see his essay "Villa Parks," ibid., n.s. 8 (Nov. 1858): 495–96, and "Landscape Gardening. Llewellyn Park," *Crayon* 4 (Aug. 1857): 248. For an assessment of Daniels's career see C. M. Hovey, "The Progress of Horticulture," *Magazine of Horticulture* 27 (Jan. 1861): 13, and Peter B. Mead, "Editor's Table," *Horticulturist*, n.s., 14 (Feb. 1864): 71.

27. Manhattan [Howard Daniels], *Plan for Central Park*, in New York (City), Board of Commissioners of the Central Park, *Catalogue of Plans for the Improvement of the Central Park* (New York, 1858). Quoted material in this paragraph appears on pages 3, 5–7, 10, 18–19.

28. Swann, in *Inaugural Ceremonies*, pp. 28, 30; Daniels, "A Public Park for Baltimore," pp. 436–38; Hovey, "The Progress of Horticulture," p. 13. See also Hovey's remarks on Druid Hill in "New York Central Park," *Magazine of Horticulture* 26 (Dec. 1860): 530.

29. Howard Daniels, "First Annual Report of the Landscape Gardener of Druid Hill Park," in Baltimore, Park Commission, *First Annual Report*, pp. 444–45, passim; Baltimore, Park Commission, *Second Annual Report* (Baltimore, 1862), p. 4.

30. Hovey, "New York Central Park," p. 530; Howard Daniels, "Second Annual Report of the Landscape Gardener of Druid Hill Park," in Baltimore, Park Commission, *Second Annual Report*, pp. 21–23; Daniels, "First Annual Report," p. 459.

When Olmsted visited Druid Hill in 1877, thirteen years after Daniels's death, he reported: "The scenery is very park-like, the trees charming—the work atrociously bad. So bad that I could do nothing with it. It is hopeless. Every bit of work has been done with ingeniously bad intention." Olmsted to Mary P. Olmsted, July 31, 1877.

31. Daniels, "First Annual Report," p. 460.

32. Daniels "Second Annual Report," p. 30.

33. Baltimore, Park Commission, *First Annual Report*, p. 436; David Murray, *A Plan for a Park for the City of Albany* (Albany, 1863), p. 9; Providence, Public Park Association, *Parks of Leading Cities of this Country; Their Advantages. Parks of Providence* (Providence, 1887), p. 24; Swann, in *Inaugural Ceremonies*, p. 19.

34. Ralph Foster Weld, *Brooklyn Village, 1816–1834* (1938; rpt. ed., New York, 1970), pp. 15–16, 27–28. For a general history of Brooklyn at this time see Henry R. Stiles, *A History of the City of Brooklyn. Including the Old Town and Village of Brooklyn, The Town of Bushwick, and the Village and City of Williamsburg*, 3 vols. (Brooklyn, 1867–70).

35. Donald Simon, "The Public Park Movement in Brooklyn, 1824–1873," (Ph.D. dissertation, New York University, 1972), pp. 38–63, 190–99, 234, passim.

36. Ibid.; Stiles, *History of the City of Brooklyn*, 3: 618.

37. Simon, "Public Park Movement in Brooklyn," passim; George W. Cullum, *Biographical Register of the Officers and Graduates of the United States Military Academy...*, 2 vols. (New York, 1868), 2: 202–3; *Dictionary of American Biography*, s.v. "Viele, Egbert Ludovicus."

38. Egbert L. Viele, "Prospect Park. Report of Egbert L. Viele, Esq.," in Brooklyn, Commissioners of Prospect Park, *First Annual Report* (Brooklyn, 1861), pp. 36–42.

39. Ibid.

40. James S. T. Stranahan, in Brooklyn, Park Commission, *Second Annual Report* (Brooklyn, 1862), p. 4, and *Fourth Annual Report* (Brooklyn, 1864), p. 1.

41. Vaux to Olmsted, Sept. 17, 1864; Simon, "Public Park Movement in Brooklyn," passim; *Dictionary of American Biography,* s.v. "Stranahan, James Samuel Thomas."

42. Vaux to James S. T. Stranahan, Jan. 10, 1865; Vaux to Olmsted, Jan. 9, 1865; Olmsted to Vaux, Mar. 12, 1865.

43. Vaux to Olmsted, Mar. 12, 1865, and Feb. 26, 1865; Olmsted to Mary P. Olmsted, Feb. 27, 1865; Olmsted to Vaux, Mar. 12, 1865, and May 10, 1865; Resolution appointing Olmsted, Vaux & Co. landscape architects to the Brooklyn Park Commission, May 29, 1865, manuscript copy in the Olmsted Papers.

44. Olmsted, Vaux & Co., "Report of the Landscape Architects," *Sixth Annual Report of the Commissioners of Prospect Park* [1866], in Brooklyn, Park Commission, *Annual Reports, 1861–1873*...(Brooklyn, 1873), p. 92.

45. Ibid., pp. 93–95.

46. Ibid., pp. 95–97.

47. Ibid., pp. 111–12.

48. Ibid., pp. 100–101.

49. Ibid., p. 100.

50. Ibid., pp. 104–5.

51. Ibid., pp. 108, 97, 110.

52. Olmsted, "Park," in George Ripley and Charles A. Dana, eds., *The New American Cyclopaedia: A Popular Dictionary of General Knowledge,* 16 vols., 2nd ed. (New York, 1875), s.v. "Park"; Robert Morris Copeland to Olmsted, May 23, 1869; Charles Sprague Sargent, "Prospect Park," *Garden and Forest* 1 (July 4, 1888): 217.

53. *Papers of Frederick Law Olmsted,* 3: 214; Olmsted and Vaux, "Report of the Landscape Architects, 1866," p. 111.

54. Ibid., pp. 112–13.

VII. Parks, Parkways, and Park Systems

The epigraph is from Olmsted, Vaux & Co. to William Dorsheimer, Esq., Oct. 1, 1868, in *First Annual Report of the Buffalo Park Commissioners, January, 1871* (Buffalo, 1871), p. 12.

1. Frederick Law Olmsted, *Public Parks: Being Two Papers Read Before the American Social Science Association in 1870 and 1880, Entitled, Respectively, Public Parks and the Enlargement of Towns and A Consideration of the Justifying Value of a Public Park* (Brookline, Mass., 1902), pp. 65–66; Olmsted to William Robinson, May 17, 1872.

2. Olmsted, Vaux & Co., "Preliminary Report to the Commissioners for Laying Out a Park in Brooklyn, New York," in *Landscape into Cityscape: Frederick Law Olmsted's Plans for a Greater New York,* ed. Albert Fein (Ithaca, 1967), pp. 126–27.

3. Olmsted, Vaux & Co., "Report of the Landscape Architects and Superintendents to the President of the Board of Commissioners of Prospect Park, Brooklyn," in Fein, *Landscape into Cityscape,* pp. 135–48.

4. Ibid., pp. 132, 149–52, 158–64.

5. Ibid., pp. 159–62.

6. John Bogart to Olmsted, Nov. 10, 1869; O. C. Bullard to Olmsted, Apr. 21, 1870; Olmsted to F. Knapp, July 11, 1870.

7. Olmsted to Mary P. Olmsted, Aug. 27, 1868; Charles E. Beveridge, "Buffalo's Park and Parkway System," in Reyner Banham, et al., *Buffalo Architecture: A Guide* (Cambridge, Mass., 1981), p. 15.

8. Olmsted, Vaux & Co., *Preliminary Report Respecting a Public Park in Buffalo, and a Copy of the Act of the Legislature Authorizing its Establishment* (Buffalo, 1869), pp. 15–16, 13–14.

9. Ibid., pp. 20–21ff.

10. Ibid., pp. 13–14, 18, 23–24.

11. Ibid., pp. 19–20; Beveridge, "Buffalo's Park and Parkway System," pp. 17–18.

12. Olmsted, Vaux & Co., *Preliminary Report Respecting a Park in Buffalo*, p. 25.

13. Olmsted to F. C. Rogers, Apr. 26, 1875.

14. Olmsted to George E. Waring, Apr. 13, 1876.

15. Glen E. Holt, "Private Plans for Public Spaces: The Origins of Chicago's Park System, 1850-1875," *Chicago History* 8 (Fall 1979): 173-84; Daniel M. Bluestone, "Olmsted's Boston and Other Park Places," *Reviews in American History* 11 (Dec. 1983): 531–36; Michael P. McCarthy, "Politics and the Parks: Chicago Businessmen and the Recreation Movement," *Journal of the Illinois State Historical Society* 63 (Summer 1972): 158–72; Olmsted to Alfred T. Field, Apr. 11, 1871; A. T. Andreas, *History of Chicago: From the Earliest Period to the Present Time...*, 3 vols. (Chicago, 1884–86), 3: 167–71; Victoria Post Ranney, *Olmsted in Chicago* (Chicago, 1972), pp. 15–25.

16. H. W. S. Cleveland, *The Public Grounds of Chicago: How to Give Them Character and Expression* (Chicago, 1869), pp. 19, 15, 17, passim; idem, *Landscape Architecture As Applied to the Wants of the West*, ed. Roy Lubove (1873; Pittsburgh, 1965), pp. 23–25.

17. Olmsted, Vaux & Co., *Report Accompanying Plan for Laying Out the South Park* (Chicago, 1871). p. 7; Ranney, *Olmsted in Chicago*, pp. 15–25; Theodore Turak, "William LeBaron Jenney: Pioneer of Chicago's West Parks," *Inland Architect* 25 (Mar. 1981): 38–45. Holt, "Private Plans for Public Spaces," pp. 178–80, points out that a third commission was responsible for administering Lincoln Park.

18. Turak, "William LeBaron Jenney," p. 39; Holt, "Private Plans for Public Spaces," pp. 178–80.

19. Olmsted, Vaux & Co., *Report Accompanying Plan for the South Park*, pp. 12–15, 18–20, 27.

20. Ibid., pp. 25, 27–29, passim.

21. Turak, "William LeBaron Jenney," pp. 41–43.

22. Ibid., pp. 39, 45.

23. Holt, "Private Plans for Public Spaces," pp. 181–82.

24. Cynthia Zaitzevsky, *Frederick Law Olmsted and the Boston Park System* (Cambridge, Mass., 1982), pp. 33–34; H. W. S. Cleveland, *Landscape Architecture Applied to the West*, pp. 38ff.

25. Zaitzevsky, *Olmsted and the Boston Park System*, pp. 34–38; H.W.S. Cleveland, *Public Grounds of Chicago*, pp. 8–12.

26. Zaitzevsky, *Olmsted and the Boston Park System*, pp. 35–38; [Robert M. Copeland], Editorial, *Boston Daily Advertiser*, Oct. 16, 1873, quoted in ibid., p. 18.

27. Olmsted, *Public Parks*, p. 30; James Houghton to Olmsted, Jan. 28, 1870, and Feb. 14, 1870.

28. Zaitzevsky, *Olmsted and the Boston Park System*, p. 37.

29. Robert M. Copeland, *The Most Beautiful City in America: Essay and Plan for the Improvement of the City of Boston* (Boston, 1872), passim; Zaitzevsky, *Olmsted and the Boston Park System*, pp. 38–41.

30. Zaitzevsky, *Olmsted and the Boston Park System*, p. 41.

31. Ibid., pp. 41–47.

32. Ibid., pp. 46–47, 51–64.

33. Olmsted to Charles H. Dalton, May 17, 1881.

34. Olmsted, *Notes on the Plan of Franklin Park and Related Matters*, in

Boston, Department of Parks, *Eleventh Annual Report of the Board of Commissioners of the Department of Parks for the Year 1885* (Boston, 1886), pp. 51–63.

35. Zaitzevsky, *Olmsted and the Boston Park System*, passim; Charles Eliot, quoted in Charles William Eliot, *Charles Eliot, Landscape Architect* (Boston, 1902), pp. 356–57.

36. Zaitzevsky, *Olmsted and the Boston Park System*, p. 118–23; Charles Eliot, "The Waverly Oaks: A Plan for their Preservation by the People," *Garden and Forest* 3 (Mar. 1890): 118; see also Norman T. Newton, *Design on the Land: The Development of Landscape Architecture* (Cambridge, Mass., 1971), pp. 318–36.

37. Zaitzevsky, *Olmsted and the Boston Park System*, pp. 118–23; Newton, *Design on the Land*, pp. 320–32.

38. Charles Sprague Sargent, "Prospect Park," *Garden and Forest* 1 (July 4, 1888): 217–18.

VIII. Urban Decentralization and the Domestic Landscape

The epigraph is from Frederick Law Olmsted to Charles Loring Brace, Mar. 7, 1882.

1. [Richard Morris Hunt], *Designs for the Gateways of the Southern Entrances to the Central Park. By Richard M. Hunt, Member of the American Institute of Architects. With a Description of the Designs, and a Letter in Relation to Them, Addressed to the Commissioners of the Central Park* (New York, 1866), p. 15; Carl W. Condit, *The Port of New York: A History of the Rail Terminal System from the Beginnings to Pennsylvania Station* (New York, 1980), p. 79.

2. On Haussmann, see David H. Pinkney, *Napoleon III and the Rebuilding of Paris* (Princeton, 1958), passim; Olmsted, Vaux & Co., "Report of the Landscape Architects and Superintendents to the President of the Board of Commissioners of Prospect Park, Brooklyn," Jan. 1, 1868, in *Landscape into Cityscape: Frederick Law Olmsted's Plans for a Greater New York*, ed. Albert Fein (Ithaca, 1967), pp. 158–62.

3. Kenneth T. Jackson, "The Crabgrass Frontier: 150 Years of Suburban Growth in America," in Raymond A. Mohl and James F. Richardson, eds., *The Urban Experience: Themes in American History* (Belmont, Calif., 1973), pp. 199–200. On urban transportation systems, see especially George R. Taylor, "The Beginnings of Mass Transportation in Urban America," *Smithsonian Journal of History* 1 (Summer and Autumn 1966); Kenneth T. Jackson, "Urban Decentralization in the Nineteenth Century: A Statistical Inquiry," in Leo F. Schnore, ed., *The New Urban History: Quantitative Explorations by American Historians* (Princeton, 1975), pp. 110–14.

4. *The Boston Common, Or Rural Walks in Cities. By a Friend of Improvement* (Boston, 1838), pp. 41–42; Taylor, "The Beginnings of Mass Transportation in Urban America," part 1, pp. 39–40; Sam Bass Warner, Jr., "If All the World Were Philadelphia: A Scaffolding for Urban History," *American Historical Review* 74 (Oct. 1968): 26–43; David Ward, *Cities and Immigrants: A Geography of Change in Nineteenth-Century America* (New York, 1971), pp. 85–102.

5. See, for example, Sam Bass Warner, Jr., *Streetcar Suburbs: The Process of Growth in Boston, 1870–1900* (Cambridge, Mass., 1962); Charles Lockwood, *Manhattan Moves Uptown: An Illustrated History* (Boston, 1976); Sidney George Fisher, *A Philadelphia Perspective: The Diary of Sidney George Fisher Covering the Years 1834–1871*, ed. Nicholas B. Wainwright (Philadelphia, 1967), p. 202.

6. The literature on urban transportation systems is large and increasing, but see especially Taylor, "The Beginnings of Mass Transportation in Urban America"; Harry James Carman, *The Street Surface Railway Franchises of New York City*, Studies in History, Economics, and Public Law 88 (New York,

1919); Charles J. Kennedy, "Commuter Service in the Boston Area, 1835–1860," *Business History Review* 36 (Summer 1962): 153–70; Joel Arthur Tarr, "From City to Suburb: The 'Moral' Influence of Transportation Technology," in Alexander B. Callow, Jr., ed., *American Urban History: An Interpretative Reader with Commentaries*, 2nd ed. (New York, 1973), pp. 202–12; idem, *Transportation Innovation and Changing Spatial Patterns in Pittsburgh, 1850–1934* (Chicago, 1978); and Glen E. Holt, "The Changing Perception of Urban Pathology: An Essay on the Development of Mass Transit in the United States," in Kenneth T. Jackson and Stanley Schultz, eds., *Cities in American History* (New York, 1972), pp. 324–43. The Baltimore *Sun* is quoted in Holt, "Changing Perception of Urban Pathology," p. 325; Lyell is quoted in Taylor, "Beginnings of Mass Transportation in Urban America," part 1, p. 48.

7. Fisher, *A Philadelphia Perspective*, pp. 277, 327–28.

8. Lewis Mumford, *The City in History: Its Origins, Its Transformations, and Its Prospects* (New York, 1961), pp. 458–65, 503–9; Ralph Waldo Emerson, "The Young American," in *Emerson's Complete Works*, Riverside Edition, 12 vols. (Boston, 1888–93), 1: 344; H. W. S. Cleveland, "Landscape Gardening," *Christian Examiner* 58 (May 1855): 386.

9. [Andrew Jackson Downing], "Domestic Notices. Suburban Embellishments," *Horticulturist* 6 (Feb. 1851): 98; [Andrew Jackson Downing], "Hints to Rural Improvers," ibid. 3 (July 1848): 10; Kennedy, "Commuter Service in the Boston Area," p. 162.

10. Fredrika Bremer, *Homes of the New World: Impressions of America*, trans. Mary Howitt, 2 vols. (New York, 1853), 1: 52; Dauphin, "The Village of Rahway," *New-York Daily Tribune*, Sept. 18, 1850; Lady Emmeline Stuart Wortley, *Travels in the United States, etc. During 1849 and 1850* (New York, 1851), p. 16; Sidney Denise Maxwell, *The Suburbs of Cincinnati: Sketches Historical and Descriptive* (Cincinnati, 1870), p. 186.

11. [William J. Stillman], "Sketchings," *Crayon* 1 (Jan. 3, 1855): 11; [Andrew Jackson Downing], "Our Country Villages," *Horticulturist* 4 (June 1850): 539–40.

12. [Downing], "Our Country Villages," pp. 539–40; John Randel is quoted in New York (City), Common Council, *Manual of the Corporation of the City of New York, 1864*, comp. D. T. Valentine (New York, 1864), p. 878.

13. See the "Map of Village Lots and Cottage Sites at Dearman, Westchester Co., . . . ," Archives of the Hudson River Museum, Yonkers, New York. I am indebted to John Zukowsky for bringing this map to my attention.

14. [Downing], "Our Country Villages," pp. 539–40.

15. [George W. Curtis], "Editor's Easy Chair," *Harper's New Monthly Magazine* 7 (June 1853): 129–30; Henry W. Cleaveland, William Backus, and Samuel D. Backus, *Village and Farm Cottages*, reprint edition, with a new introduction by David Schuyler (1856; Watkins Glen, N.Y., 1982), pp. 24–25, 29; H.W.S. Cleveland, "Landscape Gardening," p. 389; [John Jay Smith], "Parks Versus Villages," *Horticulturist*, n.s., 6 (Apr. 1856): 153–55; H. W. S. Cleveland, *Landscape Architecture As Applied to the Wants of the West*, ed. Roy Lubove (1873; Pittsburgh, 1965), pp. 33–36; [Downing], "Hints to Rural Improvers," p. 9.

16. [Downing], "Our Country Villages," pp. 540–41; [J. J. Smith], "Parks Versus Villages," pp. 154–55. The idea of locating a suburban village around a park was not new, of course. John Nash's Regent's Park was surrounded by residential terraces, and the town of Birkenhead, near Liverpool, paid for the cost of its park through the sale of adjacent lots. See [Olmsted], *Walks and Talks of an American Farmer in England*, 2 vols. (New York, 1852), 1: 78–83.

17. See, for example, Cleaveland, et al., *Village and Farm Cottages*,

pp. 12–14, and R. Richard Wohl, "The 'Country Boy' Myth and Its Place in American Urban Culture: The Nineteenth-Century Contribution," ed. Moses Rischin, *Perspectives in American History* 3 (1969): 82–95.

18. [William M. Shinn, Trustee], *Constitution of Evergreen Hamlet* (Pittsburgh, 1851), pp. 1–8; Charles C. Arensberg, "Evergreen Hamlet," *Western Pennsylvania Historical Magazine* 38 (Fall–Winter 1955): 117–33.

19. "Llewellyn Park. Country Homes for City People. A Private Park of 750 Acres; 10 Miles of Drives and Walks; A 'Ramble' of 50 Acres; Only 60 Minutes from New York," real estate prospectus, copy in the Olmsted Papers.

20. Jane B. Davies, "Llewellyn Park in West Orange, New Jersey," *Antiques* 107 (Jan. 1975): 142–58; Richard Guy Wilson, "Idealism and the Origin of the First American Suburb: Llewellyn Park, New Jersey," *American Art Journal* 11 (Fall 1979): 79–90; Henry Winthrop Sargent, "Historical Notices," in Andrew Jackson Downing, *A Treatise on the Theory and Practice of Landscape Gardening, Adapted to North America . . .*, 6th ed. (New York, 1859), pp. 568–71; "Landscape-Gardening. Llewellyn Park," *Crayon* 4 (Aug. 1857): 248; "Rural Taste in North America," *Christian Examiner* 69 (Nov. 1860): 350.

21. Davies, "Llewellyn Park in West Orange, New Jersey," p. 143; Sargent, "Historical Notices," pp. 569–70; "Landscape-Gardening. Llewellyn Park," p. 248. See also Howard Daniels, "Villa Parks," *Horticulturist*, n.s., 8 (Nov. 1858): 495–96. Although this essay does not mention Llewellyn Park by name, Daniels was undoubtedly referring to it when he wrote: "The park should be laid out as the grand central feature of the enterprise, having fine drives, broad walks, verdant lawns, play grounds for the children, &c., and should contain the finest trees and shrubs that can be cultivated. The improvements should be made to produce the greatest possible number of fine scenes, each having a distinctive character of its own, forming a complete picture of itself."

22. "Llewellyn Park. Country Homes for City People"; Davies, "Llewellyn Park in West Orange, New Jersey," p. 144.

23. Nathaniel Parker Willis, *Out-Doors at Idlewild* (New York, 1855), pp. 17–25.

24. *Description of Irving Park, Tarrytown; The Property of Charles H. Lyon* (New York, 1859), pp. 5–16; "Irving Park, Tarrytown," *Harper's Weekly* 4 (Jan. 28, 1860): 52; John Jay Smith, "Editor's Table," *Horticulturist*, n.s., 9 (June 1859): 292. I am indebted to Jon A. Peterson for bringing the *Description of Irving Park* to my attention.

25. Wilson, "Idealism and the Origin of the Suburb," p. 83; *Description of Irving Park*, p. 10.

26. Allan Nevins, *The War for the Union*, vol. 3: *The Organized War, 1863–1864* (New York, 1971), pp. 212–70.

27. Olmsted, Vaux & Co. to the Riverside Improvement Company, Dec. 1, 1868; Olmsted to Calvert Vaux, Aug. 29, 1868; L. W. Murray to Edward Everett Hale, Dec. 29, 1868, Edward Everett Hale Papers, New York State Library, Albany.

28. Olmsted, Vaux & Co., *Preliminary Report Upon the Proposed Suburban Village at Riverside, Near Chicago* (New York, 1868), pp. 7, 25–26; Olmsted to Vaux, Mar. 12, 1865; Olmsted to Edward Everett Hale, Oct. 21, 1869, Hale Papers.

29. Olmsted, Vaux & Co., "Preliminary Report to the Commissioners for Laying Out a Park in Brooklyn," in Fein, *Landscape into Cityscape*, pp. 98–101, 106–7; Olmsted, Vaux & Co., *Preliminary Report Upon the Proposed Suburban Village at Riverside*, pp. 26, 7, 25.

30. Olmsted, Vaux & Co., *Preliminary Report Upon the Proposed Suburban Village at Riverside*, pp. 4, 5, 7.

31. Ibid., pp. 8–14.

32. Ibid., pp. 16–17, 24–25.

33. Everett Chamberlain, *Chicago and its Suburbs* (Chicago, 1874), pp. 414–16; Howard K. Menhinick, "Riverside Sixty Years Later," *Landscape Architecture* 22 (Jan. 1932): 109–17; Victoria Post Ranney, *Olmsted in Chicago* (Chicago, 1972), pp. 11–15.

34. Olmsted, Vaux & Co., *Preliminary Report Upon the Proposed Suburban Village at Riverside*, p. 28.

35. Chamberlain, *Chicago and its Suburbs*, p. 415; Vaux to Olmsted, June 18, 1869; Olmsted to Emery E. Childs, Oct. 28, 1869; Vaux to Olmsted, Oct. 30 [1869], Apr. 11, 1870; Olmsted, Vaux & Co. to Childs, Apr. 30, 1870; Olmsted to Edward Everett Hale, Oct. 21, 1869, Hale Papers.

36. Menhinick, "Riverside Sixty Years Later," pp. 109–17.

37. Olmsted, et al., "Report to the Staten Island Improvement Commission of a Preliminary Scheme of Improvements," in Fein, *Landscape into Cityscape*, p. 182.

38. Warner, *Streetcar Suburbs*, p. 3.

39. Ibid.; Philippe Ariès, "The Family and the City," *Daedalus* 106 (Spring 1977): 227–35; Kirk Jeffrey, "The Family as Utopian Retreat from the City: The Nineteenth-Century Contribution," *Soundings* 55 (Spring 1972): 21–41. Charles Loring Brace's book was entitled *The Dangerous Classes of New York, and Twenty Years Work Among Them* (New York, 1872).

IX. The New City: A House with Many Rooms

The epigraph is from Frederick Law Olmsted and J.J.R. Croes, "Report of the Landscape Architect and the Civil and Topographical Engineer, Accompanying a Plan for Laying Out that Part of the Twenty-fourth Ward Lying West of the Riverdale Road," Nov. 21, 1876, in *Landscape into Cityscape: Frederick Law Olmsted's Plans for a Greater New York*, ed. Albert Fein (Ithaca, 1967), p. 359.

1. Kenneth T. Jackson, "The Crabgrass Frontier: 150 Years of Suburban Growth in America," in Raymond A. Mohl and James F. Richardson, eds. *The Urban Experience: Themes in American History* (Belmont, Calif. 1973), passim; Olmsted to Edward Everett Hale, Oct. 21, 1869, Edward Everett Hale Papers, New York State Library, Albany. On Hyde Park see Jean F. Block, *Hyde Park Houses: An Informal History, 1856–1910* (Chicago, 1978).

2. Olmsted to Hale, Oct. 21, 1869, Hale Papers.

3. Olmsted, *Public Parks: Being Two Papers Read Before the American Social Science Association in 1870 and 1880, Entitled, Respectively, Public Parks and the Enlargement of Towns and A Consideration of the Justifying Value of a Public Park* (Brookline, Mass., 1902), pp. 8, 20–21, 14.

4. Ibid., pp. 14–20, 23.

5. Ibid., pp. 23–24, 32–33, 45.

6. Ibid., p. 30.

7. Olmsted and J.J.R. Croes, "Preliminary Report of the Landscape Architect and the Civil and Topographical Engineer, upon the Laying Out of the Twenty-third and Twenty-fourth Wards," Nov. 15, 1876, in Fein *Landscape into Cityscape*, p. 352.

8. Ibid., pp. 352–57; Olmsted, "The Future of New-York," *New-York Daily Tribune*, Dec. 28, 1879.

9. Olmsted and Croes, "Preliminary Report," p. 353; Olmsted, "Observations on the Future of New-York," manuscript draft, 1879.

10. Olmsted and Croes, "Preliminary Report," pp. 353, 356; Olmsted, "Observations on the Future of New-York."

11. Olmsted, "Observations on the Future of New-York"; Olmsted, *Public Parks*, pp. 27–32.

12. Olmsted and Calvert Vaux, "Report of the Landscape Architects and Superintendents to the President of the Board of Commissioners of Prospect Park, Brooklyn," Jan. 1, 1868, in Fein, *Landscape into Cityscape*, pp. 140–43; Olmsted, *Public Parks*, pp. 27–33; Olmsted, "The Shaping of Towns," *American Architect and Building News* 2 (1877): 195.

13. Olmsted, "Passages in the Life of an Unpractical Man," manuscript draft, c. 1878.

14. Olmsted and Croes, "Preliminary Report," p. 352.

15. Henry Hill Elliott to Olmsted, n.d. [Summer 1860]; Olmsted to Elliott, Aug. 27, 1860, in *The Papers of Frederick Law Olmsted*, vol. 3: *Creating Central Park, 1857–1861*, ed. Charles E. Beveridge and David Schuyler (Baltimore, 1983), pp. 259–66; Olmsted to John Olmsted, July 22, 1860, in ibid., pp. 256–57.

16. Olmsted to Elliott, Aug. 27, 1860, in *Papers of Frederick Law Olmsted*, 3: 264.

17. Ibid., pp. 262–65.

18. Ibid., pp. 265–66.

19. Andrew Haswell Green later prepared an extensive report for laying out the Washington Heights area. That report was published in New York (City), Board of Commissioners of the Central Park, *Tenth Annual Report* (New York, 1866).

20. Olmsted, et al., "Report to the Staten Island Improvement Commission of a Preliminary Scheme of Improvements," in Fein, *Landscape into Cityscape*, pp. 173–283.

21. William H. Grant, an engineer employed by the Department of Public Parks, reported in 1873 that the population of the Twenty-third and Twenty-fourth wards was 30,742 in 1870, while Manhattan's was 942,292, and that the value of assessed property in the Bronx was 9.8 million dollars, while Manhattan's was 836.7 million dollars. William H. Grant, "Report of the Chief Engineer of the Civil and Topographical Divison," in New York (City), Department of Public Parks, *Third Annual Report*, Dec. 31, 1873 (New York, 1874), p. 232.

22. William Irwin to Olmsted, Nov. 5, 1875; New York (City), Department of Public Parks, *Minutes*, Nov. 5, 1875, May 20, 1874, and Nov. 12, 1875.

23. Olmsted and Croes, "Preliminary Report," pp. 356–57.

24. Olmsted and J.J.R. Croes, "Communication from the Landscape Architect and the Civil and Topographical Engineer, in relation to the proposed plan for laying out the Central District of the Twenty-third and Twenty-fourth Wards, lying east of Jerome Avenue, and west of Third Avenue and the Harlem Railroad," Nov. 7, 1877, in New York (City), Department of Public Parks, *Documents*, doc. 76, pp. 3–11, 12.

25. Olmsted and Croes, "Preliminary Report," pp. 357–58; Olmsted and J.J.R. Croes, "Report of the Landscape Architect and the Civil and Topographical Engineer," Nov. 21, 1876, in Fein, *Landscape into Cityscape*, pp. 360–62, 364–65.

26. Olmsted and Croes, "Preliminary Report" and "Communication," passim.

27. Olmsted and J.J.R. Croes, "Document No. 75 of the Board of the Department of Public Parks: Report of the Landscape Architect and the Civil and Topographical Engineer, Accompanying a Plan for Local Steam Transit Routes in the Twenty-third and Twenty-fourth Wards," Mar. 20, 1877, in Fein, *Landscape into Cityscape*, pp. 375–82.

28. Edith Wharton, *A Backward Glance* (New York, 1934), p. 55.

29. Henry G. Stebbins, "Report of Commissioner Stebbins upon the

plans for Laying Out that part of the Twenty-fourth Ward lying west of River-dale Road," in New York (City), Department of Public Parks, *Documents,* doc. 74, part 1 (Feb. 28, 1877), pp. 7–12; *Public Improvements in the City of New York. A Communication from Andrew H. Green to Wm. A. Booth, Esq., and Others,* Sept. 28, 1874, pp. 9, 21.

30. John C. Olmsted to Frederick Law Olmsted, Jr., Oct. 1, 1913.

31. Ibid.

32. See New York (State), Commission to Select and Locate Lands for Public Parks in the 23d and 24th Wards of New York City, *Report to the New York State Legislature* (New York, 1884).

X. Transformation: The Neoclassical Cityscape

The epigraph is from Montgomery Schuyler, "The Art of City-Making," *Architectural Record* 12 (May 1902): 1.

1. Henry W. Bellows, "Cities and Parks: With Special Reference to the New York Central Park," *Atlantic Monthly* 7 (Apr. 1861): 416–29; James Fenimore Cooper, *The Pioneers; Or, The Sources of the Susquehanna* (1823; New York, 1964), passim. See also Frederick Law Olmsted and Jonathan Baxter Harrison, *Observations on the Treatment of Public Plantations, More Especially Relating to the Use of the Axe,* in *Frederick Law Olmsted: Landscape Architect, 1822–1903,* ed. Frederick Law Olmsted, Jr., and Theodora Kimball, 2 vols. (New York, 1922–28), 2: 362–75.

2. Bellows, "Cities and Parks," pp. 416–29; Olmsted, Vaux & Co. to the Chairman of the Committee on Plans of the Park Commission of Philadelphia, Dec. 4, 1867.

3. Henry W. Bellows, "The Townward Tendency," *The City: An Illustrated Magazine* 1 (Jan. 1872): 40; idem, "City and Country," *Nation* 5 (Sept. 26, 1867): 257.

4. Henry W. Bellows, "The Townward Tendency," *Every Saturday: An Illustrated Weekly Journal* 3 (Oct. 21, 1871): 402.

5. Ibid.

6. Bellows, "The Townward Tendency," *The City,* pp. 38–40.

7. Mariana Griswold Van Rensselaer, "Recent Architecture in America. 3, Commercial Buildings," *The Century Illustrated Monthly Magazine* 28 (Aug. 1884): 511–23; idem, "Recent Architecture in America. 2, Public Buildings (Continued)," ibid. 28 (July 1884): 323–34. See also idem, "Recent Architecture in America. 1, Public Buildings," ibid. 28 (May 1884): 48–67.

8. Paul Boyer, *Urban Masses and Moral Order in America, 1820–1920* (Cambridge, Mass., 1978), pp. 123–31, 175–87.

9. James F. Muirhead, *The Land of Contrasts* (London, 1898); Larzer Ziff, *The American 1890s: Life and Times of a Lost Generation* (New York, 1966), pp. 3–23; Theodore Roosevelt, "The Strenuous Life," in Roderick Nash, ed., *The Call of the Wild, 1900–1916* (New York, 1970), pp. 79–84; Lewis Mumford, "The Intolerable City," *Harper's Monthly* 62 (Feb. 1926): 283–93. See also John Higham, "The Reorientation of American Culture in the 1890's," in John Higham, *Writing American History: Essays on Modern Scholarship* (Bloomington, Ind., 1970), pp. 73–102; and John F. Kasson, *Amusing the Million: Coney Island at the Turn of the Century* (New York, 1978), passim.

10. Thomas Bender and William R. Taylor, "Culture and Architecture: Some Aesthetic Tensions in the Shaping of Modern New York City," in William Sharpe and Leonard Wallock, eds. *Visions of the Modern City: Essays in History, Art, and Literature* (New York, 1983), pp. 200–203; Robert A. M. Stern, et al., *New York 1900: Metropolitan Architecture and Urbanism, 1890–1915* (New York, 1983), pp. 164–67; Olmsted, "The Future of New-York," *New-York*

Daily Tribune, Dec. 28, 1879; Olmsted, "Observations on the Future of New-York," manuscript draft, 1879.

11. Boyer, *Urban Masses and Moral Order*, p. 254, passim; Bender and W. R. Taylor, "Culture and Architecture," p. 186. See also David C. Hammack, *Power and Society: Greater New York at the Turn of the Century* (New York, 1982), passim.

12. M. Schuyler, "The Art of City-Making," p. 2; Bender and W. R. Taylor, "Culture and Architecture," pp. 190–98; John Wellborn Root, quoted in Boyer, *Urban Masses and Moral Order*, p. 270.

13. John Y. Culyer to Olmsted, Dec. 18, 1886. See also Galen Cranz, *The Politics of Park Design: A History of Urban Parks in America* (Cambridge, Mass., 1982), passim.

14. Olmsted to A. A. Smith, Oct. 18, 1886; C. C. Martin to Olmsted, June 1, 1888; Olmsted to John C. Olmsted, Oct. 30, 1888.

15. Olmsted to Henry Van Brunt, Jan. 22, 1891. The historical literature on recreation is growing rapidly, but see especially Roy Rosenzweig, *Eight Hours for What We Will: Workers and Leisure in an Industrial City, 1870–1920* (Cambridge, 1983), pp. 127–52, and Stephen Hardy, *How Boston Played: Sport, Recreation, and Community, 1865–1915* (Boston, 1982), passim.

16. Charles Sprague Sargent, "Prospect Park," *Garden and Forest* 1 (July 4, 1888): 217–18; Richard Guy Wilson, et al., *American Renaissance, 1876–1917* (Brooklyn, 1979), p. 13; Brooklyn, Park Commission, *Twenty-Seventh Annual Report* (Brooklyn 1888), p. 28.

17. Kasson, *Amusing the Million*, p. 19; Henry Adams, *The Education of Henry Adams*, ed. Ernest Samuels (1918; Boston, 1979), p. 343; Montgomery Schuyler, "Last Words About the World's Fair," in Montgomery Schuyler, *American Architecture and Other Writings*, ed. William H. Jordy and Ralph Coe, 2 vols. (Cambridge, Mass., 1961), 2: 574.

18. Kasson, *Amusing the Million*, pp. 11–22; Bender and W. R. Taylor, "Culture and Architecture," pp. 189–91; Thomas Bender, *Toward an Urban Vision: Ideas and Institutions in Nineteenth-Century America* (Lexington, Ky., 1975), pp. 184–87; Boyer, *Urban Masses and Moral Order*, p. 356, n. 26; Wilson, *American Renaissance*, pp. 87–92.

19. McKim, Mead & White, *A Monograph of the Works of McKim, Mead & White, 1879–1915*, new ed. (1915; New York, 1977), p. 21, plates 20, 21; Olmsted to Frank Squier, July 6, 1895, Olmsted Associates Papers, Manuscript Division, Library of Congress, Washington, D.C.

20. Clay Lancaster, *Prospect Park Handbook* (1967; New York, 1972), pp. 69–78, passim.

21. Boyer, *Urban Masses and Moral Order*, p. 273; Daniel H. Burnham and Edward H. Bennett, *Plan of Chicago* (1909; New York, 1970), pp. 110–15; Wilson, *American Renaissance*, pp. 75, 81.

22. Burnham and Bennett, *Plan of Chicago*, passim; Wilson, *American Renaissance*, p. 21; Thomas Hines, *Burnham of Chicago: Architect and Planner* (New York, 1974), pp. 158–96.

23. Jon Alvah Peterson, "The City Beautiful Movement: Forgotten Origins and Lost Meanings," *Journal of Urban History* 2 (Aug. 1976): 415–34; idem, "The Origins of the Comprehensive City Planning Ideal in the United States, 1840–1911," (Ph.D. dissertation, Harvard University, 1967); Stern, *New York 1900*, pp. 27–34.

24. Stern, *New York 1900*, pp. 27–34.

25. Ibid.

26. Ibid.; Bender and W. R. Taylor, "Culture and Architecture," pp. 186–96.

27. Wilson, *American Renaissance*, p. 12, passim.

28. Jon Alvah Peterson, "The Nation's First Comprehensive City Plan: A Political Analysis of the McMillan Plan for Washington, D.C., 1900–1902," *Journal of the American Planning Association* 51 (Spring 1985): 134–50; Charles Moore, ed., *The Improvement of the Park System of the District of Columbia* (Washington, D.C., 1902).

BIBLIOGRAPHICAL ESSAY

The history of American cities in the nineteenth century is a vast and growing field of investigation. While no precise beginning to its scholarship can be fixed, the writings of Frederick Law Olmsted, Henry W. Bellows, Charles Loring Brace, and members of the American Social Science Association in the second half of the nineteenth century surely form the first chapter of modern historical writing on American cities. Contemporary historians are particularly indebted to Olmsted's colleague, sanitary engineer George E. Waring, Jr., who compiled the social statistics of cities for the United States Census of 1880. With the rise of university education at the end of the century, a series of monographs, most notably Adna Ferrin Weber's classic *The Growth of Cities in the Nineteenth Century: A Study in Statistics* (New York, 1899), investigated conditions of life in cities. One early study that was of particular value in preparing this book is Harry James Carman's *The Street Surface Railroad Franchises of New York City*, Studies in History, Economics, and Public Law 88 (New York, 1919).

Recent works devoted to nineteenth-century cities are legion, but this book owes a special debt to Thomas Bender, *Toward an Urban Vision: Ideas and Institutions in Nineteenth-Century America* (Lexington, Ky., 1975); Paul Boyer, *Urban Masses and Moral Order in America, 1820–1920* (Cambridge, Mass., 1978); Gunther Barth, *City People: The Rise of Modern City Culture in Nineteenth-Century America* (New York, 1980); and Neil Harris, *The Artist in American Society: The Formative Years, 1790–1860* (New York, 1966). My approach to urban form has benefited greatly from the research of historical geographers, especially Allan R. Pred, writing in *The Spatial Dynamics of United States Urban-Industrial Growth, 1800–1914* (Cambridge, Mass., 1966) and *Urban Growth and the Circulation of Information: The United States System of Cities, 1790–1840* (Cambridge, Mass., 1973); and David Ward, author of *Cities and Immigrants: A Geography of Change in Nineteenth-Century America* (New York, 1971). I have also learned much from the works of historians of city planning, particularly those of John W. Reps, *The Making of Urban America: A History of City Planning in the United States* (Princeton, 1965) and *Monumental Washington: The Planning and Development of the Capital Center* (Princeton, 1967); Mel Scott, Jr., *American City Planning since 1890* (Berkeley and Los Angeles, 1969); and Jon Alvah Peterson, "The Origins of the Comprehensive City Planning Ideal in the United States, 1840–1911," Ph.D. dissertation, Harvard University, 1967.

Any historian pursuing a study of nineteenth-century city planning, the development of landscape architecture, or the career of Frederick Law Olmsted consults the massive collection of Olmsted's papers, and the even more intimidating collection of Olmsted Associates Papers, housed at the Manuscript Division of the Library of Congress. Included in these collections are reports and correspondence chronicling the majority of public and private design projects undertaken in the United States during the nineteenth century.

Printed collections of Olmsted's writings include *Frederick Law Olmsted: Landscape Architect, 1822–1903*, ed. Frederick Law Olmsted, Jr., and Theodora Kimball, 2 vols. (New York, 1922–28); *Landscape into Cityscape: Frederick Law Olmsted's Plans for a Greater New York*, ed. Albert Fein (Ithaca, 1967); *Civilizing American Cities: A Selection of Frederick Law Olmsted's Writings on City Landscapes*, ed. S. B. Sutton (Cambridge, Mass., 1971), which unfortunately presents only portions of important documents; and *The Papers of Frederick Law Olmsted*, ed. Charles Capen McLaughlin, Charles E. Beveridge, and David Schuyler, 3 vols. to date (Baltimore, 1977–).

Major works on Olmsted include Broadus Mitchell, *Frederick Law Olmsted: Critic of the Old South* (Baltimore, 1922); Albert Fein, *Frederick Law Olmsted and the American Environmental Tradition* (New York, 1972); Laura Wood Roper, *FLO: A Biography of Frederick Law Olmsted* (Baltimore, 1973); Elizabeth Stevenson, *Park Maker: A Life of Frederick Law Olmsted* (New York, 1977); Dana F. White and Victor A. Kramer, eds., *Olmsted South: Old South Critic/New South Planner* (Westport, Conn., 1979); and especially Charles E. Beveridge, "Frederick Law Olmsted: The Formative Years, 1822–1865," Ph.D. dissertation, University of Wisconsin, 1966. See also his "Frederick Law Olmsted's Theory of Landscape Design," *Nineteenth Century* 3 (Summer 1977): 38–43. Cynthia Zaitzevsky's *Frederick Law Olmsted and the Boston Park System* (Cambridge, Mass., 1982) is a richly detailed and imaginative work.

Books of more specialized interest or ones principally devoted to illustrations include Julius Gy. Fabos, et al., *Frederick Law Olmsted, Sr.: Founder of Landscape Architecture in America* (Amherst, 1968); Elizabeth Barlow, *Frederick Law Olmsted's New York* (New York, 1972); Richard S. Wurman, *The Nature of Recreation: A Handbook in Honor of Frederick Law Olmsted* (Cambridge, Mass., 1972); and Bruce Kelly, et al., *Art of the Olmsted Landscape*, 2 vols. (New York, 1981).

As Olmsted's career has attracted increasing attention, historians have begun to debate his motivation and vision. Albert Fein, for example, presents Olmsted as a liberal social activist in *Frederick Law Olmsted and the American Environmental Tradition* and in his introduction to *Landscape into Cityscape*. Geoffrey Blodgett offers a more persuasive interpretation in his essay "Frederick Law Olmsted: Landscape Architecture as Conservative Reform," *Journal of American History* 62 (Mar. 1976): 869–89, as does Thomas Bender in *Toward an Urban Vision*. See also Roy Lubove, "Social History and the History of Landscape Architecture," *Journal of Social History* 8 (Winter 1975): 268–75. Important for an understanding of the intellectual and cultural context in which Olmsted worked are Daniel Walker Howe, *The Political Culture of the American Whigs* (Chicago, 1979); Boyer's *Urban Masses and Moral Order in America*; Stowe Persons, *The Decline of American Gentility* (New York, 1973); and Geoffrey Blodgett, *The Gentle Reformers: Massachusetts Democrats in the Cleveland Era* (Cambridge, Mass., 1966).

For biographical and interpretive studies of other landscape architects a good general reference is Norman T. Newton, *Design on the Land: The Development of Landscape Architecture* (Cambridge, Mass., 1971). The most comprehensive treatment of Downing's career remains George B. Tatum, "Andrew Jackson Downing: Arbiter of American Taste, 1815–1852," Ph.D. dissertation, Princeton University, 1950. On Vaux see Dennis Stedman Francis and Joy M. Kestenbaum, "Calvert Vaux," *The MacMillan Encyclopaedia of Architects*, 4 vols. (New York, 1982), 2: 303–4; [C. Bowyer Vaux], "Calvert Vaux, Designer of Parks," *Park International* 1 (Sept. 1920): 138–43; and John David Sigle, "Calvert Vaux: An American Architect," M.A. thesis, University of Virginia, 1967. The best source of information on the career of H. W. S. Cleveland is Roy Lubove's introduction to the new edition of Cleveland's *Landscape Architecture As Applied to the Wants of the West* (1873; Pittsburgh, 1965). Charles W. Eliot presents an affectionate and appreciative biography of his son in *Charles Eliot: Landscape Architect* (Boston, 1902).

The best general history of urban parks is George F. Chadwick, *The Park and the Town: Public Landscapes in the Nineteenth and Twentieth Centuries* (New York, 1966), which is especially useful for its information on contemporary developments in Europe. I clearly disagree with Galen Cranz's static interpretation of park planning in the second half of the nineteenth century as presented in *The Politics of Park Design: A History of Urban Parks in America* (Cambridge, Mass., 1982). See also Robert C. Wendling, comp., *Parks and Recreation in the United States: A Bibliography* (Monticello, Ill., 1981).

Public documents and histories of individual parks and park systems are important sources of information. Predictably, of all nineteenth-century parks, New York's Central Park has received the most attention. Essential to its study are the published *Documents* and *Minutes* of the Board of Commissioners of the Central Park (1857–70), as well as the contemporary newspapers and the records of the New York City Board of Aldermen and Common Council. Also useful in examining the 1850s and 1860s is New York (City), Common Council, *Manual of the Corporation of the City of New York*, comp. D. T. Valentine, which reprints numerous important documents. For general histories of the park see Clarence C. Cook, *A Description of the New York Central Park* (1869; New York, 1972); Gherardi Davis, *The Establishment of Public Parks in the City of New York* (New York, 1897); Henry Hope Reed and Sophia Duckworth, *Central Park: A History and a Guide* (New York, 1967); Elizabeth Barlow, *The Central Park Book* (New York, 1977); M. M. Graff, *The Men Who Made Central Park* (New York, 1982); and especially *The Papers of Frederick Law Olmsted*, vol. 3, *Creating Central Park, 1857–1861*, ed. Charles E. Beveridge and David Schuyler (Baltimore, 1983). Other helpful works on New York are Fein, ed., *Landscape into Cityscape*; Barlow, *Frederick Law Olmsted's New York*; and Kelly, et al., *Art of the Olmsted Landscape*. Robert A. Caro's *The Power Broker: Robert Moses and the Fall of New York* (New York, 1974) chronicles the impact of twentieth-century recreation and transportation on nineteenth-century parks. Every student who works in New York materials owes a tremendous debt to I. N. Phelps Stokes, *The Iconography of Manhattan Island, 1498–1909*, 6 vols. (New York, 1915–28). Also important are Edward K. Spann, *The New Metropolis: New York City, 1840–1857* (New York, 1981); David C. Hammack, *Power and Society: Greater New York at the Turn of the Century* (New York, 1982); Robert A. M. Stern, et al., *New York 1900: Metropolitan Architecture and Urbanism, 1890–1915* (New York, 1983); John A. Kouwenhoven, *The Columbia Historical Portrait of New York: An Essay in Graphic History*...(Garden City, N.Y., 1953); and Charles Lockwood, *Manhattan Moves Uptown: An Illustrated History* (Boston, 1976).

Less has been written about park systems in other cities. Brooklyn's Prospect Park, for example, has long remained in the shadow of its more famous neighbor. But public records again provide much useful information, particularly the *Annual Reports* of the Brooklyn Park Commission. Also important, especially for its research in local newspapers of the time, is Donald Simon, "The Public Park Movement in Brooklyn, 1824–1873," Ph.D. dissertation, New York University, 1972. M. M. Graff, *The Making of Prospect Park: Notes for a Projected Historical Study* (New York, 1982), is an attempt by a longtime friend of New York's parks to distribute credit to Olmsted's associates, but the pamphlet is deeply flawed.

Charles E. Beveridge's "Buffalo's Park and Parkway System," in Reyner Banham, et al., *Buffalo Architecture: A Guide* (Cambridge, Mass., 1981), is the best history of Buffalo's public spaces, as Cynthia Zaitzevsky's *Olmsted and the Boston Park System* is for that city. Little of consequence has been written about Philadelphia's or Baltimore's parks, which makes reliance on public records and newspapers essential; but see Esther M. Klein, *Fairmount Park: A History and a Guidebook* (Bryn Mawr, 1974); Theo B. White, *Fairmount, Philadelphia's Park, A History* (Philadelphia, 1975); and John V. Kelly, *Public Parks of Baltimore, No. 4, Druid Hill Park: Events Resulting in its Acquirement, and Method of Financing* (Baltimore, 1929).

For information on Chicago's park system see Michael P. McCarthy,

"Politics and the Parks: Chicago Businessmen and the Recreation Movement," *Journal of the Illinois State Historical Society* 63 (Summer 1972): 158-72; Victoria Post Ranney, *Olmsted in Chicago* (Chicago, 1972); Glen E. Holt, "Private Plans for Public Spaces: The Origins of Chicago's Park System, 1850-1875," *Chicago History* 8 (Fall 1979): 173-84; Theodore Turak, "William LeBaron Jenney: Pioneer of Chicago's West Parks," *Inland Architect* 25 (Mar. 1981): 38-45; and Daniel M. Bluestone, "Olmsted's Boston and Other Park Places," *Reviews in American History* 11 (Dec. 1983): 531-36 as well as his "Landscape and Culture in Nineteenth-Century Chicago," Ph.D. dissertation, University of Chicago, 1984. Two important general histories of the city are Bessie Louise Pierce, *A History of Chicago*, 3 vols. (New York, 1937-57), and Harold M. Mayer and Richard C. Wade, *Chicago: Growth of a Metropolis* (Chicago, 1969).

Several recent studies of recreation, particularly among working-class residents of cities, emphasize the disparity between planning ideals and popular use. See, for example, Stephen Hardy, *How Boston Played: Sport, Recreation, and Community, 1865-1915* (Boston, 1982), and Roy Rosenzweig, *Eight Hours for What We Will: Workers and Leisure in an Industrial City, 1870-1920* (Cambridge, Mass., 1983).

During the last two decades historians have begun examining the processes of urban decentralization and suburbanization. Sam Bass Warner, Jr., *Streetcar Suburbs: The Process of Growth in Boston, 1870-1900* (Cambridge, Mass., 1962) is a pathbreaking examination of urban expansion and architectural development. See also George R. Taylor, "The Beginnings of Mass Transportation in Urban America," *Smithsonian Journal of History* 1 (Summer 1966): 35-50 and ibid. 1 (Autumn 1966): 31-52; Charles J. Kennedy, "Commuter Service in the Boston Area, 1835-1860," *Business History Review* 36 (Summer 1962): 153-70; Kenneth T. Jackson's "The Crabgrass Frontier: 150 Years of Suburban Growth in America," in Raymond A. Mohl and James F. Richardson, eds., *The Urban Experience: Themes in American History* (Belmont, Calif., 1973), and idem, "Urban Decentralization in the Nineteenth Century: A Statistical Inquiry," in Leo F. Schnore, ed., *The New Urban History: Quantitative Explorations by American Historians* (Princeton, 1975). Also helpful on urban decentralization and suburbanization are two works by Joel Arthur Tarr, "From City to Suburb: The 'Moral' Influence of Transportation Technology," in Alexander B. Callow, Jr., ed., *American Urban History: An Interpretative Reader with Commentaries*, 2nd ed. (New York, 1973) and *Transportation Innovation and Changing Spatial Patterns in Pittsburgh, 1850-1934* (Chicago, 1978); as well as Glen E. Holt's "The Changing Perception of Urban Pathology: An Essay on the Development of Mass Transit in the United States," in Kenneth T. Jackson and Stanley Schultz, eds., *Cities in American History* (New York, 1972). Of similar importance are Henry

Claxton Binford, "The Suburban Enterprise: Jacksonian Towns and Boston Commuters, 1815–1860," Ph.D. dissertation, Harvard University, 1973; Jon C. Teaford, *City and Suburb: The Political Fragmentation of Metropolitan America, 1850–1970* (Baltimore, 1979); Robert A.M. Stern, *The Anglo-American Suburb* (London, 1981); and Peter O. Muller, "The Evolution of American Suburbs: A Geographical Interpretation," *Urbanism Past and Present* 4 (Winter/Spring 1977): 1–10. Kenneth Jackson's eagerly anticipated *Crabgrass Frontier: The Suburbanization of the United States* (New York, 1985) had not yet been published when this book went to press.

Much of what I have learned about suburbanization and the history of specific nineteenth-century communities is the result of extensive research in contemporary manuscripts, newspapers, periodicals, and design reports. Histories of individual cities and their suburbs include the following: Sidney Denise Maxwell, *The Suburbs of Cincinnati: Sketches Historical and Descriptive* (Cincinnati, 1870); Everett Chamberlain, *Chicago and its Suburbs* (Chicago, 1874); Howard K. Menhinick, "Riverside Sixty Years Later," *Landscape Architecture* 22 (Jan. 1932): 109–17; Jane B. Davies, "Llewellyn Park in West Orange, New Jersey," *Antiques* 107 (Jan. 1975): 142–58; Jean F. Block, *Hyde Park Houses: An Informal History, 1856–1910* (Chicago, 1978); Richard Guy Wilson, "Idealism and the Origin of the First American Suburb: Llewellyn Park, New Jersey," *American Art Journal* 11 (Fall 1979): 79–90. The recent study that parallels my interpretation of suburbanization is John Archer, "Country and City in the American Romantic Suburb," *Journal of the Society of Architectural Historians* 42 (May 1983): 139–56.

In recent years historians have published an impressive number of books and articles on such subjects as social mobility, family structure, urban technology and the delivery of services, the creation of urban cultural institutions, and the rise of modern recreation. While this book focuses on city form as the expression of a specific set of cultural values, I hope it is evident how important this body of scholarship has been to my thinking about cities.

INDEX